THE ENCYCLOPEDIA OF THE
WORLD'S
SPECIAL
FORCES

TACTICS • HISTORY • STRATEGY • WEAPONS

THE ENCYCLOPEDIA OF THE
WORLD'S SPECIAL FORCES

TACTICS • HISTORY • STRATEGY • WEAPONS
FOREWORD BY MAJOR MIKE MCKINNEY, USAF SPECIAL OPERATIONS

MIKE RYAN, CHRIS MANN, AND ALEXANDER STILWELL

BARNES
&NOBLE
BOOKS
NEW YORK

This edition published by Barnes & Noble Inc.,
by arrangement with Amber Books Ltd
2003 Barnes & Noble Books

10 9 8 7 6 5 4 3 2 1

ISBN: 0-7607-3939-0

Library of Congress Cataloging-in-Publication Data
available upon request.

Editorial and design by:
Amber Books Ltd
Bradley's Close
74–77 White Lion Street
London N1 9PF
www.amberbooks.co.uk

Project Editor: Mariano Kälfors
Editor: Caroline Curtis
Design: Brian Rust

Picture credits:
TRH Pictures: 8, 11(b), 12 (t), 14, 28, 29, 30 (t.r), 31(b), 32(both), 33, 35, 46, 54, 55, 64, 66, 67(both), 68, 73(both), 76, 77, 79, 80, 81, 82, 85(U.S. Army), 87(t)(U.S. Navy), (U.S. Army)(b), 89(U.S. Army), 90(D.O.D), 91(U.S. Air Force), 92(U.S. Navy), 93(D.O.D.), 95(t), 96(U.S. Army), 100, 104, 111(t), 112(l), 113(t), 118, 120(t), 130, 131(both), 132, 133, 134, 137(D.O.D.), 138, 144, 147(U.S. Navy), 149, 154, 161, 162(both), 163, 164(b), 167(both), 180(t), 186(U.S. Navy), 187(D.O.D./U.S.M.C.), 188(U.S. Navy), 189(U.S. Navy), 190(U.S. Navy), 194–195(U.S. Air Force), 196(both), 198(b), 200, 201(t), 214(t)(D.O.D.), 218(t), 223(I.W.M.), 225(t), 225(b)(U.S. Air Force), 226, 228, 229, 230, 232(both), 236(b), 238(U.S. Army), 239, 240(U.S. Army), 241(both)(D.O.D), 242(t)(U.S. Air Force), 244(both);
Private Collection: 11 (t), 12 (b), 13 (t & b.r), 102, 103(b);
Amber Books: 13(b.l), 3 (l), 31(t.l), 36(t), 37, 40, 41, 42, 65(l), 72(b), 74(l), 78, 94, 95(b), 98–99, 109(r), 119(t), 135, 146, 175, 181, 182, 192(b), 199(both), 201(b.l, b.r), 204(t), 212, 213(both), 235, 236(t);
Istituto Geografico DeAgostini S.p.A: 105, 185(t), 191;
POPPERFOTO: 16 (both), 20, 23 (both), 35(t), 36(b), 38, 39(both), 38, 39(both), 44, 45, 49, 50(both), 51(both), 57, 63(both), 65(r), 86, 88, 103(t), 106, 107, 109(l), 110, 111(b), 114, 115(r),116, 117, 119(b), 120(b), 121, 127(b), 128, 129, 139, 141, 143, 156, 159, 160(both), 164(t), 171, 177(both), 178(both), 179(t), 183, 184, 197, 198(t), 203, 204(b), 205, 206, 207, 208, 209, 210, 211, 243;
Corbis: 18(both), 19, 58, 71, 72(t), 157, 158, 174;
PA Photos: 21, 34, 47, 48, 56, 57(b), 113(b), 115(b), 124, 125, 155, 166, 169, 170, 172, 173, 180(b);
Military Picture Library International: 25, 26, 27(both), 43, 59, 60, 61(both), 62, 70, 74(r), 75, 83, 84(both), 112(r), 122, 126, 127(t), 179(b), 182(t), 220–221, 222, 223(t), 231, 233, 234, 237, 242(b);
United States Department of Defense: 97, 108, 193, 214(b), 215, 216, 217, 218(b), 219(both).

(t)=top; (b)=bottom; (l)=left; (r)=right.

Printed in Italy

CONTENTS

SPECIAL FORCES AT SEA 144

SPECIAL FORCES IN THE AIR 194

SPECIAL FORCES TRAINING 220

FOREWORD

Special forces hold a unique place in military history. Operating on the fringe of conventional military theory, the details of their missions are often kept in the shadows. Unfortunately, this secrecy has led to a misunderstanding of their impact on the battlefield. The use of special forces can have dramatic strategic effects, as witnessed at Entebbe, Son Tay, Eben Emael, and Saint Nazaire. These names are just a few examples of special operations missions that have gained a mystique in military history. The world gained a glimpse into the unique capabilities of special forces during Operation Enduring Freedom in Afghanistan. The photos of US Special Forces soldiers on horseback, riding into battle alongside Northern Alliance allies, illustrate the range of diversity for these highly-skilled professionals. Special forces units from several nations conducted direct action raids, special reconnaissance, psychological operations, unconventional warfare, and airborne assault missions, directly contributing to the destruction of Taliban and Al Qaeda forces. The conflict in Afghanistan proved to be a tremendous success for Special Forces largely because they were able to employ in the classical manner in which they are trained. They are a true force multiplier for commanders and can be considered the original 'smart weapons'.

One trait binding special forces soldiers of all nations together is an overwhelming sense of dedication to this unique brand of warfare. What's important to remember is that members of all special forces units are volunteers, a fact that is especially vital in a time of declining military force structures. Some volunteer for the excitement, others feel a calling to the profession. Being a member of a special forces unit means dedicating oneself to a high standard of professionalism and expertise. What makes a special forces soldier different lies in the philosophy. Every special forces soldier is selected based upon his ability to lead and handle pressure. After a rigorous selection process, the lifestyle is one of constant training and readiness. Unlike conventional military forces, special forces must be ready to act in times of peace and war. Some units, like the Green Berets or British SAS, become masters of many skills, while others focus on a particular area of interest, such as counterterrorism. Regardless of their specialty, they are supreme experts at their craft. The world they live in is deadly serious and each member recognizes the outcome of failure. This is the very reason why special forces missions are considered 'high-risk/high-gain', and usually limits when and where they are employed.

Many of the units found in this book have never been written about before, and you get an inside look into what makes them tick. Their selection, training, skills and equipment are presented in exacting detail. With the publication of *The Encyclopedia of the World's Special Forces*, you get a better understanding of just what it takes to be a member of these elite forces.

Major Mike McKinney
USAF Special Operations

SPECIAL FORCES ON LAND

Following the tragic events of 11 September 2001, the words 'special forces' have dominated the world's headlines as they are seen as the key tool in future warfare against both terrorists and conventional forces alike. Their ability to deploy unseen and unheard gives their governments a powerful weapon that is both efficient and effective, as no one knows when or where they will strike.

Left: French Foreign Legionnaires from the 6ème Regiment Étrangere de Genie standing to attention during Desert Storm in 1991.

ALGERIA
Algerian Airborne Commando Division

Since independence in 1962 Algeria has had a long struggle to keep its terrorist factions in check. Little is known of its airborne special forces unit apart from its dedicated role to counter the numerous attacks and bombings of government forces.

Algeria has a long and bloody history of internal turmoil that has kept its armed forces, and indeed those of the French, extremely busy for many decades. France granted Algeria its independence in July 1962, and since then the country has struggled to keep terrorist factions in check. There have been numerous bombings and attacks on government forces in recent years, and it was these that prompted the formation of a dedicated counterterrorist unit.

Although little is known of its strength or capabilities, the unit is part of a new airborne special forces division within the Algerian Army and replaces the 1st, 2nd and 3rd parachute commando battalions formed in 1962. Algeria's first special forces unit was the 19th Algerian Parachute Battalion, formed by the French Army in 1954.

After independence, Algeria turned to the Soviet Union for its training and equipment, and much of its new airborne operational doctrine is now based on Russian practices, rather than French. The Algerian special forces have been involved in combat outside Algeria: they are known to have deployed a battalion to Fayid, Egypt, for raids across the Suez Canal against the IDF during the War of Attrition.

ARGENTINA
Brigada del Ejercito 601 and 602
Brigada Especial Operativa Halcon

Two army commando brigades and the dedicated anti-terrorist unit Brigada Halcon, under the control of the police, form Argentina's special forces capabilities.

Argentina first set up a special forces capability with American assistance in the 1960s, with the formation of a commando brigade that was modelled along US Ranger lines. Known as Brigada del Ejercito 601, this force quickly gained respect amongst the Argentine armed forces, and this led to the formation of a second brigade, the 602nd. All members of the brigade undergo parachute training at the Catamarca Airborne School, and they crosstrain with other special forces units. The 601st saw action during the Falklands War (1982) on Mount Kent, where its members fought running battles with the British SAS.

Standard equipment for the Brigada del Ejercito includes sniper rifles, assault weapons fitted with high-quality night-vision devices, and very high-quality combat clothing.

BRIGADA ESPECIAL OPERATIVA HALCON

Formed in 1986 to combat terrorism, the Brigada Especial Operativa Halcon (Falcon Special Operations Brigade) is a police unit directly under the command of the Buenos Aires police department. With a make-up very similar to that of a military CRW team, the Brigada Halcon consists of 75 operators who are subdivided into five 15-man teams. Each team consists

of two snipers, eight assaulters, one negotiator, an intelligence specialist, a communications specialist, a medic and an EOD specialist. Training comprises three two-month courses, which cover shooting, parachuting, offensive driving, sniping, intelligence gathering, use of explosives and helicopter insertion. In addition to its anti-terrorist role, the unit provides bodyguards for VIPs because of Argentina's current state of economic crisis. The Brigada Halcon utilizes both local- and foreign-manufactured clothing and protective gear.

Weapons include the Franchi SPAS 12 shotgun; Glock 17 pistol; and HK G3 GS/1 for sniping.

AUSTRALIA
Special Air Service Regiment (SASR)

Australia's SASR has a long and proud history dating back to fighting the Japanese during World War II. They are organized along the same lines as the British SAS, with whom they maintain close ties. The SASR recently saw action cooperating with US special forces in Afghanistan.

The Australian Special Air Service Regiment, based at Campbell Barracks, Swanbourne, has an operational strength of around 600 men and is made up of six squadrons – three Sabre, one signals, one operational support, one base – and a Regimental Headquarters (RHQ).

To ensure maximum operational efficiency at any given time, the three Sabre squadrons work on a three-year cycle, which provides both training and operational experience. In the first year of a typical squadron cycle, new recruits are processed and worked up, while more experienced troopers develop new skills and attend refresher courses. The second year of

Below: A well-armed Australian 6x6 Perentie LRPV shows off its impressive armament of two 7.62mm (0.3in) GPMGs.

Above: SASR soldiers part of a peace-keeping force in East Timor secure a landing zone close to the border in 1999.

the cycle sees the squadron train for its overt military responsibilities, including special operations in conventional warfare. This provides a good contrast to the third and final year of the cycle, which involves training for covert operations. The base squadron provides logistical and administrative support, while the SASR's operational support squadron evaluates new equipment and provides specialist training for new tactics, techniques and procedures. In addition to this, 152 Signals Squadron (SASR) provides a highly capable communications network.

The SASR has a long and proud history. The first Australian SAS squadrons were formed during World War II to fight the Japanese behind their own lines, a task they performed with great success. After the war ended, they were disbanded in the

same way as the British SAS and were not reformed until 1949. For three years, the unit was known as the 1st SAS Company and operated out of Swanbourne. In 1951, it was incorporated into the Royal Australian Regiment (RAR) as an airborne platoon; however, this arrangement was far from ideal, and, in 1957, it broke away to become the 1st Special Air Service Company. The unit quickly grew in size and capability, and in 1964 became the 1st Special Air Service Regiment (SASR), the title it holds to this day.

The SASR mirrors the British SAS in many ways, the two having worked together over many years, both in training and in combat. The strength of this special relationship was ably demonstrated in the jungles of Borneo from February 1965 to August 1966: British and Australian SAS troopers fought side by side against Indonesian forces in difficult and demanding conditions. This experience proved to be of immense value to the SASR, which soon found itself involved in another difficult operation in Vietnam, fighting in support of the US Armed Forces. The SASR originally deployed to Vietnam in 1962 as part of the Australian Army Training Team. As this controversial and increasingly unpopular war dragged on, it became necessary to raise another squadron in July 1966, which brought the SASR up to an operational strength of three Sabre squadrons. Up until 1971, the squadrons were rotated after each had completed two tours of Vietnam.

The SASR developed a fearsome reputation: its troopers were known as tough and tenacious fighters who never quit, and the Viet Cong tended to avoid them.

After Vietnam, the SASR was forced to disband one of its Sabre squadrons. However, it was reformed in 1982 following a terrorist bomb attack on the Sydney Hilton Hotel on

Above: A potential Australian SASR soldier takes a quick break during the individual endurance and navigation phase of the SASR's selection course.

Below: SASR soldiers part of Operation Enduring Freedom search a cave in Afghanistan during a routine sweep-and-clear operation.

Right: An SASR trooper questions an Afghani about Al Qaeda activity in the area following a series of air strikes by American B-52 bombers.

13 February 1978. Within days of the attack, the SASR was formally designated the national counter-terrorist unit and immediately set up the TAG/OAT groups as a reaction force. From 1982, the SASR expanded rapidly and soon found itself needing a dedicated signals squadron. In response, 152 Signals Squadron was formed and set about providing each Sabre squadron with a signals troop to enable better communications while on operations. The Gulf War in 1991 led to the deployment of one SASR squadron in support of the Allied Coalition force. This force of 110 men joined up with the New Zealand SAS to form the ANZAC SAS Squadron, which worked alongside both British and US special forces against Iraq. In recent years, the SASR has been involved in operations in East Timor and Afghanistan, and has performed superbly in both.

The SASR wear standard Australian Army combat uniforms, with only their sand-coloured beret, cap badge and wings differentiating them from any other conventional army unit. Standard weapons include the locally produced F-88 Austeyr assault rifle; the M16A2; M249 Minimi SAW; and various 40mm (1.57in) grenade launchers. As with the British SAS, the SASR makes good use of its Land Rover long-range patrol vehicles and operates a large fleet of specially developed vehicles which are 6 x 6 rather than 4 x 4 in configuration. Known as the Land Rover Perentie within the SASR, this excellent vehicle is ideal for operating in Australia's vast and varied landscape and has proved very successful in supporting the SASR in its operations in Afghanistan.

Left: An Australian SAS trooper in standard camouflage uniform with a sweatrag wrapped around his head. He is armed with an M16A1.

Right: LT COL Rowan Tink shown presented with the United States Bronze Star for commanding operations with the Special Air Service in Afganistan, 2002.

AUSTRIA ≡
Gendarmerieeinsatzkommando (GEK) 'Cobra' Jagdkommando

Austria's special forces are made up of the anti-terrorist unit GEK 'Cobra' and an elite commando unit. The units maintain close ties with each other and train regularly with Germany's GSG-9.

The history of Austria's Gendarmerieeinsatzkommando 'Cobra' dates back to 1973, when a unit known as Gendarmeriekommando Bad Voslau was formed in response to Palestinian terrorists who posed a threat to Jewish immigrants living and travelling through Austria. The unit was deployed on several occasions when terrorists seized a number of hostages and demanded millions of dollars for their safe return. In one incident, the infamous Carlos the Jackal received a multimillion-dollar ransom in exchange for the safe return of a number of government ministers who had been taken hostage during a meeting of OPEC countries.

With terrorism on the increase within Europe, it was felt that the current unit was inadequate for its role and that a new force was needed. In 1978, Gendarmerieeinsatzkommando (GEK) 'Cobra' was formed to replace Gendarmeriekommando Bad Voslau. Its first commandant, Oberst Johannes Pechter, had close ties with Germany's GSG-9 and Israel's Sayeret Mat'kal and crosstrained with both of these excellent units to ensure that his force was up to the standard of some of the best in the world. Not content simply to take ideas from elsewhere, GEK has also developed excellent skills in specific areas of anti-terrorist operations, including ropework and building assaults.

Typical weapons include the Glock 17 pistol; Steyr 5.56 AUG assault rifle; and Steyr 7.62 police rifle for sniping.

JAGDKOMMANDO

The Jagdkommando are located in Wiener Neustadt, which is just south of Vienna and is manned by highly motivated volunteers rather than national service conscripts. To join this elite force, volunteers must be both physically and mentally fit and have no previous criminal convictions.

Aptitude training requires that each candidate undergo a 24km (15-mile) march in three and a half hours carrying a 10kg (22lb) pack and personal weapon; a 5km (3-mile) run in less than 24 minutes; a suspended traverse along a 30m (98ft) sloping rope; a dive from a 10m (33ft) tower; and a 30-minute nonstop swim.

If they are successful in passing the initial assessment, all potential commandos are required to complete basic military and preparatory cadre training prior to undertaking a specialized 22-week commando course. During this part of the training, potential commandos learn parachuting (including free fall), close-quarter combat, alpine operations, demolitions, sniping, amphibious warfare, first aid and survival techniques. After completion of the course, newly qualified commandos can look forward to working with other special forces, including their own GEK 'Cobra', Germany's GSG-9 and the United States' Delta Force.

Left: A GEK operator using a Steyr sniper rifle observes a potential target during a training exercise.

BELGIUM ▮▮
Équipes Specialisées de Reconnaissance (ESR)
Escadron Special d'Intervention (ESI)

Belgium's elite long-range reconnaisance unit, ESR, has now disbanded but its operatives
continue to train Belgium's reconnaissance teams. The ESI form Belgium's anti-terrorist arm.

Although the ESR (Equipes Specialisées de Reconnaissance – Specialized Reconnaissance Teams) were officially disbanded in June 1994, they warrant a mention because many former members are now assigned to the Para-Commandos as instructors for future Belgian long-range reconnaissance teams.

The ESR were first formed in 1961 for the demanding role of deep reconnaissance behind enemy lines. Their primary mission was to gather intelligence data and transmit it back to their operational HQ for evaluation. The Belgium Government steadfastly denied the existence of the ESR, even when 12 members defended the Belgium Embassy in Kinshasa, Zaire, from rebel attack. The ESR also deployed to Sarajevo as a close protection force to the Belgian General Briquemont, who was Commander in Chief for the 'Blue Helmets' in Sarajevo. In Somalia, 28 ESRs were discreetly deployed to monitor Somali warlords, in particular General Muhammad Said Hersi. The final operation that the ESR performed before being disbanded took place in Rwanda, where they were part of Operation Silver Back, a rescue mission set up to secure the safe evacuation of European nationals from the wartorn nation.

The ESI (Escadron Special d'Intervention) was formed after the terrorist attack on Israeli athletes in Munich during the 1972 Olympic Games. Originally called Le Group Diane, this title was changed to ESI in 1974 to better reflect the unit's operational role as an anti-terrorist force. Despite the name change, however, the Belgium media still refer to the unit as the Diane. ESI doctrine is to be proactive rather than reactive and, as a result, the unit is used in an aggressive way, performing both anti- and counterterrorist roles. Not only do they take active measures to counter terrorist incidents, but they also aim to prevent terrorists striking in the first place.

Service within ESI is voluntary, and all potential candidates must undergo a tough selection process before they can be considered for active service. This process last for two weeks and has a high failure rate: almost half the number of candidates fail to reach the end of the course. Those that do pass the selection phase move on to three months of intensive training before they become qualified operators. ESI also allows females to serve in the unit, but only in observation and undercover roles. This operational flexibility allows the unit to perform other duties, such as fighting narcotics traffickers and their criminal gangs.

ESI training involves making tactical use of high-speed vehicles in both defensive and offensive modes. Current vehicles include Mercedes sedans; 4 x 4 Range Rovers; and unmarked vans.

Weapons used include the HK MP5; Sako TRG-21 sniper rifle; Glock 17; Browning 9mm (0.35in) pistol; and Remington 12-gauge shotguns.

BRAZIL ◉
1st Special Forces Battalion

Failure rate for admittance to Brazil's special forces is high. Their survival skills are considerable,
being constantly deployed on long-range patrols deep within the Amazon rainforest.

Rio de Janeiro is home to the 1st Special Forces Battalion, Brazil's leading special forces unit. The formation of this unit came about in 1953, after an aircraft on an internal flight was hijacked over the Amazon.

In 1983, a detachment from the 1st Special Forces Battalion was assigned to anti-terrorist duties, a role that it

Right: Brazilian commandos parachute into the Piranha-infested waters of the Rio Negro located near the jungle warfare centre at Manaus.

maintains to this day. All members of the unit are volunteers and undergo a 14-day selection course, which is arduous, to say the least, and has a failure rate of almost 90 per cent. Those that pass then go to a 13-week counterterrorist training course, held at a secret base located near Rio de Janeiro. The training undertaken is very similar to that of the US Delta Force and includes parachuting, heliborne insertion, fast roping, marksmanship and close-quarter combat. Teams within the counterterrorist detachment tend to be large because they will often be required to carry out long-range patrols deep within the Brazilian rainforest; in some cases, these patrols can be as large as 24 men.

Although Brazil needed American assistance to set up its original parachute training school and special forces unit, it now operates independently of outside help; however, it does maintain an association with the US 1st SFOD-D,

7th Special Forces Group and Portuguese GOE. Within Brazil, the 1st Special Forces Battalion trains with other elite army units that have a counterterrorist capability. They also work closely with the federal and state police, as well as the Brazilian Navy's GRUMEC unit.

Weapons used include the HK MP5; M16A2; Remington M870;

ENARM Pentagun; HK PSG 1; and Colt .45 pistol. In addition to firearms, the counterterrorist detachment also practises unarmed combat with knives and machetes.

Below: Brazilian commandos mount an assault on a fortified barracks during a training exercise at Brazil's jungle warfare centre in Manaus.

CANADA 🇨🇦
Joint Task Force Two (JTF-2)

*Canada remains secretive about its special forces unit, but are known to have recently deployed
in Kosovo and Afghanistan in co-operation with American and British special forces.*

Joint Task Force Two (JTF-2) was set up in April 1993 following the disbandment of the Royal Canadian Mounted Police's (RCMP's) Special Emergency Response Team (SERT). Reliable information about this unit is hard to verify, as the Canadian Armed Forces (CAF) are reluctant to discuss its very existence. This is understandable as the greatest enemy of the CAF has not been terrorism, but rather the constant defence cuts by anti-militarist politicians. In response, CAF's attitude has been that the less known about its

armed forces, the better – especially its special forces and their activities.

JTF-2 is very secretive about its size, training, operational roles and even location. Its estimated operational strength is around 200 operators plus support personnel, making it self-sufficient and independent. The role of JTF-2 seems to be one of reconnaissance and counterterrorism, as the RCMP and CSIS carry out all intelligence gathering both in Canada and overseas. JTF-2 works very closely with the British SAS and US Delta

Force, having operated with both of them in Kosovo and Afghanistan. Although JTF-2 is still a relatively new unit compared to other more established Western special forces organizations, there is no doubting its dedication and professionalism. Many of its operators have come from disbanded units such as the once proud Canadian Airborne Regiment.

Weapons used include the Colt M4; M16A2; HK MP5; 40mm (1.57in) grenade launcher; and Browning 9mm (0.35in) HP pistol.

CHILE 🇨🇱
1st Battalion Airborne Forces
Unidad Anti-Terroristes (UAT)

*Chile's special forces were first trained by American instructors, and have since maintained close
links with the US. The UAT are tasked with anti-terrorist duties.*

Chile's involvement in special forces began in 1965 with the opening of the Parachute and Special Forces School at Peldehue. The facility had US instructors who helped to form Chile's first special forces unit, the 1st Battalion Airborne Forces, raised on 2 April 1968 and operational two years later. Both a special forces unit and a paratroop battalion, it has a rigorous selection process. Those who pass can look forward to more training in other South American countries, as well as the United States. The unit played a major part in the 1973 overthrow of the Allende regime, then went on to

fight communist insurgents operating in the Andes. The Chilean forces' command structure is unusual in that one parachute battalion is under Air Force control, while the Boinas Negras Special Forces Commando Battalion is under command of the Army.

Weapons used include the M16; HK MP5; Remington M870 shotgun; Colt .45; M203 grenade launcher; and the Corvo (a curved jungle knife).

UNIDAD ANTI-TERRORISTES (UAT)
Located near Tobalaba Airport in Santiago is Chile's UAT, a unit primarily tasked with anti-terrorist and hostage

rescue duties. Its 120 operators are subdivided into seven-man teams, all commanded by an officer. Potential recruits must undergo the Chilean Army's Commando Course. Newly qualified operators move on to more advanced training, including close-quarter battle, marksmanship, unarmed combat and parachuting. Further training includes exercises with other South American special forces and specialized training in the United States.

Weapons used include the M16; Colt .45; 40mm (1.57in) grenade launcher; and a variety of foreign submachine guns.

CHINA
6th Special Warfare Group
8th Special Warfare Group
12th Special Warfare SF Detachment

China's army, man for man, is the largest in the world and subsequently have several special forces units at her disposal. They remain secretive about their operations but are known to regularly deploy on reconnaissance and intelligence gathering missions across borders.

China has the largest armed forces in the world, with some two million men and women serving with the People's Liberation Army (PLA) alone. They also have at their disposal a large number of special forces who are organized into spearhead units for large-scale assaults prior to the arrival of conventional forces. These units are known in China as the 6th Special Warfare Group and 8th Special Warfare Group, and, although they are not as

Right: Chinese special forces are seen here arresting illegal immigrants in the region near Shenzhen during a routine border patrol in March 2001.

Left: Members of Chinese special forces rigorously practise unarmed combat until it becomes second nature. This style of fighting is an intrinsic facet of the Chinese special forces soldier's arsenal.

experienced or refined as Western special forces units, China is learning fast the value of such units and their role in modern warfare.

The first special forces were disaffected members of the Kuomintang Army who decided to remain on the Chinese mainland following the Nationalists' defeat and departure to Taiwan. Having been parachute-trained by US forces, they quickly set about building up an impressive airborne capability, which

Operations

Although China is very secretive about the role of its special forces and their operations over the past few decades, it is known that they have mounted a number of low-key operations in neighbouring countries for reconnaissance and intelligence-gathering purposes. Units of the Special Warfare Group were also tasked with guarding the US Orion spyplane that was forced to land in China following a collision with a Chinese fighter aircraft in 2001. This incident led to a serious political crisis, which at one stage threatened to lead to military action, as China refused to release the captured American aircrew. The crisis was eventually resolved peacefully following intense diplomatic negotiations that secured the release of both the aircraft and its crew.

Chinese nationals have also been seen in Afghanistan, observing the operations of both British and American forces. When questioned about their presence in the region, the men stated that they were journalists reporting the war. However, it is generally believed that they were members of a Chinese special forces reconnaissance unit sent to gather intelligence on Western forces operating in the region because a small number of Chinese nationals were known to be fighting for the Al Qaeda/Taliban forces. Such an operation is no different to those carried out by both British and American special forces during the Soviet occupation of Afghanistan in the 1980s.

mini-submarines for covert insertion (as operated by North Korea against its southern neighbour) because China's long-range airborne special forces capability is limited.

Despite its essentially secretive attitude, China does procure services from many countries, and, during its bid for the 2008 Olympic Games, it sought advice from a number of Western governments on counter-terrorist tactics, techniques and procedures for use by its 12th Special Warfare SF Detachment.

China also procures military hardware from many countries; however, it is typically reluctant to discuss exactly what equipment is purchased for its special forces. Weapons used are known to include licensed copies of the Kalashnikov AK-47, AK-74 and AKS-74; and Dragunov SVD. In addition, China has also illegally copied a number of modern Western weapons, although their build quality is questionable.

amounted to three full divisions. First seeing action in Korea, this massive force then went on to oppose the Nationalist threat that prevailed during the 1960s, and their primary role was key point defence and the protection of the Communist Party elite, who greatly valued their services.

Modern Chinese special forces perform a variety of operational missions, including counterterrorism, long-range reconnaissance, sabotage, hostage rescue, hit-and-run operations and deep penetration warfare. In addition, China also uses a large number of combat divers, who specialize in both inshore and offshore maritime warfare. It is also highly probable that China possesses a fleet of

Right: Chinese officers discuss security concerns at a border checkpoint located near Shenzhen.

COLOMBIA

Lanceros
Agrupacion de Fuerzas Especiales Urbanas (AFEU)

Colombia's violent history led to the formation of her special forces arm, the Lanceros. Much of their operations, and that of the counter-terrorism unit AFEU, involve combating the country's drug cartels and insurgent factions.

Colombia's special forces unit, the Lanceros was formed in December 1955 during the civil war known as 'La Violencia'. The initial cadre for this unit was made up of officers from the Colombian Army who volunteered for special forces training. These men were then sent to the US Army's Ranger School for training in mobile warfare and counterinsurgency operations.

Having completed the training course, the officers set up an elite force of paratroopers who had the job of finding and eliminating the guerilla fighters that were terrorizing the country. This was a difficult task as Colombia's terrain is vast and varied, and has many natural obstacles, such as mountains and jungles, to hinder progress. The Lanceros quickly became adept at fighting in the jungle against the guerillas, but could never defeat them – there was just too many. There are essentially three main groups active in Colombia: the EPL, EPN and FARC. These groups have a combined strength of almost 5500 guerillas plus some 15,000 supporters.

The Lanceros' biggest problem is narcotics traffickers. Not only are they well equipped with modern weapons, but they are also seen by many poverty-stricken Colombians as good employers. This makes it hard for the Lanceros to acquire intelligence on the guerillas operating within areas controlled by the drug cartels. The locals are also well aware of what happens to anyone who opposes the drug barons. Fortunately for the Lanceros, help is at hand from the British SAS and US special forces, who provide both training and equipment. They also mount combined operations against the drug cartels. As much of their product ends up in the United Kingdom or the United States, it is not just the Colombian Government that wants to stop the drug trade.

All volunteers for the Lanceros are sent to the Escuela de Lanceros school for a 10-week course that involves marksmanship, martial arts, forced marches and training in airborne operations. Candidates are also trained to operate in mountain environments and attend a three-week jungle course. Although their prime mission is counterinsurgency, the Lanceros also carry out intelligence-gathering operations against the drug cartels and search-and-destroy missions on the well-camouflaged cocaine plantations scattered around Colombia.

Weapons used include the M16A2 with 40mm (1.57in) M203 grenade launcher; M249 Minimi SAW; HK MP5; Glock 17; Remington M870 shotgun; and Colt Commando.

AGRUPACION DE FUERZAS ESPECIALES URBANAS (AFEU)

The Agrupacion de Fuerzas Especiales Urbanas (AFEU) was formed on 8 April 1985, following a major terrorist

Left: A US-trained Lancero crouches in an illegal plantation of coca leaves during an anti-drug operation in southern Narino.

attack on Bogota's Palace of Justice in November 1985. Bogota's main criminal court was seized and more than 500 hostages taken by 30 heavily armed members of M-19, the 19 April Movement. Within this group were members of the Council of State and Supreme Court as well as ordinary Colombian citizens. Without any warning, elements of the Colombian Army assaulted the palace and fought a fierce gun battle with the terrorists, killing almost 20 in the process. However, there was a high price to pay for this operation: more than 50 hostages were killed (11 of them were members of the Supreme Court), as well as 11 soldiers. In response, AFEU was formed and tasked with hostage rescue and VIP protection.

The AFEU is a small unit with around 100 operators who are drawn from various elements of the armed forces and police. The unit is organized into six 15-man squads, with each squad consisting of two officers and 13 operators who are all under the direct command of the Commandante de las Fuerzas Armadas.

The selection process for the AFEU lasts for seven days, and those that are accepted for operator training move to Facatativa, near Bogota. Here they train in sniping, EOD, fast roping, heliborne operations and high-speed driving, and they also learn hostage rescue from aircraft, ships, buildings, buses and trains.

Above: Colombian special forces search a group of men in Barrancabermeja, a town located in Colombia's oil-producing region northeast of Bogota.

Weapons used include the HK MP5 submachine gun; M16 A2 assault rifle; M60 light machine gun; Beretta 92F pistol; and Browning HP pistol.

CUBA
Comando de Missiones Especiales (CME)

The Cuban special forces unit, CME, was first trained by the former Soviet Union's elite Spetsnaz unit. They maintain links with subversive groups around the world and operatives are known to train with their counterparts in Vietnam.

Cuba's CME is tasked with performing special operations both in Cuba and overseas. Its members are well trained and highly motivated operators who owe much to their former Soviet Spetsnaz instructors. CME operates under the control of the Ministry of Interior department and has many links with subversive groups around the world.

During the invasion of Grenada in 1983, US armed forces met resistance that was well coordinated and highly effective, and the suspicion is that the CME played a role in supporting the regular Cuban forces on the island. Cuba has since tried to improve its political relationship with the United States, but deep distrust remains. Following the terrible events of 11

September 2001, and the subsequent US operations in Afghanistan, Al Qaeda/Taliban forces captured in Afghanistan have been sent to a US-run holding facility in Cuba, known as Camp X-Ray. No doubt, CME takes great interest in this facility, which is right in its backyard.

Weapons used include the AK-47; M16; Colt Commando; and AK-74.

DENMARK 🇩🇰
Jaegerkorpset

Denmark maintains a small but elite ranger force, the Jaegerkorpset, who are also tasked with counterterrorist duties. They maintain good working relationships with the US Army Rangers and the British SAS.

Based at Aalborg Air Base in Northern Jutland is Denmark's Jaegerkorpset (Ranger Corp LRRP), an elite unit that is responsible for most of Denmark's counterterrorist capability and has gained a reputation for being highly skilful and capable, despite the unit's small size. The Jaegerkorpset's operational strength is estimated at around 100 men plus support personnel, and it is effectively an elite ranger force. It has strong links with both British and American special forces. Indeed, the unit was first established in 1961 after a number of Danish Army officers had passed the US Army's Ranger training course and then completed an operational attachment with the British SAS.

Candidates for the Jaegerkorpset have to undergo an eight-week patrol course. Successful completion leads to a period of further advanced training that includes parachuting, diving and airborne sniping from moving helicopters. As Denmark has no large support helicopters of its own, it is not uncommon to see British helicopters flying over Denmark on training exercises with the Jaegerkorpset, as both countries' special forces have a good working relationship.

Weapons used by the Jaegerkorpset include the HK MP5; HK PSG-1 7.62 sniper rifle; HK G41; HK 13E; and Remington M870 shotgun.

EGYPT 🇪🇬
Task Force 777

The early years of Task Force 777 were far from illustrious, as two disastrous and much publicised operations did much to damage their reputation. Training with the US Delta Force and Navy SEALs, they have since learned from mistakes and taken their place among the world's elite units.

Based near Cairo, Task Force 777 was formed in 1977 following a number of terrorist incidents that gave Egypt cause for concern. The initial force consisted of three officers, four NCOs and 40 operators who had little experience of counterterrorist operations, having fought against conventional military forces only.

Egypt's terrorist troubles began in 1972, when President Anwar El Sadat, wishing to make peace with Israel and in turn the West, ordered the expulsion of 30,000 Soviet advisers. This decision caused outrage among Arab terrorist groups, who now regarded Egypt as an enemy and vowed to attack its people. Nor were these idle threats, as Egyptian intelligence sources soon discovered.

Two Arab terrorist groups in particular gave Egypt reason to be cautious – the Abu Nidal Faction and the Popular Front for the Liberation of Palestine (PFLP). In 1978, Task Force 777 was dispatched to Cyprus after the hijacking by the PFLP of a Cyprus Air passenger aircraft en route from Cairo to Nicosia. With only an hour to prepare for such an operation, nobody thought to notify the Cypriot authorities of TF 777's imminent arrival, a simple mistake that was to have devastating consequences. As the operators of TF 777 made their way across the tarmac towards the hijacked aircraft, local police units mistook them for terrorist reinforcements and opened fire. The ensuing firefight lasted for almost 80 minutes and cost the lives of 15 TF 777 operators and several Cypriots.

As bad as this incident was for TF 777, worse was to come. The second disastrous operation for TF 777 occurred when Palestinian Abu Nidal terrorists hijacked Egyptair Flight 648 at Athens Airport and ordered the aircrew to fly to Luqa Airport in Malta. The aircraft was hijacked in revenge for Egypt's failure to protect terrorists who had seized the cruise liner *Achille Lauro*. Ironically, the aircraft hijacked was the very one used

SPECIAL FORCES ON LAND

Left: Egyptian special forces show off their free-fall skills in the Eastern Desert during a ceremony to celebrate the 25th anniversary of the October War, fought against Israel in 1973.

explosives were detonated, the force of the blast was so powerful that it blew six rows of seats out of their mountings, killing 20 passengers in the process. As if this were not enough, the operators fired indiscriminately when they stormed the aircraft, killing several more passengers and injuring a number of others. To escape this carnage, the remaining passengers ran out of the aircraft and were cut down by snipers positioned on nearby emergency vehicles who mistook them for terrorists. In all, some 57 hostages were killed, making it one of the the worst special forces' blunder ever. Needless to say, TF 777 was temporarily disbanded after this incident, pending an inquiry, although it was allowed to reform after a major change in its ranks and organization.

For understandable reasons, the new TF 777 likes to maintain a low profile and operates within Egypt as a counterterrorist unit. In recent years, it has been involved in Egypt's civil war against the 'Brotherhood' and has lost a number of operators. TF 777 now trains with a number of Western units, including the US Delta Force and SEALS, and France's GIGN.

The equipment used by TF 777 includes Mil-8 and Westland commando helicopters; unmarked vehicles for internal police support; and a small number of boats.

Weapons used by TF 777 include the HK MP5; M16 A2; Remington M870; and AK-47.

Below: Egyptian commandos storm a beach during Exercise Bright Star (October 2001).

to transport the *Achille Lauro* terrorists in the first place.

This time around, Egypt made sure that the Maltese government was aware of TF 777's involvement and that the unit was on its way in a C-130. However, upon arrival at Luqa, TF 777 made a number of fatal mistakes, and again these were to prove catastrophic. First, they failed to carry out any surveillance on the aircraft prior to assaulting it. Secondly, they failed to interview any of the hostages who had survived an attempted execution by the terrorists. Thirdly, they failed to study blueprints of the hijacked Boeing 737 aircraft. And fourthly, they did not to intend to use stun grenades to disorientate the terrorists during the initial assault phase; instead, their plan was to use a higher charge than normal to blow a hole in the aircraft's roof, the theory being that this would create an entry hole for the operators and at the same time stun the terrorists.

The reality, however, was completely different. When the

EIRE (Republic of Ireland) ■ ■
Sciathan Fianoglach an Airm (Army Rangers Wing)

The Army Rangers Wing is the Republic of Ireland's special forces arm and are also responsible for counterterrorist duties. They play an important part in providing the United Nations with part of its peacekeeping force.

Based at the Curragh Camp in County Kildare is Sciathan Fianoglach an Airm (Army Rangers Wing), the Irish counterterrorist and special operations unit. Having just 100–125 operators, this unit more than makes up for its small size by ensuring that its operators are highly professional and extremely well trained. It was first formed in the early 1970s after a cadre of around 25 suitable candidates from the Irish Army were sent to Fort Benning, Georgia, for special forces training. Once set up, this unit made contact with a number of other police and special forces units to exchange ideas on hostage rescue and counterterrorist operations.

Although the United Kingdom has a close relationship with the Republic of Ireland and provides specialized military training to the Irish Armed Forces in a number of key areas, this does not include contact and operational training with the SAS as the political situation in Northern Ireland remains unstable. Operational roles set out for the Army Rangers Wing include counterterrorism, sabotage, VIP protection, counter-insurgency operations, raiding, hostage rescue and covert reconnaissance.

The Irish Armed Forces have only 18,000 regular soldiers and 22,000 reservists, but they play an important part in supporting the United Nations on peacekeeping operations throughout the world, with the Army Rangers Wing on short notice to deploy should a crisis develop. The Irish are very proud of their special forces capability and with good reason, as every operator has had to complete a very long and highly demanding training course. Potential recruits are required to pass an arduous four-week selection course before being considered for the Rangers' six-month basic skills course, which includes weapons and explosives, hostage rescue, combat medicine, close-quarter battle, survival training, mountaineering, long-range patrolling and basic parachuting. After completion of the course, candidates can volunteer for more specialized training courses, such as HAHO and HALO operations, fast roping, EOD, combat diving, boat handling, amphibious operations and sniper training.

Weapons used include the Austrian 5.56 Steyr AUG; the M16 with M203 grenade launcher; the SIG P-226 pistol; the Remington 870; the Accuracy International AI 96 sniper rifle; and the HK MP5.

FINLAND ✚

Finland maintains a small conscript military force who are particularly renowned for their survival and reconnaissance skills in arctic conditions, a tradition dating back to World War II when elite Finnish rangers on skis would take on Soviet forces.

Although only a small country, Finland is very proud of its conscript military forces and wants to involve them more in peacekeeping operations as a means of providing operational training.

In 1996, the Finnish Defence Forces embarked on a new strategy to better prepare them for any possible conflict situation and specifically identified the need for a dedicated special forces unit. Unusually within the West, it is the first force to feature conscript volunteer rather than regular volunteers.

Volunteers undergo psychological as well as physical tests prior to being accepted for special forces training.

Successful candidates then undergo parachute and commando training before being declared operational.

Those that volunteer for ranger-type roles need to undertake further courses in reconnaissance and survival techniques, a skill for which the Finnish Army is renowned, particularly in harsh winter conditions.

FRANCE ▮ ▮
Légion Étrangère
Commandement des Operations Speciales (COS)
Groupement Speciale Autonome (GSA)
Groupe d'Intervention Gendarmerie Nationale (GIGN)

France has many special forces units at her disposal, with the illustrious Foreign Legion at the forefront of any operation. The GSA is an independent army command under the recently formed French Special Operations Command (COS). The GIGN is charged with counter-terrorism and although a police unit, has seen action around the world.

The Légion Étrangère (Foreign Legion) was formed in 1831 to help maintain control of the French colonies in North Africa. However, after a series of major actions, it soon became clear that this highly effective force had the potential to be exploited in other regions around the world. Up until 1962, its headquarters were located at Sidi Bel Abbès in Algeria; however, after Algeria was granted independence, it moved to its current location in Corsica. The Foreign Legion is largely made up of foreign mercenaries and French citizens, who are commanded by French officers. Indeed, the only language spoken within the Legion is French.

Below: Legionnaires march proudly during a victory parade in Marseille.

Above: Legionnaires from the 13ème Demi-brigade de Legion Étrangere (13e DBLE) man a .50in cal. Browning heavy machine gun at a vehicle checkpoint in Bosnia-Herzegovina.

The Foreign Legion fought with great distinction in both world wars and later in Indo-China; however, its most famous action was the defence of Dien Bien Phu in 1954, when its men fought bravely against overwhelming odds until being ordered to surrender. Although the Foreign Legion is not part of France's special forces orbit, it has been used for special forces operations around the world on behalf of France. In 1991, the Foreign Legion fought in the Gulf War as part of the Allied Coalition Force assembled against Iraq and received considerable praise for its knowledge and expertise in desert warfare.

The Foreign Legion has also had its fair share of controversy, the most famous incident being the Algerian mutiny in 1961, when a Legion regiment mutinied in support of Algerian settlers who were trying to prevent independence. Despite having an excellent combat record, the

Foreign Legion Units

The Foreign Legion operates the following combat units, each with particular responsibilities:

1er Regiment Étrangere de Cavalerie (1 REC) − based at Orange, this is part of the French 6th Light Armoured Division. It consists of three armoured car companies and a mechanized APC infantry company.

2ème Regiment Étrangere d'Infanterie (2 REI) − based at Nîmes, it has served in virtually every French colonial campaign since its formation.

3ème Regiment Étrangere d'Infanterie (3 REI) − based at Kourou in French Guyana, this is the specialist jungle warfare unit and is also responsible for defence of the French missile-launching site located there.

5ème Regiment Étrangere (5 RE) − based on French islands located in the Pacific, this unit is responsible for the French nuclear weapon test site situated on Mururoa Atoll.

6ème Regiment Étrangere de Genie (6 REG) − based in Plain d'Albion, this unit was formed in 1984 and provides engineer support for overseas detachments. In addition, the unit also has combat swimmers and underwater EOD teams that are part of Detachment d'intervention opérationnelle subaquatique.

2ème Regiment Étrangere de Parachutistes (2 REP) − based at Calvi in Corsica, this airborne commando regiment is a rapid deployment unit that comprises six companies, all with different combat specialities.

13ème Demi-brigade Legion Étrangere (13 DBLE) − based at Djibouti in Africa, this half-brigade comprises an armoured car squadron, an infantry company and a support company armed with heavy machine guns, mortars and MILAN anti-tank missiles.

Detachment de Legion Étrangere à Mayotte (DLEM) − this detachment is responsible for the island of Mayotte in the Indian Ocean.

regiment was disbanded in disgrace as an example to others.

In 1988, the French Army was reduced in size because France wanted an all-professional army like that of the British, rather than a conscript army. As part of these cutbacks, the Legion was reduced in size to 7500 men and withdrew from a number of its overseas bases.

The Foreign Legion reserves two regiments specifically for the tasks of recruiting and training: 1er Regiment étranger (1 RE), based at Aubagne,

Right: A French Legionnaire from the 2ème Regiment Étrangere de Parachutistes fires his 7.62mm (0.3in) AA52 machine gun during a training exercise in the Corsican mountains.

Below: Legionnaires from 3ème Regiment Étrangere d'Infanterie (3 REI), armed with 5.56mm (0.22in) FAMAS assault rifles, carry out a river patrol in French Guyana.

Left: A sniper from 2ème Regiment Étrangere de Parachutistes (2 REP) observes a potential target during a training exercise.

more than 100 different countries. In theory, there are no French members of the Legion, apart from officers, though many get around this ban by claiming to be French Canadian, Belgian or Swiss. Most enlist under an alias, as they are running away from someone or something; however, it should be remembered that the Legion does not accept those with a criminal record.

Once enlisted, the recruits attend a demanding three-week induction course which spells out precisely what life in the Legion involves; there are always those who have a naive and romantic vision of the Foreign Legion and what it represents. During this period, recruits may leave of their own free will, or they may be discharged if found to be unsuitable for service. Those surviving induction have to serve for a further period of at least five months before embarking on further training with 4 RE. During this time, they concentrate on physical training as well as marksmanship, and for some there are opportunities for specialist training in signalling and engineering. Those wishing to become NCOs must first attend a demanding eight-week course to qualify for promotion to corporal and a 14-week course for sergeants.

Weapons used by the French Foreign Legion include the FAMAS assault rifle; M249 Minimi light machine gun; UZI submachine gun; and HK MP5 submachine gun.

COMMANDEMENT DES OPERATIONS SPECIALES (COS)

Combat experience during the Gulf War highlighted a number of operational deficiencies in France's military capabilities, in particular

near Marseilles, is responsible for all new recruits, and 4er Regiment étranger (4 RE) at Casteinaudar, also near Marseilles, is responsible for training both recruits and NCOs. Aubagne is now considered the new

spiritual home of the French Foreign Legion, where its band and museum are located.

The Foreign Legion accepts volunteers from all over the world, and it currently contains soldiers from tactical assets, organic transport assets, operational procedures, communications, and command and control structures.

In response, France set about creating a unified command structure to bring together Army, Navy and Air Force special operations forces under one roof and make them answerable only to the Armed Forces Chief of Staff. The new command, the Commandement des Operations Speciales (COS), became operational in 1992 with a mandate that stated its primary mission:

Below: French Legionnaires take a break during operations in Lebanon in 1982.

Groupement Speciale Autonome (GSA)

Based at Pau, GSA, the Army's Special Autonomous Group, is an independent Army command within COS (French Special Operations Command). The unit consists of the DAOS special operations aviation unit, the 1er RPIMa and three support units – research and development, personnel, and training and logistics. GSA is commanded by a brigadier general and operates under the direct control of COS.

GSA is tasked with acting as a link between the French Army and COS, and is responsible for sourcing and developing new equipment for French special forces. It ensures that new equipment is compatible with that already used by other services; plans training exercises; provides administrative support; and helps to develop joint special operations doctrine. GSA also maintains stocks of specialized equipment and vehicles for rapid deployment units.

To plan, coordinate and conduct at the command level all operations carried out by units that are specifically organized, trained and equipped to attain military or paramilitary objectives as defined by the Armed Forces Chief of Staff.

Above: A Milan mounted on a French Foreign Legion jeep marks a moving target during a routine training exercise.

Above: A French Foreign Legionnaire stands on guard with his FAMAS F1 rifle, with attached bayonet, with the classic kepi hat displaying his military allegiance.

Based at Taverny, COS operates under the command of a major general or an officer of equivalent rank. It is composed of the following units:

1er Regiment parachutiste D, infanterie marine (1er RPIMa) – an Army unit that carries on the traditions of the Free French SAS units of World War II. Although only a battalion-sized force, 1er RPIMa is France's primary special operations unit and is tasked with conducting missions such as long-range reconnaissance patrolling, light strike and counterterrorism (along with GIGN). Despite its title, it has no connection to Naval infantry units.

Detachment ALAT operations speciales (DAOS) – the Army's special operations aviation unit (comparable to the US 160th SOAR), which is composed of two special operations helicopter squadrons. The first squadron operates Cougars and Pumas, while the second squadron operates armed Gazelles (soon to be replaced by the Eurocopter Tiger). (The 1er RPIMa and DAOS form a separate subcommand within COS, known as Groupement speciale autonome (GSA). GSA operates in a very similar manner to the US Army's Special Operations Command.)

Above: Seven flames and a grenade. The Legion's symbol at one time denoting all elite French forces (the French army badge has only six flames). The regiment number is usually stamped inside the grenade.

Commandement des Fusiliers marins commandos (COFUSCO) – the naval component of COS.

Groupement de Combat en milieu clos (GCMC) – a 17-man force tasked with conducting maritime counterterrorist operations.

Commando Hubert CASM (Commando Hubert: Commando d'action sous marine) – the Navy's combat diver unit and comparable to the British SBS and the US Navy SEALs.

Division des Operations speciales (DOS) – equipped with C-130 Hercules and C-160 Transall transport aircraft.

Escadrille des helicopteres speciaux (EHS) – performs both special operations and combat search and rescue (CSAR) missions in support of French and Allied forces.

Commando Parachutiste de l'air no. 10 (CPA 10) – provides a link between air and ground assets – in short, combat search and rescue, FAC, laser target designation and combat air traffic control.

In addition to these units, COS also has a research and development branch, an administrative support staff, and a sizeable group of reservists who

Below: French Legionnaires rapidly debus from a French Puma helicopter during a work-up exercise.

specialize in conducting civil affairs operations.

GROUPE D'INTERVENTION GENDARMERIE NATIONALE (GIGN)

Formed in 1974, the Groupe d'Intervention Gendarmerie Nationale (GIGN) is one of the most active police counterterrorist units in the world today. With only 87 operators, this small but highly efficient unit carried out over 650 operations between 1974 and 1985, freeing more than 500 hostages, making more than 1000 arrests and eliminating dozens of terrorists in the process. These operations did, however, come with a heavy price: five operators were killed and dozens wounded.

Above: A French Legionnaire marks his target after firing a burst from his 5.56mm (0.22in) FAMAS assault rifle. Note the weapon's built-in bipod which is designed to give the firer extra accuracy.

One of its most successful recent operations took place on 26 December 1994, after a group of Algerian terrorists hijacked an Air France airbus in Algiers and ordered it to fly to Marseilles. GIGN operators hoped for a peaceful ending; however, following the murder of three of the hostages, they had no choice but to storm the aircraft. During the rescue operation, in which 173 passengers were freed unharmed, four terrorists were shot dead and nine GIGN operators wounded. It was later discovered that the terrorists had been planning to crash the aircraft into central Paris, a plan that thankfully was foiled.

Left: A French Legionnaire from the 6ème Regiment Étrangere de Genie, frogmen unit, gives orders to his section during a long-range reconnaissance patrol mission.

Right: It's a long way down to the bottom, as this French Legionnaire is finding out. Special skills such as rappelling and abseiling are taught to Legionnaires as part of normal training, as much of their time is spent overseas where these skills often prove vital to success.

The GIGN recruits exclusively from the ranks of the Gendarmerie, and all volunteers must have an exemplary record, as well as a minimum of five years' experience before they will be considered as a potential candidate. However, even with these high standards, on average, only seven per cent of all applicants is accepted. New recruits then attend a 10-month training course before being declared operational within one of the four 15-man groups that make up the GIGN. In addition to these teams, there is a command and support group and a special hostage negotiation cell.

Although the GIGN is technically a police unit, it operates all over the world and has seen action in far flung corners of the world with French interests such as, Djibouti, Lebanon, New Caledonia, Sudan and the Island of Comoros. To help prepare them for such diverse deployments, GIGN operators regularly train in alpine, desert and urban conditions. Typical training involves parachuting; combat shooting – each operator fires some 300 rounds per day; unarmed combat; fast driving; sniping; scuba diving; and mountaineering. In addition to this training, further courses are available in HAHO/HALO operations, EOD and maritime operations.

Weapons used by the GIGN include the HK MP5 submachine gun; HK G3 assault rifle; French FAMAS assault rifle; Beretta 92F pistol; .357 magnum revolver; Remington M870 shotgun; and the Barret .50 long-range sniper rifle.

GERMANY ▬
Kommando Spezialkrafte (KSK)
Grenzschutzgruppe 9 (GSG-9)

Germany's KSK was recently formed to safeguard the country's national interests. Formed to operate in much the same global role as the more established and renowned GSG-9 counterpart, it could very well supplant the latter's overseas operations.

Based at Calw in Baden–Wurttemberg, the Kommando Spezialkrafte (KSK) was formed in 1995 primarily to protect or rescue German nationals at risk in overseas conflicts. At present, the unit is working up to its brigade strength of 1000 fully trained operators, but still has some way to go before achieving this figure. The impetus for forming the KSK dates back to 1994, when Germany found that it had no suitably trained force to rescue 11 of its nationals who were trapped during the Rwandan civil war. Fortunately for the Germans, help was at hand in the shape of Belgium and French paratroopers, who rescued the 11.

However, the German government was highly embarrassed by this incident and appointed a senior Army Brigadier to oversee the formation and development of a new special forces unit, with an operational

*Below: KSK operators practise hostage-rescue drills during manoeuvre **Schneller Adler (Fast Eagle), held in Baumholder near Kaiserslautern on 11 September 1997.** While not fully up to operational strength, some 10,000 regular soldiers of the German Army have received some degree of special forces training so that they can support the KSK on operations if the need arises. Note the operator in the middle of the group carrying an armoured shield for protection against small-calibre rounds.*

Left: A KSK soldier stands guard in a destroyed house during a one-day official visit to Kabul by German Chancellor Gerhard Schroeder on 9 May 2002.

Range Scout Companies, which were part of the three West German airborne brigades commando companies dating from the Cold War. The unit now comprises an HQ, four commando companies, a long-range reconnaissance company, a communications company and a logistics company. Each fighting company has four platoons, one of which specializes in hostage rescue, both within Germany and overseas. In addition, platoons also specialize in different areas, including airborne operations, amphibious operations, ground infiltration, and arctic or mountainous warfare.

As with many other special forces units, the KSK operates on the tried-and-tested principle of four-man teams, with the long-range reconnaissance company operating as many as 40 four-man teams at any given time, each capable of operating

independently of each other. Should an emergency develop overseas involving German nationals or interests, KSK would deploy and operate under the control of the German Crisis Section and would be responsible for conducting missions such as deep penetration raids; strategic reconnaissance; hostage rescue; counterterrorist operations; peacekeeping; the rescue and recovery of downed pilots; military crisis deterrence operations; and the defence of German or NATO territory. KSK has the means of attacking high-value targets, including enemy airfields, HQs and lines of communication, but its main operational priority is that of protecting German citizens in war or conflict zones and hostage rescue.

The KSK is not yet fully up to strength, but it still has more than enough trained operators to undertake low-level operations. This they demonstrated in 1999, when a detachment from the KSK deployed to Kosovo as a close-protection detail for high-ranking German officials. In

capability similar to that of Britain's SAS or the United States' Delta Force. The Brigadier recognized that his force would have to be capable of rapid deployment anywhere in the world at a moment's notice and that it would have to be capable of operating in any terrain, whether arctic, desert or jungle. He also understood that forming such a unit from scratch would be no easy task, and, where possible, he used existing soldiers who were mature and experienced.

Even though KSK is trained for hostage-rescue operations, it is a military unit, to be used in military operations, and not another counter-terrorist force, such as GSG-9. GSG-9 is an excellent unit, but because it is a Federal Border Guards unit it is restricted by law from operating overseas on military missions. (That said, it did break this law in 1977 when it carried out a spectacular rescue mission in Mogadishu, Somalia.) This legal restriction also applies to other elite German police units, including the SEKs (SWAT-type units).

KSK was initially formed from soldiers of the Army's two Long

Right: A GSG-9 sniper marks a potential target during a training exercise.

Above: The emblem of GSG-9.

2001, a small force was deployed to Afghanistan following the abduction of a number of German nationals by the Taliban. However, the nationals were released unharmed after intense diplomatic pressure was brought to bear on the Taliban rulers. The KSK is also known to have provided protection for German government officials taking part in the G8 summits, where the VIPs attending are possible terrorist targets.

When the KSK is fully operational, it will be organized as follows:

HQ and Signal Company – HQ Platoon, three Signal Platoons, Long Range Recon Signal Platoon (all operators being trained in SATCOM, HF, and LOS communication).

Commando/Long-Range Recon Company – HQ element, Long Range Recon Commando Platoon, Long Range Recon Platoon.

Each Commando Company consists of an HQ Platoon and four Commando Platoons, each specializing in different operational areas: land infiltration; air infiltration (HALO-capable); amphibious operations; mountainous and arctic climate operations. Each platoon consists of four teams of four men each. One man acts as team

leader, and each of the four men specialize in one of the following areas: communications, medical, explosives, or operations and intelligence. One of the four platoons is trained in conducting hostage rescue and counterterrorist operations, with some operators trained in high-speed defensive and offensive driving.

In addition, the Support Company includes a Logistics Platoon, Parachute Equipment Platoon, Maintenance and Repair Platoon, Medical Platoon and Training Platoon.

Weapons and equipment used by the KSK include HK G36 assault rifles; HK MP5 SD3 9mm (0.35in) submachine guns; HK G8 assault rifles; HK512 12-gauge shotguns; G22 sniper rifles; P8 9mm (0.35in) pistols;

HK PII underwater pistols; HK21 light machine gun; HK23 light machine guns; MG3 general-purpose machine guns; and Milan and Panzerfaust 3 anti-tank weapons.

Operators also have access to night-vision sights, tactical lights and laser-aiming devices.

Vehicles used include Mercedes Benz G Wagons, unmarked cars and Unimog two-ton trucks. Operators also practise insertion and extraction techniques using German Luftwaffe Bell 212s and Sikorsky CH-53s.

GRENZSCHUTZGRUPPE 9 (GSG-9)

GSG-9 was formed as a response to the terrorist incident at the Munich Olympics in 1972. Arab 'Black September' terrorists broke into the Olympic village, taking a number of Israeli athletes hostage and killing others. A police rescue attempt went tragically wrong and left nine hostages, four terrorists and a policeman dead. The loss of so many lives was put down to the fact that the German police were not prepared for dealing with hostage rescue situations, and this prompted the creation of a

Right: KSK operators practise a hostage rescue drill at the unit's base in Baumholder on 11 September 1997.

Mogadishu, Somalia

For GSG-9, the operation in Mogadishu, Somalia, was its finest hour. On 18 October 1977, the unit stormed a Lufthansa airliner at Mogadishu airport, killing three Palestinian terrorists and wounding one more without any losses to their own operators or the hostages on board. The operation had been well planned and executed, and it took the terrorists by surprise. In part, this success was down to the British SAS, who provided two highly trained operators equipped with stun grenades and various assault weapons. Indeed, it was an SAS operator who shot and wounded a female terrorist during the assault. The success of this operation subsequently led to a very close relationship being formed with the British SAS, a relationship that remains strong to this day.

dedicated counterterrorist force. Formed on 17 April 1973, GSG-9 is a paramilitary arm of the German police force and is organized as follows:

Commander GSG-9
Operations staff
External Advisers and Technical Support Staff (including medical personnel)
GSG-9/1 – counterterrorist assault group
GSG-9/2 – responsible for maritime anti-terrorist operations
GSG-9/3 – airborne unit para-trained in HALO and free-fall parachuting
GSG-9/4 – reserve counterterrorist assault group

At its peak, GSG-9 had an operational strength of almost 250 operators, but this figure has now been reduced to some 200 regular personnel because Germany now has the additional resources of the KSK and local police SEKs (SWAT teams). The formation of these new units has put the future of GSG-9 in doubt, for some Germans take the view that GSG-9 is now redundant, arguing that the KSK can handle hostage rescue and counter-terrorist operations both in Germany and overseas – and has the legal mandate to do so. This presents GSG-9 with a problem, as it is legally forbidden from deploying overseas on counterterrorist operations (although this injunction has been ignored on a number of occasions, as witnessed in Mogadishu, for instance).

Members of the unit are all volunteers, either from the army or border police, and undergo six months of arduous training before being declared operational. In addition to the physical training, operators are expected to have a good knowledge of both police and legal matters, and great emphasis is placed on further academic studies. The failure rate among candidates is very high: only 20 per cent of each intake is accepted. These demanding standards have made GSG-9 an outstanding modern counterterrorist force, and although its future path is uncertain, it has many friends around the world who greatly admire and respect their capabilities.

Weapons used by GSG-9 include the HK MP5; SIG SG 551-1P special operations assault rifle; HK G8 assault rifle and HK PSG-1; and Mauser SP86 and SP66 sniper rifles. Pistols used include the Ruger .357 magnum revolver; 9mm (0.35in) Glock 17; HK P7, P9 and P9S; and Walther P5 and P88 models.

GSG-9 also operates a large fleet of both marked and unmarked vehicles, including the Mercedes 280, which have special modifications that allow operators to fire through the windscreen while the car is on the move. In addition to small boats, GSG-9 has its own aviation group, the Bundesgrenzschutz-Fliegergruppe, which has some of Germany's best pilots within its ranks.

Right: A GSG-9 operative clad in classic urban-combat gear, with para-style helmet and airborne harness for fast-roping helicopter deployment.

GREECE 🇬🇷
Greek Special Forces Directorate

The Greek special forces date back to World War II and today rank among the most modern elite units around the world. They saw action in 1974 against Turkish forces in Cyprus. Though the two nations have since entered dialogue, Greece nonetheless maintains military preparedness.

The Greek Special Forces Directorate lives by the motto 'Those who dare, win'. Its special forces are amongst the most modern in the world, and they are capable of mounting land, sea and air operations on an impressive scale.

The Hellenic special forces organization was formed in Egypt following the Battle of Crete in May 1941, which forced the Hellenic Government to flee Greece and reform in the Middle East. In order to retake Crete, the Hellenic Army formed a number of new military units that were capable of operating as commandos against the occupying German and Italian forces. One of these units was the Company of the Chosen Immortals, which was established in August 1942, under the command of Major Stephanakis. Although only 200-strong when formed, this unit

operated in North Africa with the British SAS and quickly gained a fearsome reputation for its raiding techniques.

The unit was later renamed the Sacred Company, a title that had been used on four prior occasions within the Greek Army. Following their success in North Africa, the Sacred Company redeployed to Italy and the Dodecanese, where they fought many successful actions until their disbandment at the end of World War II.

During the Greek civil war (1945–50), many ex-members of the Sacred Company fought as a raiding force in a manner very similar to that of the British SAS and SBS. In 1946, a Mountain Raiding Warfare Company was formed to deal with armed communist groups that were active in the mountain areas. Eventually, its operational strength grew to 40

companies, which remained active right up until the end of the revolt in 1950. After the civil war ended, the Greeks decided to retain a special forces capability and, with American help, set about creating a Parachute School at Aspropyrgros of Attica, near Athens. In addition to airborne forces, the Greeks also set up specialist maritime units that operate under the command of the Special Forces Directorate in Thessaloniki.

During the Turkish invasion of Cyprus in 1974, Greek special forces fought running battles against the Turkish forces, and some 33 special forces soldiers lost their lives. A ceasefire was eventually negotiated by the United Nations, which led to the partitioning of the country. It was a costly war, both in political and human terms, and one that could have been avoided.

Since then, Greece and Turkey have entered dialogue over the future of Cyprus; however, in recent years there have been a number of incidents that have taken the two countries to the brink of another war. The Greeks are very mindful of Turkey's military capability and have spent considerable time and effort in recent years expanding and modernizing their special forces in preparation for any possible threat.

Left: Greek special forces on board a high-powered inflatable boat mount a mock assault off the coast near the training camp of Megalo Pefko, which is located close to Athens.

A volunteer force, the Greek Special Forces Directorate is comprised of one Ranger Regiment, one Marine Brigade, one Parachute Regiment and one Special Operations Command.

Weapons used by the Greek special forces include the M16 A2 assault rifle with M203 grenade launcher; Colt M4 assault rifle; M249 light machine gun; and HK MP5 submachine gun.

Above: Greek special forces practise maritime insertion techniques with a Chinook helicopter. If operationally viable, the helicopter can actually land in the sea to both load or unload equipment.

INDIA
Special Rangers Group

India's many ethnic groups, and ongoing disputes with Pakistant sees the SGR constantly involved in actions, most recently in the border areas near Kashmir.

India's Special Rangers Group (SGR) is a combination of military and police units, tasked with mounting anti-terrorist operations throughout India and its border areas near Kashmir. It is a massive force, with some 7000 personnel drawn from a variety of military and police backgrounds and reflecting India's ethnic mix. The Special Rangers Group has been involved in numerous

Left: An Indian commando stands guard outside the US information centre in Calcutta on 14 June 2002, following a car bomb attack on the US consulate in Karachi in neighbouring Pakistan.

actions in recent years, including the siege of the Golden Temple at Amritsar in 1986 by Sikh militants and ongoing counterinsurgency operations against terrorists and drug traffickers sponsored by Pakistan. In addition, the SRG provides protection for VIPs during high-level state visits.

Weapons

Preferred weaponry includes the Sterling 9mm (0.35in) sub-machine gun and FN FAL 7.62mm (0.3in) assault rifle.

IRAN 🇮🇷

Little is known of Iran's special forces, with one unit first set up with the help of the US. Following the fall of the Shah it disbanded, but some member stayed on to help form new units.

Iran's original special forces unit, the 25th Airborne Brigade, was set up with American assistance in the early 1970s and operated as part of the Iranian Imperial Armed Forces. Following the fall of the Shah of Iran in 1979, however, the unit was disbanded, and many of its former members were forced into exile in the West. Those that stayed behind in Iran helped to form a Special Forces Division, which comprised several new units that operated under the command and

Left: An Iranian soldier from the Iran and Iraq war. He carries a Heckler and Koch G3 but most of the weapons used by the Iranian Special Forces are nowadays more likely to be of Russian origin.

control of different elements of the Iranian Armed Forces – the regular army, the Bassidjis (irregular forces) and the Pasdaran (Islamic Revolutionary Guards – IRGC).

During the Iran–Iraq War, elements of the special forces supported the Revolutionary Guard in offensive operations; however, they achieved little success, as their skills were wasted on large-scale assaults rather than small surgical actions. Since the end of the war, Iranian special forces have operated in Lebanon, training Hizbollah guerrillas; Bosnia, gathering intelligence on US forces; and Sudan, training soldiers in sabotage and infiltration techniques).

Weapons known to be used by the Iranian Special Forces Division include the M16 assault rifle; AK-47 assault rifle; AK-74 assault rifle; SVD sniper rifle; and RPG-7.

IRAQ 🇮🇶
Republican Guard

Iraq's shock troops, the Republican Guard performed well in the Iran-Iraq war but are above all else Saddam Hussein's personal protection force.

Based in Baghdad and consisting of seven divisions are Iraq's shock troops, the Republican Guard. Originally formed to protect not just the government, but also its tanks, mechanized infantry and ground troops, the Iraqi Republican Guard performed so well during the Iran–Iraq war that it received special forces

status and found itself protecting Iraq's President Saddam Hussein. The decision to change the unit's status was also in part due to a major reorganization within the Iraqi armed forces. This change affected all aspects of the Iraqi military, including its arms suppliers, hierarchy, deployments and political character.

The Iraqi Army has an estimated strength of 1.7 million personnel, including reserves and paramilitary forces, and the Republican Guard accounts for a significant percentage of this figure. In 1987, the Iraqi Army had seven corps, five armoured divisions (each with one armoured brigade and one mechanized brigade) and three mechanized divisions (each with one armoured brigade and two or more mechanized brigades). By the end of the Iran–Iraq war, the Iraqi Army General Headquarters supervised up to 10 corps headquarters, which carried out logistical and administrative tasks as well as directing operations. Each corps commanded as many as 10

Below: An Iraqi soldier wearing the customary black beret which bears the gold eagle emblem, and Iraqi national symbol. He carries a 7.6cm (3in) AKMS assault rifle.

Republican Guard Division

A typical Republican Guard armoured division consists of the following: a divisional headquarters; two tank brigades; three tank battalions; one motorized special forces company; one mechanized infantry battalion; one engineering company; one medium rocket launcher battery; one reconnaissance platoon; one mechanized infantry brigade; three mechanized infantry battalions; one anti-tank company; one reconnaissance platoon; a divisional artillery brigade with three self-propelled artillery battalions (155mm (6.1in) SP); four self-propelled artillery battalions (two 152mm (5.98in) SP and two 122mm (4.8in) SP); three motorized special forces battalions; one anti-tank battalion; one reconnaissance battalion; and one engineer battalion.

mechanized divisions, depending on the operational situation at the time.

Within the Army, the brigade was normally the smallest unit to operate independently. Also subordinate to the General Headquarters was the corps–sized Republican Guard Forces Command, which consisted of three armoured divisions, one infantry division and one commando division, all of which operated separately from the regular army.

When Saddam Hussein invaded Kuwait in 1990, the Republican Guard played a major part in the invasion and, once operations had ceased, acted as a theatre reserve force. When Western military planners plotted the ousting of Iraqi forces from Kuwait, it appeared high on the list of targets as it posed a significant threat to Allied ground forces. From the outset of Operation Desert Storm, the Republican Guard was subjected to constant air attack, but never broke. This was a remarkable feat as its troops were deployed in open desert, where they had little or no cover; however, they stood their ground and put up stiff resistance.

During the ground invasion phase of Desert Storm, the American 24th Infantry Division encountered heavy resistance from the 47th and 49th Infantry divisions, who were part of the Nebuchadnezzar Division of the Republican Guard. In addition, the 26th Commando Brigade fought with great distinction against American infantry and armoured units. Eventually the US 1st Armored Division succeeded in defeating elements of the Tawakalna Division, while the 3rd Armored Division engaged remnants of the Tawalzalaa, Madina and Adnan divisions of the Republican Guard.

Following the end of the Gulf War, the Republican Guard was used to suppress anti-government forces as well as elements of the Iraqi Army who mounted an unsuccessful coup against Saddam. The Republican Guard has reorganized and re-equipped since the Gulf War, and it remains a potent force. It is currently commanded by Qusai Saddam Hussein, and the Chief of Staff is Staff General Ibrahim Abd Al Sattar Mohammad Al-Tikriti.

Weapons used by the Republican Guard include the AK-47 assault rifle; AK-74 assault rifle; AKSU-74 submachine gun; RPK light machine gun; Type 74 medium machine gun; and RPG-7 anti-tank rocket launcher.

ISRAEL ⬦
Sayeret Golani
Sayeret Mat'kal
Sayeret Tzanhanin

Israel's special forces are second to none. With an ongoing bloody history ever since the creation of the state, the nation maintains one of the highest levels of military preparedness in the world and is constantly in action against terrorist factions within her own borders.

Israel's special forces are amongst the most active and proficient in the world. They have to be: Israel lives under perpetual threat of violence and bloodshed. The roots of Israel's special forces history can be traced back to the 1930s, after Captain Charles Orde Wingate formed special night squads to fight an anti-guerrilla war against Arab intruders. During World War II, Palestinian Jews fought against the Axis forces in Eritrea as part of the British 51st Middle East Commando and the Special Interrogation Group in North Africa.

After failing to defeat the Israelis in the 1948–49 war, the Arabs changed their tactics and began mounting infiltration operations into Israel. Arab guerillas usually entered the country through the large and open Negev Desert, which was very hard for the Israeli forces to defend with their limited resources. To combat these infiltrations, Israel formed a number of special units. Amongst them was Unit 101, a small formation of some 60 volunteers who trained for night fighting. After less than four months, however, the unit was disbanded and its members incorporated into the first Israeli Defence Force (IDF) regiment, the 890th. This regiment eventually became the 202nd Parachute Brigade, a unit that greatly distinguished itself during the Battle of the Mitla Pass in October 1956 and subsequent spearhead actions.

Above: A soldier with the elite Israeli reconnaissance unit Sayeret Golani during the Six-Day War, when the unit captured the Syrian-held Mount Hermon.

Despite Israel's numerous successes against the Arab marauders, raids still took place, shaking the confidence of Israeli citizens and prompting the formation of special anti-guerilla units. One of the most effective units was the Shaked (Almond) reconnaissance unit, which became the first mobile Sayeret (Reconnaissance Company). The Sayeret consisted of six teams, each manned by five soldiers, a driver and an officer as commander. The Shaked became the first Sayeret to pursue terrorists through the desert using helicopters; however, these operations were reactive rather than proactive ones. To stem these raids once and for all, Israel formed a special hit squad known as Shefifon (Rattlesnake), which performed missions on behalf of IDF Intelligence.

After the Six Day War in 1967, Israel formed several Sayerets, one for each of their territorial commands. These Sayerets included Shaked, Carob (specializing in unconventional warfare in the Jordan Valley) and Walnut, which was based in the north. During the 1968–70 War of Attrition, the Sayerets carried out numerous deep penetration raids against the Arabs, while in the 1973 Yom Kippur War they fought in a more traditional manner, carrying out both reconnaissance and anti-commando missions.

After the war ended, most of the older Sayerets were disbanded, but their reputation and skills were such that every regular brigade in the IDF has since formed a specialized reconnaissance unit. One of the most famous units is the Sayeret Golani, which was formed in 1959 as 1st Golani Infantry Brigades, Special Reconnaissance Platoon (a.k.a. the Flying Leopards Unit). In combat, the unit has proven to be a great asset, as its fighting capabilities extend way beyond that of a normal dedicated reconnaissance unit. It has seen action in Israel, Lebanon, Beirut, Syria and even Uganda as part of the Entebbe operation. Sayeret Golani fought its first action in January 1960 at Tewfiq, in the Golan Heights, against Syrian mortar positions. Similar actions followed, steadily enhancing the unit's

reputation, the status of which is now almost legendary.

In the 1967 war, the unit fought alongside the Golani Brigade, when its members successfully assaulted the feared Syrian redoubt at Tel Fahar on the Golan Heights. During the War of Attrition, Sayeret Golani fought a long and frustrating operation against PLO (Palestine Liberation Organization) guerillas in the Lebanese 'Fatahland' and Gaza Strip. Their most spectacular action, however, took place during the latter stages of the 1973 Yom Kippur War, when they fought their way up the slopes of Mount Hermon to retake a strategic listening post that had fallen into the hands of the elite Syrian 82nd Paratroop Regiment. During the vicious nine-hour battle that ensued, 55 Golani soldiers were killed and a further 79 wounded before the Syrians

Above: A soldier from the elite Golani Brigade of the Israeli Defence Force (IDF) guards a position with his 5.56mm (0.22in) Galil assault rifle. Of particular interest is the fact that the soldier is left-handed and can fire his weapon from the left shoulder, a feat that is not always possible with some weapons, such as the British SA-80 assault rifle.

eventually surrendered the position – a costly victory. Among those killed was Sayeret leader Captain Vinnick (posthumously advanced to the rank of major), who was mortally wounded during the initial phase of the attack, yet continued to direct his men right up until he was removed from the battlefield by medics.

Sayeret Golani also played a major part during the Israeli invasion of Lebanon in June 1982, when the unit

Left: A patrol of Golani Brigade soldiers heads out across the Judean Desert as part of a large-scale live-fire brigade-strength exercise in 1998.

SAYERET MAT'KAL (GHQ RECON)

Formed in the late 1960s as a special commando force within the IDF's GHQ Intelligence Corps, Sayeret Mat'kal – or Unit 269 (General Staff Reconnaissance), as it is more commonly known – is a highly secretive force which has carried out many daring and often spectacular military operations since its formation, the most famous being the Entebbe rescue in 1976. Although much of its history remains unknown, some of its operations are public knowledge, such as the rescue mission performed in 1972 at Lod Airport following the hijacking of a Sabena airliner. Four Black September terrorists were killed, but all the passengers were rescued unharmed. Barely a month later, Unit 269 carried out a daring commando operation in Lebanon and kidnapped five high-level Syrian intelligence officers, the idea being to trade them for three Israeli pilots that were being held captive. In April 1973, following the murder of Israeli athletes during the 1972 Munich Olympic Games, the unit carried out a retaliation attack in Beirut against a significant number of high-ranking PLO officials, killing or seriously wounding many of them.

captured Beaufort Castle (located on top of a gorge) in a daring night assault that cost the unit its leader.

Today, Sayeret Golani is engaged in ongoing operations against Hizbollah in South Lebanon and the PLO along the Gaza Strip. In 2002, the unit found itself under intense pressure to prevent Palestinian suicide bombers entering Israel and carrying out attacks against Israeli citizens. In response, Sayeret Golani, along with many other elements of the IDF, entered Palestinian territory and mounted a series of operations to flush the terrorists out. Although certain aspects of the operation were successful, the terrorist attacks still continued, despite all the bloodshed on both sides.

For obvious reasons, the Sayeret Golani is extremely selective about its members, and it employs a gruelling selection process to weed out any unsuitable candidates. Following completion of the Gibush (selection phase), successful candidates move on

to an intensive training course that lasts for almost 20 months. Skills covered during this course include parachuting; escape and evasion; weapons familiarization, including enemy weapons; demolitions; survival; intelligence gathering; and, of course, long-range reconnaissance.

In addition, Sayeret Golani has its own urban warfare training centre, which is known as 'Hell Town'. Those candidates that successfully complete the training receive the badge of the Sayeret, a small pin with a flying tiger as an emblem.

Weapons

Weapons used by the Sayeret include the Galil assault rifle; IMI Tavor CTAR 21 assault rifle; IMI Tavor MTAR assault rifle; M16 Assault rifle; Colt M4 assault rifle; AK-47 assault rifle; Colt Commando assault rifle; Mini UZI submachine gun; M249 SAW light machine gun; FN MAG medium machine gun; Browning M2 .50 heavy machine gun; M203 grenade launcher; and Gill/Spike anti-tank missile system.

Although only a small unit, Sayeret Mat'kal operates on the A-team principle, as used by the British SAS and US Delta Force. Officially the unit is under the command of the Intelligence Branch; however, its commander answers to the Chief of Staff directly. Potential candidates for Sayeret Mat'kal are hand-picked from the IDF, as well as reservists and regular conscripts. Former members include several major-generals, two chiefs of staff and two prime ministers – an impressive pedigree.

SAYERET TZANHANIN

Sayeret Tzanhanin is a highly trained commando force that is very similar in capability to that of the US Army's Ranger Force. The unit is capable of mounting both airborne and ground insertion operations, and it has conducted numerous long-range patrols within Lebanon since the Israeli invasion of Lebanon in 1982. Its most famous mission was the raid on the Entebbe Airport in Uganda, in which it supported Sayeret Mat'kal in the rescue of 103 Jewish and Israeli hostages. During the operation, Sayeret Tzanhanin was responsible both for securing the airport against possible attack from the Ugandan Army and for placing beacons on the airport's runways because there were no lights to guide the C-130s.

During Operation Law and Order, Sayeret Tzanhanin terminated a Shi'ite Hizbollah terrorist cell that was operating from the town of Maidun. It was a bloody action that featured point-blank use of RPGs, .50 calibre machine guns, and LAW rockets. More than 50 terrorists were killed, as well as two Sayeret Tzanhanim officers and one NCO, while dozens were wounded during the operation.

During the Gibush phase, which lasts for three days and tests potential recruits rigorously for their mental and physical stamina, only about 24 potential candidates out of 100 will pass. Once through selection, candidates face the gruelling Masaa Kumta, or Beret March, an exercise that requires a 90km (56-mile) forced march with full kit over rough terrain.

Below: Israeli soldiers practise chemical and biological warfare drills until they are second nature, as they are under constant threat of attack from Iraq and the chemical warheads available for its Scud missiles.

ITALY ■ ■
Gruppo d'Intervento Speziale (GIS)

Formed in 1978, in league with a host of other special anti-terrorist units around Europe during the 1970s, the GIS is one of the world's most active counterterrorist units.

The Gruppo d'Intervento Speziale (GIS) was formed in 1978, and it is one of the world's most active counterterrorist units. Consisting of only 100 highly trained operators drawn from the Carabinieri, the GIS is engaged in almost constant operations against the Sicilian Mafia, the Red Brigade and other criminal organizations. Becoming an operator within the GIS is extremely hard, and almost 40 per cent of potential candidates fail the entry test. These tests involve exhaustive security checks, medical tests, psychiatric tests and intensive questioning by senior GIS officers.

Those that do pass the initial test move on to a two-week selection process, which is followed by a 10-month course that includes high-speed driving (on Ferrari's test track); combat shooting; and close-quarter battle. Although most GIS operations take place out of the public eye, in May 1997 its operators carried out an assault on the 99m (325ft) belltower in St Mark's Square, Venice, in front of millions of television viewers. The tower was occupied by 10 Italian separatists, who had stormed it by using an armoured vehicle as a battering ram. GIS operators using

helicopters and ground forces eventually removed the terrorists by force, giving the Italian public a spectacular show in the process.

Weapons used by the GIS include the HK MP5 submachine gun; the Beretta SC70/90 5.56 assault rifle; the HK PSG-1 sniper rifle; the Mauser SP86 7.62 sniper rifle; the Barrett M82 .50 long-range sniper rifle; the Franchi SPAS 12 and 15 12-gauge combat shotguns; the .357 magnum revolver; and the Beretta 92 SB pistol.

Below: A GIS operator marks a target with his long-range Barrett M82 .50 sniper rifle.

JAPAN
Special Assault Team

Japan's special forces unit was formed in response to a number of terrorist attacks in the early 1990s. The SAT is part of Japan's police unit as, ever since World War II, the country's constitution forbids it from maintaining an aggressive military force.

The Special Assault Team (SAT) is Japan's counterterrorist unit, and it was formed in April 1996, following a number of terrorist attacks. Some were perpetrated by the Japanese Red Army, but the most well-known attack was carried out by the Japanese Aum Shiri Kyo religious sect, which released Sarin gas on the Tokyo subway in 1995, killing 12 and wounding more than 5500. Fearing further attacks on their cities, the Japanese government decided to act swiftly and set up a SAT platoon within each of their seven prefectures (which are comparable to a state or province).

In total, the SAT has 10 platoons, each consisting of 20 operators, giving it an operational force of 200 personnel. The SAT is actually part of the Japanese National Police and not the military, as it is forbidden to have such a force. Although little is known of the SAT or its capabilities outside Japan, it is considered to be well trained and equipped, and its operators have cross-trained with the French GIGN. The SAT's biggest operation was in 2002, when Japan and South Korea co-hosted the soccer World Cup. During this premier world event, its members were tasked with protecting the various football teams and their VIP visitors: there were great fears for the footballers' safety following the events of 11 September 2001.

JORDAN
SOU 17

An elite within an elite, SOU 17 is a counterterrorist unit found within Jordan's Special Forces Brigade formed in 1971. As a result of having formed closer relations with Israel in recent years, terrorist activities have been steadily on the rise on Jordanian soil. Jordan's special forces are known to train with the US Special forces, British SAS and French GIGN.

Jordan's primary counterterrorist unit is SOU 17, and it is part of the Special Forces Brigade, which was formed in 1971. The Hashemite Kingdom of Jordan boasts one of the best trained and motivated armies in the Middle East, and its special forces are the best of the best within the Royal Jordanian Army. The Jordanian special forces can trace their history back to 1963, when a company-sized

Right: Taken on 31 December 2001, this photograph shows the lead element of 45 Jordanian special forces arriving in Mazar-I-Sharif, Afghanistan, for security duties around their humanitarian field hospital.

47

Above: Jordanian special forces arrest a terrorist suspect in Amman on 25 May 1998, following the murders of 11 people.

force was recruited from loyal Bedouin tribesmen, who volunteered to undergo parachute training and form an elite unit. This unit was of battalion strength (about 700 men), and it came under the authority of the Royal Jordanian Special Operations Command (SOC).

The SOC fought a series of actions against Palestinian guerillas at Wachdat and Amman during the Black September crisis in 1970, and its soldiers proved to be formidable

fighters. In the early 1970s, the newly formed Special Forces Brigade also found themselves involved in clashes with the Palestinian guerillas and foiled a number of their attacks.

In recent years, Jordan has formed a closer relationship with Israel, which in turn has caused anger and unrest among some of its citizens, especially with those who sympathize with the Palestinian cause. This unrest has led to a massive increase in counter-terrorist operations throughout Jordan by both SOU 17 and other units of the Special Forces Brigade, and they are greatly feared by the Palestinians.

SOU 17 operators are highly professional and crosstrain with

numerous other counterterrorist forces, including the British SAS, the French GIGN, Egypt's Task Force 777 and the US 1st SOF.

Training for SOU 17 includes sniping, demolition, heliborne assaults and close-quarter battle.

Weapons and equipment used by the SOU 17 include the HK MP5 submachine gun; M16 A2 assault rifle; M203 grenade launcher; Colt M4 Carbine; Browning HP pistol; and M60 machine gun.

Uniforms worn by the Jordanian special forces are a variation on British DPM and US woodland pattern, with counterterrorist units wearing dark blue combats.

KOREA, SOUTH
707th Special Missions Battalion

*Formed in 1972, the 707th Special Missions Battalion is South Korea's prime counterterrorist unit.
Extremely well funded the unit has access to some of the very best weaponry and equipment
available and regularly train with Australia's SASR and US Special Forces.*

Based at Songham City, southeast of Seoul, is South Korea's prime counterterrorist unit, the 707th Special Missions Battalion (SMB). Part of the Republic of Korea's Army Special Warfare Command (ROKA SOCOM), the unit was formed in 1972 following the murder of Israeli athletes at the Munich Olympic Games, and it now has an operational strength of some 250 personnel. To ensure maximum efficiency, the unit is organized into six companies, four of which act as support companies, while the other two carry out counterterrorist operations.

Each of the counterterrorist companies is made up of four 14-man operations teams, which are backed up by additional specialists, such as explosives experts and combat medics. The 707th SMB also has a team of female operatives for use in surveillance and undercover operations. In male-dominated Korean society, women can be highly effective, as they are not generally seen as posing a threat. In crisis situations, such as aircraft hijackings, women can move close to aircraft or even board them without causing any alarm.

The biggest threat to South Korea comes from its neighbour North Korea, which mounts clandestine operations deep within South Korean territory on a frequent basis. These incursions are conducted as a means of destabilizing and intimidating the South Korean Government, and the 707th SMB has been involved in a number of fire-fights against North Korean operatives. The 707th SMB has also mounted operations in North Korea against key intelligence-gathering centres and sensitive military installations as a means of preventing further attacks on South Korea. During the 1986 Asian Games, 1988 Seoul Summer Olympics and the 2002 Football World Cup, the 707th SMB was tasked with protecting VIPs and key facilities, for each event carried a high terrorist threat.

Training requirements for the 707th SMB are stringent and vigorous: only qualified special forces personnel from other units are allowed to apply as potential candidates. Those personnel wishing to apply for service in the unit need to pass an intrusive and extensive background check, then endure a gruelling 10-day selection process that eliminates almost 90 per cent of the applicants.

Special Forces operator selection and training lasts for a year and includes six months of basic infantry training and six months of special warfare training, which involves parachuting, martial arts, rappelling, mountain warfare, close-quarter battle and demolition techniques. Once qualified as operators within the 707th SMB, new members can look forward to harsh physical training work-outs, which involve swimming in freezing water without any protective clothing, as well as long runs carrying heavy backpacks. New members also undergo training in scuba diving and boating skills, as much of their work is

Right: Korean special forces take part in a civil defence exercise at a subway station in Seoul on 15 November 2001.

The 707th SMB is extremely well funded and has access to a wide variety of foreign and locally produced weapons, including the HK MP5 submachine gun; HK PSG-1 sniper rifle; RAI .50 calibre long-range sniper rifle; Daewoo K1 and K2 assault rifles; Benelli Super-90 shotgun; Colt .45 pistol; and Daewoo 9mm (0.35in) pistol. The 707th SMB also uses the following heavy weapons: the M60E3 and K3 belt-fed machine gun; the M203 grenade launcher; and the British Javelin SAM system.

In addition to their personal weapons, all special forces must reach black-belt standard in tae kwon do or a comparable martial art.

The uniform consists of a black beret with a silver special forces badge and standard Republic of Korea camouflage combat suits.

Left: A South Korean operator from the Ranger commando force participates in a counterterrorist exercise at the Seoul World Cup Stadium on 6 March 2002.

Right: South Korean commandos inspect road bridges for possible bombs on the Han River near Seoul's World Cup Stadium on 21 May 2002.

done on or near water. The 707th SMB has one of the finest training facilities in the world and includes a mock-up of a Boeing 747 airliner, multiple shooting ranges and a close-quarter battle range.

The unit works very closely with other South Korean special forces, as well as police counterterrorist units such as the Korean National Police Agency's SWAT team. The 707th SMB also has links with similar units around the world, including Australia's SASR Tactical Assault Group (TAG), Singapore's STAR team, Hong Kong's SDU and the US Army's 1st SFOD-D and the US Navy's SEAL teams.

LEBANON
101st Parachute Company

With its close links to Israel, Lebanon's special forces are primarily tasked with counterterrorist duties, with ongoing actions against terrorist factions such as Hizbollah guerrillas. The 101st Parachute Company receives substantial training and aid from the US, Britain and Israel.

Lebanon has a number of special forces units within its armed forces, most of which are airborne-trained and well equipped for modern warfare. Its primary unit is the Israeli-trained 101st Parachute Company, which is responsible for counter-insurgency operations and internal security. Following the Taif Agreement of 1989, Lebanon received substantial military training and equipment from the United States, United Kingdom and Israel, allowing the country to emerge from civil war to relative stability in a very short period of time. Israel has worked very closely with some of the Lebanese special forces, for they share a common enemy, the Palestine Liberation Organization (PLO). One of these units, the Red Berets, saw action in 1997 against Hizbollah guerrillas in the Syrian-controlled Beka'a Valley and against

Islamic terrorists in the Dinnieh hills, and it performed well.

Lebanon's special forces history dates back to the 1920s, when the French formed the Troupes speciales du Levant in Syria and Lebanon. In the early 1950s, the first commando

battalion was formed, which eventually disintegrated during the civil war because of internal sectarian issues. Once these problems were resolved, the Israelis stepped in and helped form 101st Parachute Company. Selection and training standards for the 101st are comparable to those of the Israeli para-troopers, by whom they are trained.

Weapons used by the 101st Parachute Company include the AK-47 assault rifle; AK-74 assault rifle; M16 assault rifle; Colt commando assault rifle; HK MP5 submachine gun; Browning HP pistol; and M60 medium machine gun.

Above: Lebanese operators practise a boarding operation off the coast of Beirut on 19 March 2002, prior to the start of the Arab summit on 27–28 March 2002.

Left: A Lebanese commando fires his sidearm at a target during a firepower demonstration for Jordan's King Abdullah.

LIBYA

Republican Guard

The Republican Guard is Libya's nearest equivalent to a special forces unit. Originally created and trained with the help of Spetsnaz instructors. Very little is known about the unit's skills and capabilities and their operations remain secret.

The Republican Guard is Libya's main special forces unit and was set up with the help of Russian Spetsnaz instructors. Libya does not have a counterterrorist capability as such, as terrorist groups such as the IRA (Irish Republican Army) and the PLO (Palestine Liberation Organization) have used the country as an overseas training base and view Libya as a friend and not an enemy. This may now be changing.

Libya has admitted that its agents carried out the Pan-Am Flight 103 bombing over Lockerbie, Scotland, which killed hundreds of people, and it has now offered compensation to the victims' families. Many in the West regard this less as an act of goodwill and more as an attempt to bring an end to the international economic sanctions that are crippling the country. If these sanctions are lifted, there will be conditions, one of them being the immediate suspension of support to terrorist organizations around the world.

Should Libya comply with these conditions, there will be many repercussions from its former terrorist friends, leading to the possibility of terrorist attacks against Libyan nationals or interests. If this happens, Libya has a considerable force of some 19 para-commando battalions at its disposal, plus the Republican Guard, which operates at brigade strength.

Little is known of the Republican Guard in the West; however, it can be assumed that its training includes counterinsurgency; sabotage; VIP protection; hostage rescue; and Russian-style deep penetration attacks using massive force. Libya is desperate to lose its pariah status, and it has recently purchased a significant quantity of weapons and equipment from the West in exchange for its oil. The West also has its own agenda for Libya and views its territory as a good strategic location for a US Forward Operations Base (FOB).

Weapons used by the Republican Guard include the AK-74 assault rifle; AK-47 assault rifle; RPK light machine gun; Type 74 medium machine gun; and RPG-7 man portable anti-tank rocket launcher, which can also be used against low-flying helicopters.

MOROCCO

The Royal Guard

Morocco's special forces, the Royal Guard, are much influenced by the French Army, Morocco having been a French colony. The unit saw action during the Yom Kippur War in 1973, siding with Syria against Israel.

The Royal Guard was formed in response to a requirement for a highly trained unit that was capable of rapid deployment. It consists of one infantry battalion that is mechanized and two cavalry squadrons that are capable of reconnaissance and light strike roles. Most aspects of the Moroccan armed forces have a French influence, as many of its soldiers served in the French Army up until 1956, including their special forces.

At present, Morocco has two paratroop brigades and six commando battalions in service, as well as a number of specialized support units.

During the Yom Kippur War in 1973, a force of Moroccan para-commandos under Syrian command fought against the Israelis on the slopes of Mount Hermon in the Golan Heights. In 1976, elements of the Moroccan special forces fought Mauritanian forces in the Western Sahara and against the Polisario around Bir Enzaran.

In addition to these actions, Moroccan commando units were also deployed to Zaire in 1977 for a large-scale operation.

NEW ZEALAND
New Zealand Special Air Service Squadron

Small but elite, the NZSAS have much in common with the British SAS and Australian SASR, and maintains close links with them. The unit has seen action since it was created in 1954, including operations in Vietnam between 1968–1971, and more recently in Afghanistan.

Based at Whenuapai, and comprising only five troops (120 men) and a HQ, is New Zealand's small but highly effective 1st Special Air Service Squadron. The NZSAS was first formed in 1954 to operate alongside the British SAS during the Malayan Emergency; however, problems with selection and training delayed this deployment until 1957. After serving with distinction in Malaya, the unit was disbanded, then reformed at troop-strength only. The NZSAS did try to increase its numbers, but was unsuccessful because the Defence Department preferred them to remain a small but well trained unit. It did, however, allow them to undergo parachute training in Australia prior to New Zealand forming its own training school near Auckland.

In 1962, New Zealand sent a small detachment of around 35 men to Korat in Thailand to work alongside US forces, who were training the Thai Rangers in anti-guerilla warfare. In 1963, the Squadron changed its name to the 1st SAS Rangers Squadron in commemoration of two Ranger formations that fought in the Maori Wars. The next deployment for the unit was in Brunei in 1965, where they fought alongside the British SAS against Indonesian insurgents, an experience that would prove invaluable because the unit soon found itself fighting in Vietnam in support of the Australian SAS Regiment. This was the last war New Zealand sent combat troops to fight in. From their first deployment in November 1968 to

their withdrawal in February 1971, each troop from the Squadron served out a one-year tour before being rotated, which ensured maximum operational efficiency. The SRS fought with great distinction in Vietnam and gained enormous respect from their enemies, the NVA (North Vietnamese Army), for their jungle warfare skills.

In 1978, the designation of the unit was changed yet again, from the 1st Rangers Squadron to the 1st SAS Squadron, based in Papakura. In 1991, both the Australian and New Zealand SAS linked up again to form the ANZAC element of the Allied Coalition Force that fought against Iraq during the Gulf War.

Following the terrible events of 11 September 2001, elements of the 1st SAS Squadron were deployed to Afghanistan in support of the Australian SASR and British SAS, who were engaged in a series of operations against the Al Qaeda and Taliban forces. The Kiwis (as New Zealanders are nicknamed) were highly praised by the United States for their hard work in Afghanistan, although it must be

said that their government was heavily criticized for failing to provide sufficient funding during this long and difficult operation.

New Zealand is very secretive about its SAS Squadron and refuses to discuss any aspects of its training or operational capabilities. However, they are believed to be capable of the following missions: counterterrorism; long range reconnaissance; counter-insurgency; sabotage; hostage rescue; and hit-and-run operations.

Selection and training requirements for the New Zealand SAS are every bit as tough and demanding as for their Australian and British counterparts and highly competetive as there are very few vacancies available each year for new recruits. As a result, many of the better candidates either join the British SAS directly (if eligible) or apply for an exchange posting. Apart from their training opportunities with the British SAS and Australian SASR, the 1st SAS Squadron also crosstrains with a number of other elite units from Asian countries, including Indonesia, Thailand and Singapore.

Uniform and Weapons

Members of the 1st SAS Squadron wear uniforms and combats very similar to those of the British SAS Regiment, including the famous sand-coloured beret.

Weapons and equipment favoured by the 1st SAS Squadron include the M16 A2 assault rifle with M203 grenade launcher; M249 Minimi squad automatic weapon; Heckler & Koch MP5 submachine gun; PSG-1 sniper rifle; FN 7.62mm (0.3in) SLR; and Remington M870 shotgun.

THE NETHERLANDS ▬
Bijzondere Bijstands Eenheid (BBE)

The BBE is the Dutch counterterrorist unit and is made up of volunteers from the Royal Dutch Marines. Its most famous operations involved freeing 200 hostages from terrorists in 1977.

The Bijzondere Bijstands Eenheid (BBE – Close Combat Unit) is the Netherland's main counterterrorist unit. The BBE is highly unusual in that it is an ad hoc unit, formed only when needed for terrorist-related incidents. It is made up of around 100 volunteers who are drawn from the elite Royal Dutch Marines and make up a force of three platoons, each containing specialists in EOD, sniping, communications and combat medicine. The platoons are then subdivided into five-man teams. Potential candidates have to undergo 48 weeks of intensive training before they are accepted into this small but highly professional unit.

In addition to the Marines, the BBE also has a group of psychologists available who specialize in hostage situations and are available to the unit at short notice. The BBE has seen action on a number of occasions, the first being in October 1977, when the unit regained control of Scheverngen prison following a revolt by interned Palestinian terrorists. Despite the fact that the terrorists were armed, the BBE used only stun grenades and hand-to-hand combat, preferring to capture rather than kill.

The most famous BBE operation, however, was carried out on 11 June 1977, when a group of South Moluccan terrorists seized more than 200 hostages and held them captive on board a train and in a schoolhouse. Creating a spectacular diversion that involved two F-104 Starfighters buzzing the train at low altitude and at supersonic speed (resulting in the terrorists being disorientated by the sonic boom), the BBE launched simultaneous assaults on the train and schoolhouse. During the assault on the train, which was supported by members of the British SAS, the BBE killed six terrorists and, unfortunately, two hostages before they were able to free the remaining hostages.

In the early 1990s, members of the BBE were deployed to the Adriatic as boarding parties ready to search ships attempting to break the Serbian arms embargo; however, they were never utilized in this role.

Weapons used include the HK MP5 submachine gun; HK G3 assault rifle; Steyr SSG; SIG Sauer P-226 pistol; and Colt .357 magnum revolver.

Below: Dutch special forces practise a building entry during a routine training exercise. Note the operators have fastened two magazines together on their HK-MP5s for extra firepower and rapid reloading.

NORWAY 🇳🇴
Finnmark 7th Jaeger Company

Norway's elite 7th Jaeger Company are highly trained experts at arctic guerrilla warfare with survival skills in the cold to match. They are known to work closely and train with the British Royal Marines.

The 7th Jaeger Company is part of Norway's Finnmark Regiment and plays a key role in the country's defence strategy. As a small country, Norway recognizes that its military capabilities are limited and that its best means of survival rests in fighting a guerrilla war, rather than a conventional one. Hence the formation of the 7th Jaeger Company.

The role of the 7th Jaegers is to stay behind enemy lines and cause disruption to their forces and operations by means of sabotage and harassment. Their main area of operations is likely to be in the northern part of Norway, which is covered in snow for almost eight months of the year and is heavily forested, making it ideal for the camouflage and concealment of both men and equipment.

The 7th Jaeger Company is divided into four platoons (troops), a command/mortar troop and three rifle troops, each containing three eight-man teams. These teams are highly mobile and use cross-country skis and white Yamaha snowmobiles to carry weapons and equipment over rough terrain. The 7th Jaegers are experts in arctic warfare and are able to survive and fight in conditions that would restrict any other force. Because they must be able to operate independently for up to two weeks without resupply, members of the unit are highly trained in the use of small arms, sabotage techniques, communications, survival, combat medicine, reconnaissance and hit-and-run operations. Should a resupply be necessary, the 7th Jaegers

Left: A Norwegian Carl Gustav team makes its way through soft snow during an arctic warfare exercise.

Above: A fire support team manually marks a target during arctic warfare training, as optic sights are prone to misting up under extreme temperature conditions.

can call in Bell 412 helicopters from the Royal Norwegian Air Force.

Although most of the 7th Jaegers training is carried out with other Norwegian units, they are also known to work very closely with the British Royal Marines, who are also experts in arctic warfare.

Weapons used by the 7th Jaeger Company include the HK G3 assault rifle; HK MP5 submachine gun; and Vapensmia A/S NM-149 sniper rifle. Heavy weapons include the Carl Gustav 84mm (3.31in) anti-tank weapon; 40mm (1.57in) grenade launcher; RO 81mm Mortar; ERYX anti-tank missile system; and the Stinger MANPADs. Air support is available from RNAF F-16s.

PAKISTAN
Special Services Group (Army) – SSG (A)

Pakistan's special forces, the SSG (A), perform commando operations behind enemy lines, and are trained in guerrilla warfare tactics.

Pakistan's Special Services Group, SSG (A), consists of three battalions and an independent counterterrorist company. The primary role of the SSG is to support conventional units in mounting commando operations behind enemy lines and to assist the intelligence services in counter-insurgency missions. It is also alleged to train guerrilla forces for operations in India and Afghanistan, something that Pakistan vehemently denies. The SSG (A) is also unusual in that its missions are tasked not by the Army, but by Pakistan's three intelligence bodies – Military Intelligence (MI); the Directorate of Inter-Services Intelligence (ISI); and the Intelligence Bureau (IB).

Weapons used by the Special Services Group include the HK MP5 submachine gun; Remington 870 shotgun; and Glock 17 pistol. In addition, all SSG operators are proficient in unarmed combat and various martial arts.

Above: SSG soldiers march past military VIPs during a full dress parade rehearsal in Pakistan's capital, Islamabad.

THE PHILIPPINES
Special Forces Regiment (Airborne)

Dating back to 1962, the SFR is the Philippines' special forces unit. The unit has never involved itself in any large-scale conventional warfare but sees constant action against guerrilla insurgents, pirate marauders and more recently Al Qaeda linked terrorists.

The Special Forces Regiment (Airborne) is the Philippines' primary special forces unit and is tasked with performing unconventional warfare and counterinsurgency and counterterrorist operations. The SFR can trace its history back to 1962, when a unit called the Special Forces Group (Airborne) PA was formed after the withdrawal of US military support in 1962. The unit had the role of home defence and counterinsurgency, and it grew rapidly until it became clear that the size of the unit was simply too big for its intended operational role. It was renamed the Home Defense Forces Group (Airborne), a title that better reflected its capabilities.

As the unit continued to develop its range of core skills, including scuba diving and HALO parachute infiltration, it suffered a severe setback when it lost almost 70 per cent of its entire

Right: Filipino special forces stand guard in front of the US embassy in Manila during a protest against the presence of 1000 US military personnel in the southern Philippines. Their mission is to train and advise the Philippine military on matters relating to fighting the Al Qaeda–linked Abu Sayyaf group.

force to a peacekeeping mission in Vietnam, reducing its strength to that of a company.

In 1973, the unit started to expand again until it reached an operational strength of five combat companies and one HQ company, and reverted back to its original name, the Special Forces Group (Airborne). On 16 November 1989, the unit changed its name again, this time to the Special Forces Regiment (Airborne) and became subordinate to the Special Operations Command, PA. According to SOC's mission statement, the operational role of the SFR is to develop, organize, train, equip, command and control indigenous paramilitary forces; to provide mobile training teams (MTTs)

to organize, train and advise cadres of conventional forces tasked to administer paramilitary forces; to conduct denial operations to prevent enemy access, influence and control over a particular area of strategic value; to perform PSYOP, civil action operations and humanitarian assistance; to provide strike operations by special forces or jointly

with indigenous troops; to provide forward air control for air missions; to undertake sabotage, subversion and abduction of selected personnel; and search and recovery operations.

The SFR has never been involved in a large-scale conventional war with another country, but its forces have been involved in numerous contacts with guerrilla insurgents and pirate marauders, who rob and kidnap foreign tourists. Since 11 September 2001, the SFR and US special forces have been involved in extensive combat operations against both local guerrilla forces and Al Qaeda terrorists who have fled Afghanistan.

Weapons used include the M16 A2 assault rifle; Colt Commando assault rifle; HK MP5 submachine gun; Remington 870 shotgun; Ultimax and M249 SAW light machine guns; M60 medium machine gun; M203 grenade launcher; 81mm (3.19in) mortar; and M2 .50 heavy machine gun.

Left: A Philippine counterterrorist unit shows off its range of powerful assault weapons during a parade marking the activation of the Philippine Army's Special Operations Command (SOCOM).

PORTUGAL
Grupo de Operacoes Especiais (GOE)

The GOE or Special Operations Group is Portugal's main special forces unit. Created in 1979, it is similar in structure and operation to the British SAS and runs a lengthy and rigorous training period for potential members.

The Portuguese Grupo de Operacoes Especiais (GOE) was formed in December 1979, a response to the seizing of Israeli athletes at the 1972 Munich Olympics – an event that inspired every European country to create a counterterrorist capability. The GOE has close ties with the British SAS and has set up its force of 150 operators in a structure that is very similar to that of the SAS.

Training for the GOE is extremely demanding, and potential volunteers must survive a brutal and harsh eight-month training course before being allowed to join the unit. Subjects covered during the course include tubular assault (in other words, attacking aircraft, trains and buses); house clearing; maritime operations; and VIP protection.

The GOE has been involved in only one operation so far, when a group of terrorists seized the Turkish Embassy in Lisbon. The incident ended when the terrorists blew up themselves and two hostages before the GOE could intervene.

Weapons used by the GOE include the HK MP5 submachine gun; HK 502 12-gauge shotgun; HK PSG-1; Galil 7.62mm (0.3in) sniper rifles; and Browning, SIG and Glock pistols.

Vehicles used by the GOE include specially modified Range Rovers and Mercedes Benz marked and unmarked cars, which have platforms and hoists fitted to make aircraft and building assaults safer and faster.

Below: Portuguese special forces on parade in Lisbon, Portugal.

RUSSIA ▬
Spetsnaz

At the height of the cold war Spetsnaz operatives were the most feared of all special forces units from the former Soviet bloc. Experts at sabotage and reconnaissance, their original purpose was to pave the way for a main Soviet attack of western Europe. After the break-up of the Soviet Union the unit has since restructured to operate more like the US Delta Force and British SAS.

At the height of the Cold War, the mere mention of the Spetsnaz would send shivers down the spines of Western soldiers: this unknown and unseen enemy had a fearsome reputation. Meaning 'special purpose', the word 'Spetsnaz' is taken from the Russian words *spetsialnoe naznachenie* and is the most commonly used designation for describing Russian special forces. Other names are sometimes used, such as *reydoviki* (meaning 'raid'), to describe diversionary, sabotage and reconnaissance troops.

Spetsnaz operates under the command and control of the Soviet General Staff's main Intelligence Directorate (Glavnoe Razvedyvatelnoe Upravlenie, GRU) and has no Western equivalent. Its main purpose is to carry out what the Russians term 'special reconnaissance' (*Spetsialnaya Razvedka*). This is defined as reconnaissance carried out to subvert the political, economic and military potential and morale of a probable or actual enemy. This includes acquiring intelligence on major economic and military installations and either destroying them or putting them out of action; organizing sabotage and acts of subversion; carrying out punitive operations against rebels; conducting

Right: Spetsnaz operators practise heliborne insertion techniques with a Russian Mil-8 Hip transport helicopter. The operator on the ground has earthed the abseiling rope to prevent build-up of static electricity.

Selection and Training

Spetsnaz selection and training requirements are extremely demanding. Potential Reydoviki conscripts must be physically fit, intelligent and politically reliable before they will even be considered as Spetsnaz candidates. Once approved for the induction phase, conscripts have to sign a loyalty oath, in which they acknowledge their awareness of the death penalty for anyone who betrays the Spetsnaz. After the induction phase, some of the brighter conscripts will be selected for NCO training. Those that pass the six-month course graduate as NCOs, while those that fail revert back to the rank of private soldier.

In addition to their basic military training, all conscripts receive specialized instruction in hand-to-hand combat; silent killing techniques; parachuting, including HALO techniques; infiltration techniques, including defeat of alarm systems and locks; sabotage; demolition; foreign languages; survival; rappelling; sniping; reconnaissance; map reading; foreign weapons; foreign vehicle operation; and foreign tactics, techniques and procedures.

During the training phase, conscripts face obstacle courses and long, gruelling marches, many of which are conducted in full chemical warfare protective clothing, including gas masks. Most of the physical training is extremely harsh, and conscripts are often denied rations so that they have to forage for food themselves. However, there are also good opportunities for conscripts to travel to foreign countries as part of the Russian Olympic team and enjoy good food and good living while carrying out adventure training, such as mountain climbing and skiing. Once through specialized training, the conscripts face a series of battlefield exercises, which test their skills to the limit. These exercises take place in very realistic environments, such as mock Cruise missile bases, NATO airfields and communications facilities, and they involve the use of explosives and live rounds.

propaganda; and forming and training insurgent detachments.

In more general terms, the main missions of the Spetsnaz forces are sabotage and reconnaissance, although they are known to have carried out insurgent training in Africa and Cuba. During the Cold War, their main purpose was described as 'diversionary reconnaissance' (*diversiya rezvedka*), which essentially meant carrying out sabotage operations against vital Western installations, such as Cruise missile sites and bridges, in advance of a main attack force. Other missions envisaged at the time included laying mines on likely tank routes, killing NATO pilots in their accommodation blocks, marking suitable insertion sites for paratroopers and transport helicopters, and assassinating senior NATO commanders.

Although these practices were never used against European nations, many Spetsnaz tactics, techniques and procedures were tested for real during

Below: Spetsnaz unarmed combat experts put on a demonstration of close-quarter fighting techniques for a motorized infantry unit in Afghanistan. The Spetsnaz are particularly renowned for their ability to kill or maim opponents using hands or feet.

Above: Young recruits to the Spetsnaz pose with their Kalashnikov AKS74 5.45mm (0.21in) rifles with fixed bayonets for a photograph during a break in training at their base near Moscow.

Right: A Spetsnaz patrol armed with Kalashnikov AK-74 5.45mm (0.21in) automatic rifles mounts a security operation along the border Russia shares with Finland.

the Soviet invasion of Afghanistan in 1979, when Spetsnaz units spearheaded the main invasion force and were highly successful.

Spetsnaz units are trained to infiltrate enemy territory by many methods, both overt and covert, and can operate up to 1000km (620 miles) behind enemy lines without support.

Although their primary role is to locate targets for other forces (whether paratroopers, strategic bombers or armoured units), they can if necessary launch attacks themselves. Typical targets include mobile missile sites, Cruise missile bases, integrated air defence systems, radar sites, command and control facilities, airfields, ports and lines of communication.

The basic Spetsnaz unit comprises a team of eight to ten soldiers commanded by an officer. Within each team, there is a specialist in communications, reconnaissance, sniping and explosives, and every member of the

Known Spetsnaz Units

Razvedchiki – one battalion divided into two companies (one for airborne and one for LRRP operations).
Rejdoviki – a brigade-sized formation that operates in battalion- or company-sized reconnaissance units.
Vysotniki – a brigade-sized formation that operates in small 11-man units, performing SAS-style missions.

Below: Spetsnaz operators practise unarmed combat as a matter of routine, using hands, feet or any weapon that is available to them.

team has been crosstrained to ensure that a mission can continue even if a specialist is lost.

Modern Russian forces are structured in operational fronts that each contain a Spetsnaz brigade. Each brigade consists of three to five battalions, a signal company, a support unit and a HQ company, which equates to a wartime strength of some 1300 men capable of deploying 100 operational teams. In addition to the brigade units, most Russian armies also have a Spetsnaz presence of several companies, which gives them a force of 115 men or 15 operational teams. Each company is organized in a similar manner to that of a brigade, and it contains three Spetsnaz platoons, a communications platoon and a support unit. Apart from the Brigade and Army Spetsnaz, there are a number of other units operating directly under the command of the GRU and Naval Spetsnaz brigade, giving a peacetime strength of some 15,000 personnel.

As most Spetsnaz missions take place deep behind enemy lines, soldiers tend to be lightly armed and carry only a small selection of weaponry. A typical soldier will carry either an AK-74 or AN-94 assault rifle, a silenced 9mm (0.35in) pistol, ammunition, a knife and up to 10 grenades. In addition, each team carries an SVD sniper rifle, RPG-16 grenade launcher, under-rifle grenade launcher, SA-14 MANPADs, plastic

Above: A Russian commando walks past a burning obstacle on the Balashikha training ground near Moscow.

explosives, anti-personnel mines and an R–350M burst transmission radio, which has a range of some 1000km (620 miles).

Spetsnaz units can only be successful if they are in possession of good intelligence, and it is for this reason that they report directly to the GRU and, to some degree, the second directorate of the front staff, which is responsible for intelligence matters. Within this group, there are separate

Right: Russian military training is not only rigorous, but also harsh and cruel when compared to that of Western forces, as can be seen clearly on the faces of these commando recruits.

departments to process agent intelligence, signals intelligence and Spetsnaz intelligence – normally gathered via sleeper agents or operatives posing as truck drivers, for example, or athletes travelling overseas.

Much has changed amongst the Russian military since the end of the Cold War, including the manner in which Spetsnaz units operate in Europe. It should be borne in mind, however, that despite Russia's parlous financial state its Spetsnaz units still receive generous funding and are now training and re-equipping to operate more like the British SAS and US Delta Force.

Spetsnaz training now includes tubular work; counterterrorism; urban warfare training, based on lessons learned in Chechnya; and mobility warfare (vehicle-based).

Left: A Spetsnaz observation post with laser rangefinder.

SAUDI ARABIA
Special Forces Brigade

The Saudi Special Forces Brigade has received much support from US forces since the Gulf War and, with the country's resources, can afford the very best arms and equipment.

The Saudi Special Forces Brigade is made up of two airborne and airmobile battalions, which are grouped together with three parachute-trained special forces companies and a Royal Guards Regiment with three battalions. It is a complicated setup that sometimes causes confusion, for each unit is under the command of a different Ministry. The Special Forces Brigade receives considerable support from US forces, receiving specialized training and advice on special forces tactics, techniques and procedures, as Saudi Arabia has little experience of operating outside its own territory.

Operations known to have involved Saudi forces include the invasion of Kuwait in 1961, when a company-strength battle group supported British Royal Marine Commandos against Iraqi forces. Another key operation occurred during the 1973 Arab–Israeli War, when Saudi special forces operated alongside Syrian forces on the Golan Heights.

During the Gulf War in 1991, the Saudi Special Forces Brigade helped Allied Coalition forces to defend key installations from possible ground attack. It is also believed to have been involved in the expulsion of Iraqi forces from Kuwait City, although this has always been denied. The Special Forces Brigade is well trained and equipped for modern warfare, and it is keen to play its part in protecting Saudi Arabia from any possible terrorist or conventional threat.

Weapons used include the HK MP5 submachine gun; M16 A2 assault rifle with M203 grenade launcher; M249 Minimi SAW; and Remington M870 shotgun.

SOUTH AFRICA
South African Special Forces Brigade

An amalgamation of the 'Recce' Commando units dating back to the late 1970s, the South African Special Forces Brigade was formed in 1996. Its members have seen action in neighbouring countries such as Angola and Namibia.

The South African Special Forces operate to the following mandate:

Special Forces as a Strategic Force carries out special operations independently or in cooperation with other state departments or Services, achieve national objectives, internally or externally in peace and war. Such operations will be executed in accordance with the constitution of the RSA, the White Paper on Defence, the Defence Review and international law, with oversight and approval at the highest operational level.

The South African Special Forces Brigade was formed in 1996, and is an amalgamation of the famous South African 'Recce' units that served with great distinction in Angola during the late 1970s and early 1980s. The Brigade can trace its history back to 1 October 1972, when a specialist unit was formed in Durban known as 1 Reconnaissance Commando. The need for such a unit had long been recognized within the South African Defence Force (SADF), as the airborne forces were becoming more engaged in conventional warfare, rather than special forces operations.

Below: South African special forces practise a hostage rescue operation at an army base in Phalaborwa, located north of Johannesburg.

Above: A typical Recce Commando armed with an Israeli 5.56mm (0.22in) Galil rifle and carrying two rifle grenades, a smoke canister and a water bottle.

Left: The South African Special Forces excel in tracking, survival and engagement in the African bush. Here a team on patrol out in the savannah remain vigilant by their camp fire.

The 1 Reconnaissance Commando was set up along the same lines as the British SAS and was tasked with mounting long-range reconnaissance patrols (LRRPs) deep behind enemy lines, as well as hit-and-run operations. The 1 Reconnaissance Commando proved to be a very capable and useful unit, and this quickly led to the formation of additional 'Recce' Commandos, such as 4 Recce, which was based at Langebaan in the Cape and which specialized in amphibious operations.

In 1981, the special forces became an independent organization that was answerable only to the SADF and not the Army. Ten years later, in 1991, there were to be more significant changes for the Recce Commandos as the HQ element of the Special Forces was disbanded and a Directorate of Reconnaissance formed in its place, which answered only to the chief of the Army. Just as the Special Forces were adapting to their new set-up, there was yet another name change – to 45 Parachute Brigade. This meant that all Reconnaissance Commando units had to add the prefix '45' to their unit number. Thus 1 Reconnaissance Commando became known as 451 Reconnaissance Commando.

In 1996, the Recces were subjected to another name change and became known as the Special Forces Brigade, a name held to this day. In terms of operational experience, there are very few units around the world that can match the Recces and their formidable reputation. The Recces played a major part in defeating the terrorist group SWAPO (South West Africa's People's Organization), which wanted Namibia to be separated from South Africa.

The SWAPO guerillas were well trained and equipped, and they were a formidable enemy. When on patrol behind their lines, the Recces painted their faces black to pass themselves off as guerilla fighters. In 1979, SWAPO guerillas mounted a major attack against South African Forces, but it was repulsed by the Recces and other conventional forces. In 1982, the Recces took part in Operation Mebos, a deep penetration raid within Angola that destroyed SWAPO's headquarters and much of its terrorist infrastructure. In 1994, the Recces entered Angola on horseback and cut off most SWAPO supply lines, which helped to bring about the group's defeat.

Like many special forces around the world, the Recces find themselves under constant pressure to carry out missions that are technically out of their operational remit. Their key operational role is that of strategic intelligence gathering, although they have performed tactical intelligence-gathering missions on numerous occasions, especially in Angola. Highly trained and well armed, they are too valuable to be risked in direct combat missions, and they now operate more in a covert observation role (as per their remit).

The SADF never discusses any operational or tactical aspects of the Special Forces Brigade – secrecy is everything. However, it is known that the Recces have great experience in inserting small teams of men behind enemy lines by various means, including helicopters, parachute, horseback, small vehicles, boats and – their main method – by foot. Recce teams vary in size and composition, but the average size of an LRRP (Long-Range Reconnaissance Patrol) team is six soldiers, each man having a specialist combat skill. A typical patrol includes a tracker, sniper, medic, navigator, signaller and explosives expert. In addition to this type of patrol, the Recces have also been known to deploy small two-man teams on covert observation missions deep behind enemy lines.

SPAIN

Tercio de Extranjeros (The Spanish Legion)

Ardent admirers of the French Foreign Legion, Spain formed its own equivalent in 1920, with the key difference being that the majority of its members are Spanish. The unit fought under General Franco in the Spanish Civil War and afterwards saw action in Morocco against insurgents.

The Spanish Legion, or Tercio de Extranjeros (Regiment of Foreigners), was formed in 1920 to suppress dissidents in the protectorate of Spanish Morocco, where the Spanish conscript army of the day was struggling to keep control. The Spanish were great admirers of the French Foreign Legion and decided to form an equivalent unit of their own, but with some key differences. The French Foreign Legion consists mainly of foreigners, while the Spanish Legion is almost 90 per cent Spanish.

During the Spanish Civil War, General Franco's Nationalist forces had 18 Legion battalions available to act as a spearhead force. After the war ended, the Legion was reduced in size to six battalions, which were posted back to Morocco to continue operations against local insurgents.

These operations continued until Spain granted most of Morocco its independence, apart from two enclaves in northern Morocco, Ceuta (held by

Right: A Spanish Legionnaire armed with a HK 9mm (0.35in) MP5A2 submachine gun poses for the camera in a clearly staged shot. The soldier has taped together two magazines for rapid reloading.

Left: A Spanish Legionnaire takes up a defensive position on the flat roof of a low-level building.

the Spanish since 1580) and one centred on the port of Melilla, where Legion units are still based.

As with their French counterparts, training for the Spanish Legion is harsh and at times brutal, with new recruits being pushed to the edge of their physical limits. The initial training phase, however, lasts for only three months; for a modern soldier, this is now seen as totally inadequate and is currently under review. Discipline within the Legion is also very strict,

Unit Deployment

The Tercio de Extranjeros is part of Spain's Rapid Reaction Force and consists of some 7000 men, who are deployed as follows:

1st Tercio Gran Capitan (HQ Melilla) – 1st, 2nd and 3rd Banderas.

2nd Tercio Duque de Alba (HQ Ceuta) – 4th, 5th and 6th Banderas.

3rd Tercio Don Juan de Austria (HQ Fuerteventura, Canary Islands) – 7th and 8th Banderas and 1st light Cavalry Group.

4th Tercio Alejandro de Farnesio (HQ Ronda in Malaga) – 9th and 10th Banderas.

Banderas de Operaciones Especiales (BOEL) – this special forces battalion has capabilities in mountaineering, long-range reconnaissance, parachuting and amphibious operations.

with harsh punishments for those members who fail to adhere to the Legion's code of conduct.

Below: A Spanish machine-gun team lets rip on a live fire exercise.

The Legion is an all-volunteer force, and recruits sign up for an initial three years of service, which can be extended if required. Leaving the Legion early is almost impossible to do legally. Potential officers for the Legion must first become Spanish citizens, and those who are ex-Legionnaires can reach the rank of major only.

The Spanish Legion comprises four *tercios* (regiments), each of which contain four *banderas* (battalions); however, it has only one special operations unit – the BOEL, which consists of some 500 men and is a battalion within the 4th Tercio Alejandro de Farnesio (the 4th Alexander Farnesio Regiment), which is based in Ronda, Malaga.

The BOEL unit is trained in scuba; sabotage and demolitions; arctic and mountain warfare; long-range reconnaissance; parachute and HALO techniques; and counterterrorism.

Weapons used by the Spanish Legion include the CETME assault rifle; Ameli light machine gun; and SB 40 LAG automatic grenade launcher.

SWEDEN 🇸🇪

Försvarsmaktens Särskilda Skydds Grupp (SSG) – Special Protection Group

Sweden's special forces unit, the SSG or Special Protection Group, maintains strict confidentiality about its operations. Members are recruited from the Swedish army's elite ranger units and are known to train with the US Delta Force and British SAS.

Sweden's Forsvarsmaktens Sarskilda Skydds Grupp (SSG – Special Protection Group) was formed in the early 1990s as a special forces unit equivalent to Britain's SAS or the United States' Delta Force. Although Sweden pursues a stated policy of neutrality, its government is well aware of the threat of terrorism and has taken preventative action to ensure the safety of Swedish citizens both in Sweden and abroad.

The SSG recruits primarily from Sweden's elite Ranger unit, as well as other specialized units within the Swedish military and paramilitary forces. Sweden is very secretive about its military capabilities and has released very little information about the SSG

and its true operational roles. Both former and current members of the unit are prevented from speaking about its size, organization and training, and they have to sign a legal document that expressly forbids them from revealing any information.

The name Special Protection Group implies defensive rather than offensive operations, so it can be assumed that the unit protects vital installations, high-ranking military officials and Swedish citizens. Apart from the Ranger training that most SSG candidates will have undertaken, new members of the unit receive training in static line parachuting, HALO and HAHO parachuting, explosives handling, unarmed combat,

sniping, VIP protection, combat diving and small-boat operations. All SSG members are trained to the same skill level before they are assigned to their respective units.

Once assigned to their unit, new members are required to specialize in a skill such as combat diving, sniping, HAHO/HALO operations, EOD, combat medicine, or communications. SSG members also train with other special forces, including the British SAS and US Delta Force, and they undertake specialist training courses within both the United Kingdom and the United States.

Weapons used by the SSG include the AK5 assault rifle; HK MP5; PSG-90 sniper rifle; and SIG P226 pistol.

SWITZERLAND ✚
FSK-17

Switzerland's special forces unit is actually part of the Swiss Air Force, having once been known as the Fallschirm-Grenadiers (Parachute Grenadiers). Members of FSK-17 operate in four-man teams similar to the British SAS.

FSK-17 is Switzerland's main special forces unit and is part of the Swiss Air Force, rather than the Swiss Army.

Formed in the early 1970s and originally known as the Fallschirm-Grenadiers (Parachute Grenadiers) of the Swiss Air Force, the unit changed its name in 1980 to the Fernspah-

Grenadiers and was given the role of long-range reconnaissance patrolling. It is generally known in Switzerland as FSK-17 and comprises some 100 personnel of various ranks, who are divided between three platoons, but operate in four-man teams. Members of FSK-17 are highly trained in military skills that include intelligence

gathering; demolitions; close-quarter battle; survival skills; and parachuting – both static line and free fall. The unit has also pioneered its own Tactical Diamond insertion technique.

Weapons used by FSK-17 include the HK MP5 submachine gun; the SIG-P228 pistol; and various knives and grenades.

SYRIA

14th Special Forces Division

Syria has the best trained and equipped armed forces in the Arab World. The 14th Special Forces Divison saw action against Israel in the Yom Kippur War.

The Syrian armed forces have probably the best trained and equipped army in the Arab world, with a special forces capability that is legendary. Within Syria, the special forces are known as the Al-Wahdat al-Khassa (Special Units) and operate under the umbrella of the 14th Special Forces Division, which is based in Lebanon, its four special forces regiments – the 35th, 46th, 54th and 55th – all being located in the Beirut area. There is also the 44th Special Forces Regiment near Shikka, the 53rd south of Haibi near Tripoli, and the 41st and 804th east of Juniya. Each

regiment consists of three para-trained companies, which are supported by an anti-tank company, a mortar company and a machine-gun platoon.

In addition to the 14th SFD, Syria also has an airborne rapid deployment brigade and the Saraya al Difa (Defence Companies), a small paratroop battalion. Since their formation in 1958, the Syrian special forces have fought in numerous actions against Israel, the most famous being the assault on the IDF monitoring station on top of Mount Hermon in the Golan Heights during the Yom Kippur War. Elements of the 14th SFD also fought against

the Palestine Liberation Organization (PLO) in Lebanon and performed extremely well, considering the difficult urban conditions in which they had to operate.

Selection and training standards within the Syrian special forces are extremely high: only the best and most reliable soldiers from its armed forces are put forward for consideration as possible commandos.

Weapons used by the 14th Special Forces Group include the AK-74 assault rifle; AK-47 assault rifle; M23/25 submachine gun; SSG69 sniper rifle; and RPG-7.

TAIWAN

1st Special Forces Group

The 1st Special Forces Group, started in 1958, was Taiwan's very first special forces unit. Other specialized units have since come into existence.

Taiwan's special forces were initially formed after the end of World War II, with American help. This eventually resulted in the formation of the 1st Special Forces Group in 1958.

Since then, a number of other units have been formed, including the following:

• 1st Peace Preservation Police Corps Special Weapons and Tactics Unit (SWAT)
• Military Police Special Service Company – 100 personnel
• Airborne and Special Warfare

Command Special Operations Unit – 100 personnel, who train with both Delta Force and the US Rangers
• Chinese Marine Corps Special Operations Unit – 100 personnel responsible for maritime security

All of these units operate under the command and control of Security Task Force HQ, which is answerable to the Taiwanese prime minister.

Right: Taiwanese special forces stop in the jungle for a radio check during a routine patrol.

TURKEY

1st, 2nd, and 3rd Commando Brigade

Turkey's army is one of the world's largest. It has three separate Commando Brigades, one airborne, one para-commando and one para-marine, which are responsible for its special forces operations. The units saw action during the invasion of Cyprus in 1974.

With a million personnel, Turkey has one of the largest armed forces in the world. It has a large number of special forces which can deploy at very short notice.

Turkey's special forces organization consists of three airborne brigades, each containing 5000 men, and one counterterrorist battalion of some 150 operators.

A member of NATO, Turkey's special forces equipment and training is based on Western standards, such as those of the SAS and Delta Force.

Turkey's special forces history dates back to 1949, when US forces began supplying and training the Turkish Army. This eventually led to the

Below: Turkish army special forces in training in November 1993.

formation of the 1st Airborne Platoon of the Guards Regiment, which was followed in 1958 by a 2nd Airborne Platoon and in 1963 by a 3rd platoon. All of these units saw extensive action in 1974 during the Turkish invasion of Cyprus, which quickly led to the formation of two further brigades.

After further reorganization within the Turkish armed forces, the brigades' responsibilities were split again between one airborne, one para-commando and one para-marine, with each newly formed brigade having its own support company and, in the case of the airborne brigade, its own artillery company.

Left: Turkish special forces work up in preparation for operations against the Kurds.

UNITED KINGDOM 🇬🇧
Special Air Service (SAS)
Special Boat Service (SBS)

The British SAS needs little introduction as one of the best special forces unit in the world. Owing to intense public interest its secrecy has been much compromised in the last twenty years. Its naval equivalent, the SBS, still maintains a relatively low profile by comparison.

The SAS is the most feared and respected special forces unit in the world, with numerous imitators but few equals. Based at Credenhill, Hereford, 22 Special Air Service Regiment (SAS) is one of the most highly trained special forces units in the world. Its reputation is legendary, and the unit certainly lives up to its motto 'Who dares wins'. Prior to 5 May 1980, very few people around the world knew anything about the SAS or even of its existence. However, everything changed on that eventful day when millions of people around the world watched on live television as men wearing black overalls, respirators and body armour, and armed with HK MP5s, Browning HP pistols and stun grenades, stormed the Iranian Embassy in London to rescue a number of hostages, killing five terrorists in the process.

The old saying 'any publicity is good publicity' does not apply to special forces, which like to work in the shadows, and this exposure created a perception of a large unit manned by supermen. The reality is somewhat different: the SAS comprises only one

Right: The winged dagger of the SAS.

Above: An excellent shot of a heavily armed SAS Jeep on patrol in the North African desert during World War II.

Right: David Stirling (far right), founder of the SAS, poses with a well-armed SAS patrol during operations in North Africa.

regular regiment (22 SAS) and two part-time TA (Territorial Army) regiments (21 SAS Artists Rifles and 23 SAS), which are supported by 264 Signal Squadron (a regular unit attached to 22 SAS) and 63 Signal Squadron (a TA unit that supports both 21 and 23 SAS).

The SAS has some 700 highly trained operators within its ranks, who are divided between four Sabre (fighting) squadrons. Each squadron consists of four 16-man troops, who normally deploy on operations as four-man teams or eight-man patrols,

Left: A soldier from the 22 SAS Regiment deployed to Oman in 1958 at the request of the Omani Sultan to help quell rebel forces. He carries a 7.62mm (0.3in) L4A4 light machine gun.

formed a unit called L Detachment, Special Air Service Brigade. Despite its grand title, the unit was little more than a handful of unconventional soldiers, thrown together to form a new unit as part of a massive deception plan. As a means of further confusing the Germans, the name Special Air Service Brigade was created for a bogus formation of parachute and glider units that were supposedly deployed in the Middle East as part of an invasion force. In Stirling's words, the SAS was formed:

...firstly [to] raid in depth behind enemy lines, attacking HQ nerve centres, landing grounds, supply lines and so on; and secondly [for] the mounting of sustained strategic activity from secret bases within hostile territory and, if the opportunity existed, recruiting, training, arming and coordinating local guerilla elements. Within the British Army there was intense suspicion of the SAS and its unique capabilities and the doubts about them never really went away. Even when the SAS was successful it was never enough for its critics

who despised the idea of small unconventional units that seemed to be totally autonomous. The SAS, however, did have friends in high places who were so pleased with their performance in North Africa and the Mediterranean that they agreed to form a new force for operations in north-west Europe.

By 1944, the SAS had become a brigade and consisted of two British

Right: An SAS trooper from 22 SAS demonstrates the technique of 'tree jumping' during a training session in England, prior to operational deployment in Malaya. This tactic was first developed and used for operations against communist terrorists who were located deep within the jungles of Malaya, as this was the only quick method of reaching them prior to the introduction of the helicopter.

depending on tactical requirements. In addition to the Sabre squadrons, the SAS also has the support of a HQ squadron, Operations Research Wing, Planning and Intelligence Unit, Training Wing, and various attached personnel, including medics, drivers, cooks, EOD specialists and engineers. Control of the three SAS regiments and their support units is in the hands of the Director of Special Forces.

The SAS can trace its history back to 1941, when Colonel David Stirling

regiments (1 & 2 SAS), two French regiments (3 & 4 SAS), one Belgian squadron (5 SAS) and a number of signal squadrons. After the war ended, the SAS was disbanded, along with a number of other elite units that had served their country well throughout the war. The SAS, however, did not go quietly and fought a campaign within the Ministry of Defence to be reformed. In part they were successful, and they were allowed to reform in 1950 as the TA Artists Rifles, a part-time unit that was to eventually become the 21st Special Air Service Regiment (Artists Rifles) Volunteers.

Not content with being just a TA unit, the SAS saw an opportunity during the Malayan Emergency in 1952 to form a regular SAS unit, when the highly successful Malayan Scouts were looking for a new name that would be more representative of their role. Once agreed, the unit became the Malayan Scouts (SAS), later to be redesignated the 22nd Special Air Service Regiment. The SAS was now back in business.

Since reforming in Malaya, the SAS has participated in more wars and conflicts than any other special forces unit in the world, and it is the most combat-experienced.

What follows is a chronology of known SAS operations in the period 1941–2002:

Above: A patrol from 22nd Special Air Service Regiment (22 SAS) holds a briefing near a jungle drop zone off the Bentong Gap road in December 1952, during operations against communist terrorists.

1941
North Africa
The SAS is formed to carry out hit-and-run attacks on German and Italian airfields. It enjoys great success.

1942
North Africa
Further attacks on German and Italian airfields meet with great success, but other raids on Axis shipping in harbour end in failure or are aborted.

Above: SAS troopers in Oman prepare for a hostage rescue mission in Iraq during the Gulf War. The operation was later aborted however.

1943
Europe
Operations in Italy, Sardinia and Sicily include attacks on railway lines, communications and airfields, and the rescue of prisoners of war (POWs).

1944
Europe
Numerous operations in France and Italy include intelligence gathering, attacks on road and rail communications, and harassment of Axis forces.

1945
Europe
Attacks and support missions are carried out in various countries, including Italy, Germany, Holland and Norway.

1950–60
Malaya
The SAS is reformed to fight Communist terrorists in Malaya, following the murder of British citizens and their employees. This period was known as the Malayan Emergency and resulted in the SAS becoming highly skilled in jungle warfare.

1958–9
Jebel Akhdar, Oman
Two SAS squadrons are deployed to Oman to put down a rebellion on the formidable natural fortress of the Jebel Akhdar.

1963–6
Borneo
The SAS finds itself back in the jungle, fighting Indonesian forces and rebel guerillas who are opposed to the formation of the Federation of Malaysia.

1964–7
Aden

'Keeni-Meeni' operations are mounted in the Radfan area against tribesmen and guerillas.

1969–94
Northern Ireland

The SAS supports the British Army and the Royal Ulster Constabulary (RUC) in Northern Ireland by mounting intelligence gathering and anti-terrorist operations against the IRA and its supporters. The operations result in both SAS and IRA fatalities. The most successful is the ambush of IRA terrorists at Loughall, which results in the complete annihilation of the East Tyrone Brigade.

1970–76
Oman

The SAS is sent on a mission to Oman to defeat communist guerillas who are attempting to overthrow the Omani government. This particular operation also features an extremely successful 'hearts and minds' campaign designed to persuade other Omanis not to join in the insurgency.

1980
London

Under the gaze of the world's media, Operation Nimrod is launched to release hostages held in the Iranian Embassy in London, and to kill or capture the terrorists responsible. The operation's success brings the SAS worldwide acclaim and attention, and Operation Nimrod is now viewed as a textbook example of how to execute a hostage-rescue mission.

1981
Gambia

Following a coup in the Gambia, the SAS helps to restore President Jawara to power.

Below: The famous SAS patrol Bravo Two-Zero poses for a photo prior to its ill-fated mission in Iraq during the 1991 Gulf War. Note their heavy firepower, equivalent to that carried by 100 regular soldiers.

Above: The SAS Winged Dagger badge with the regiment's motto, 'Who Dares Wins' – one they certainly live up to.

Weapons

Weapons used by the SAS include the HK MP5 submachine gun (entire range); HK53 submachine gun; Ingram Model-10 submachine gun; UZI submachine gun; M16 A2 assault rifle with 40mm (1.57in) M203 grenade launcher; Colt M4 carbine; Colt Commando assault rifle; HK G3 assault rifle; HK G8 assault rifle; HK G41 assault rifle; FN 7.62mm (0.3in) SLR (no longer used by the British Army, but still used by the SAS for certain operations); Steyr AUG assault rifle; SA-80A2 assault rifle (used by TA SAS only); SA-80A2 LSW (light support weapon – used by TA SAS only); M249 Minimi light machine gun; Ameli light machine gun; HK13E light machine gun; Ultimax 100 light machine gun; 7.62mm (0.3in) GPMG; Browning M2 .50 heavy machine gun; Accuracy International PM sniper rifle; Tikka M55 sniper rifle; SSG 3000 sniper rifle; Barret .50 long-range sniper rifle; Franchi SPAS 12 combat shotgun; Franchi SPAS 15 combat shotgun; Remington 870 combat shotgun; Browning HP pistol; Glock 18 pistol; and SIG 226 and 228 pistols.

Heavy weapons include the LAW 80 anti-tank rocket launcher; M72 anti-tank rocket launcher; Milan anti-tank missile; 81mm (3.19in) mortar; Javelin MANPADs (man-portable air defence system); FIM-92 A Singer MANPADs; MK-19 automatic grenade launcher; SB 40 LAG automatic grenade launcher; and 20mm (0.79in) AMW (Anti-Material Weapon).

Vehicles used include the Land Rover 90 ('Dinkies'); Land Rover 110; Land Rover SOV (special operations vehicle); and LSV (light strike vehicle).

The SAS are well known for their armed vehicles. As well as numerous unmarked vehicles, they often use some of the following vehicle-mounted weapons: Browning M2; GPMG; M249 Minimi; 25mm (0.98in) cannon; Milan; TOW; MK-19 40mm (1.57in) grenade launcher; 0.5 GAU-19 three-barrel machine gun; 51mm (2.01in) and 81mm (3.19) mortars; Argocat mini-ATV (all-terrain vehicle); Harley-Davidson track bike; Quad ATV; Unimog utility truck; DAF utility truck; Pinzgauer lightweight utility truck; and Range Rover.

In addition to their large fleet of ground vehicles, the SAS also operates a fleet of small boats, including the Rigid Raider, Klepper canoe, Gemini, Zodiac and submersible recovery craft. The SAS also has its own fleet of Agusta A-109A light utility helicopters, two of which were captured from the Argentinian forces during the Falklands War in 1982. These are flown by pilots of 8 Flight AAC (Army Air Corps) and are painted in civilian colours for discreetly transporting counterterrorist operators within the United Kingdom.

1982

Falkland Islands

The SAS is deployed to the Falkland Islands to carry out intelligence and raiding operations against Argentinian forces occupying the island illegally. Key operations are the retaking of Grytviken, South Georgia and the Pebble Island raid. Although highly successful during this war, the SAS loses 18 men in a non–combat-related helicopter crash.

1989

Columbia

22 SAS is deployed to Colombia, to take part in the anti-cocaine war, after the British government receives a request for military assistance. This includes training for Colombian forces and missions against the drug barons.

1990–91

The Persian Gulf

The SAS is deployed to the Gulf, in support of the UN-led campaign to remove Iraq from Kuwait. It operates primarily in Iraq on missions against the Iraqis' Scud missiles and their support infrastructure. Highly successful, it operates in ways very similar to the original SAS in North Africa.

1994–5

Bosnia

Teams are deployed to Bosnia in small numbers to gain intelligence on the Serbian forces and to provide target designation for RAF strike aircraft.

1997

Peru

A six-man SAS team is sent to Lima, Peru, following the takeover of the Japanese Ambassador's residence in January 1997. It worked alongside operators from the US Delta Force.

1998

The Persian Gulf

In February, a squadron is deployed to the Gulf when Saddam Hussein threatens to start another war. It is tasked with reconnaissance missions and the rescue of downed pilots.

1998

Albania

In March, a four-man team is deployed to Albania, to rescue British aid worker Robert Welch. The team locate him

and secure his rescue by driving to the coast using Land Rovers. Upon arrival they are met by two helicopters. One provides a security force at the rendez-vous point, while the other extracts the rescue team and their vehicles.

1999

Kosovo

Following the invasion of Kosovo by Serbian forces, the SAS is deployed to assist in finding targets for NATO aircraft and to rescue downed aircrew. It also provides support to the Kosovo Liberation Army (KLA) and helps to apprehend Serbian war criminals.

2000

Sierra Leone

Initially, the SAS are called in to provide an overt presence in Sierra Leone, in

Above: An SAS team sets up an observation post during the Gulf War, in anticipation of forthcoming operations.

support of a UN peacekeeping effort. However, a number of British soldiers are captured and held hostage by a ruthless militia known as the 'West Side Boys'. In response, the SAS launches a spectacular rescue operation in conjunction with 1 Para, and it secures the release of the hostages for the loss of one soldier.

2001

Afghanistan

Following the terrorist attack on the United States on 11 September 2001, the SAS is deployed to Afghanistan in support of UK operations against terrorism. It carries out reconnaissance

and targeting missions for US forces against Taliban and Al Qaeda soldiers and their equipment. In addition, it provides support to the Northern Alliance and helps to find safe areas for the delivery of humanitarian aid. Playing a key role in this war, it is extremely successful, operating in very difficult and demanding conditions.

2002
Somalia
Small teams are deployed to search for Osama Bin Laden, and members of his Al-Qaeda terrorist network, who had fled from Afghanistan in 2001.

SAS troopers generally wear standard British Army DPM combats while training, together with their famous

sand-coloured beret and winged dagger badge. However, while on operations, troopers are allowed to wear virtually anything they like, and they are given complete freedom in their choice of weaponry.

Troopers generally try to wear clothing that is as comfortable and practical as possible for the environmental conditions within which they are operating. If feasible, they will even dress in the same manner as the local population of the area in which they are operating, to blend in as best as they can and avoid attracting attention. This particular tactic worked extremely well in Afghanistan, where SAS Gurkhas were used for reconnaissance missions as their facial features are very similar to those of local Afghanis.

Above: SAS troopers pose in front of their heavily armed Land Rover during operations in Iraq. Apart from updated equipment, little has changed in the principles of desert warfare since World War II.

For counterterrorist operations, however, troopers wear black nomex clothing, which allows them to be seen more easily by their colleagues while operating in smoke- or dust-filled rooms, and the visual effects of which are also extremely intimidating. In addition, they wear Avon S10 respirators and bulletproof assault vests that have pockets for stun grenades, spare magazines and a knife. They also attach spare magazines to their wrists for quick reloads, and these are known as wrist rockets.

SPECIAL BOAT SERVICE (SBS)

Based in Poole, Dorset, the Special Boat Service (SBS) is the naval equivalent of the SAS, and it warrants a mention in the land section as most of its recent operations have taken place on land rather than at sea. (For a full history, refer to the Special Forces at Sea section.)

This change in operational responsibility is due to the fact that the SBS now comes under a general UK

Below: The SAS made particularly good use of motorcycles during the Gulf War, often using them for scouting and liaison duties as they were far more practical for this role than heavy vehicles.

Special Forces umbrella and plays an important part in supporting the SAS during times of conflict. This move has not gone down well with the SBS, which fears that its identity is being eroded to the point that the SBS will become a maritime squadron within the SAS orbit. Indeed, in the late 1990s, the unit's name changed from Special Boat Squadron to Special Boat Service, a title it previously held during World War II.

The SBS is concerned by a further issue, namely maritime operations, for the SAS already has its own boat troop. At one time, the general rule between the two forces was that the SAS handled all maritime operations above

the surface, while the SBS took care of everything underwater – sabotage, equipment recovery and underwater demolitions. This area of responsibility has now blurred, with both units capable of carrying out maritime operations as and when required.

Part of the reason behind these changes relates to the fact that the SAS is understrength at present and cannot meet all of its operational requirements. This is understandable, as the SAS and SBS have both been involved in numerous conflicts in recent years, including operations carried out in the Persian Gulf, Bosnia, East Timor, Albania, Kosovo, Sierra Leone, Afghanistan and Somalia, as well as

ongoing internal security operations in Northern Ireland.

The SBS tends to operate in the shadows, and it is very secretive about its exact roles. The unit's operational strength is some 120 regular operators, plus a small part-time reserve unit that is highly professional and extremely well trained. Although the SBS is considerably smaller than the SAS, many operations and missions credited to the SAS have in fact been carried out by the SBS.

During the Gulf War in 1991, SBS units were inserted behind enemy lines to destroy some of Iraq's underground communications systems, which were essential for supplying targeting data to the mobile Scud launchers that plagued the coalition forces.

In 1999, both the SBS and SAS fought side by side in Sierra Leone against a ruthless bunch of armed rebels, known locally as the 'West Side Boys', who had taken a small group of British soldiers hostage. During the subsequent rescue mission, more than 80 rebels were killed for the loss of one SAS trooper, and all the hostages were released unharmed.

Above: An SAS trooper wades through a wadi, or flooded watercourse, after finding a safe route for his Land Rover.

The biggest deployment for the SBS thus far has been in Afghanistan as part of Operation Enduring Freedom, following events on 11 September 2001. First deployed to Bagram Airbase in Northern Afghanistan, the SBS was acting in support of US forces who were hunting Al Qaeda/Taliban forces known to be operating in the area. Following a number of military actions by both the British and

American forces who were acting in support of the Northern Alliance, the Al Qaeda/Taliban forces surrendered and were taken to a fortress just outside Mazar-e-Sharif.

A few days later, the prisoners overpowered their guards, and a fierce battle took place before order could be restored by British and American special forces. During the insurrection, hundreds of lives were lost, including those of a number of US personnel who were within the fortress.

It was later revealed by the US Department of Defense that, at the height of the revolt, six SBS troopers stormed the fortress and charged a force of some 200 prisoners who were trying to kill American forces trapped within the Mazar-e-Sharif compound. Despite being totally outnumbered, they drove the prisoners away and rescued the Americans from their predicament. In recognition of their bravery, President George W. Bush awarded the SBS troopers the Congressional Medal of Honor.

As SBS operations continued in Afghanistan, MI6, Britain's intelligence service, identified a valley where it was believed that Osama bin Laden, the Al Qaeda leader, was in hiding. In response, two SBS Squadrons containing 60 troopers were deployed in the valley with orders to either capture or kill him. As the troopers awaited further instructions, orders came through from the British government that they were to withdraw from the valley and allow American forces to carry out the operation instead. As the SBS withdrew from their position, there was a delay in the American deployment, one which was to have devastating consequences.

As it transpired, in between the British withdrawal and the arrival of the American forces, Osama bin Laden slipped out of the valley unnoticed

and made his way to neighbouring Pakistan, where border security was slack. Unaware that Osama bin Laden had already gone, America launched Operation Anaconda, which ran into trouble almost from its very

Above: Members of the Royal Marines SBS board an RAF Hastings in 1952 for a parachute insertion into the English Channel. The SBS has an equally illustrious history as the SAS and have worked together time and time again.

beginning. By mistake, US forces landed right in the middle of the valley, instead of its outside, and all hell broke loose at once.

As the US forces attempted to fight their way out of the valley, they sustained heavy casualties – 11 killed, 88 wounded and two Chinooks shot down, plus a number of other helicopters so badly damaged that they had to be sent back to the United States for repair.

Although the Americans inflicted hundreds of casualties on the enemy forces, their own forces were neither trained nor prepared for such warfare. Following an urgent request for assistance from the US government, Britain deployed more than 1800 Royal Marines to the area, along with a force of SBS personnel. For several weeks, the force carried out intensive search operations in the valley; however, there was no reported contact with any enemy forces.

The SBS possesses an enviable reputation amongst other special forces right around the world, and it will no doubt fight extremely hard to maintain both its independence and its identity in the future, despite ever growing rumours of merging the unit with the SAS.

Weapons used by the SBS include the M16A2 with M203 grenade launcher; Colt M4; Colt Commando; M249 Minimi; SA 80 A2; HK MP5 (all versions); HK G3; Steyr AUG; Remington M870; Barret 50; and Browning HP.

Above: SBS frogmen prepare to jump from an RAF Hastings in 1952.

Above: The SBS badge with the unit's motto, 'Not by strength by guile'.

UNITED STATES OF AMERICA 🇺🇸
US Special Operations Command (USSOCOM)
US Army Special Operations Command (USASOC)
75th Ranger Regiment
Green Berets

The United States Armed Forces special forces operations are organized under the USSOCOM. The USASOC is the Army component of the USSOCOM and elite units within USASOC include the Special Forces Group, more famously known as the Green Berets during the Vietnam conflict, and the 75th Ranger Regiment, the oldest regiment in the US Army.

Special forces have been a part of American history since the 17th century, when Major Robert Rogers decided that unconventional warfare had a place within the American armed forces of the day and set about forming America's first special forces unit, the Rangers. Although individual officers and men have used unconventional tactics and strategies for hundreds of years, it became apparent only during World War II that there was a need for official recognition of such forces. Although the United States had the Office of Strategic Services (OSS) to coordinate unconventional warfare during the war, its scope was acknowledged to be limited, a fact that eventually led to formation of the 10th Special Forces Group in the early 1950s.

It was only when the United States became involved in Vietnam that things started to change. This was partly a result of President Kennedy's interest in Special Operations Forces (SOF), and it was he who allowed the 'Green Berets' (a unit he established) to wear the distinctive beret for which they are now famous. After the Vietnam war

Below: A US special forces operator is seen here using his boat as cover during a training exercise.

ended, SOF capability declined within the US Army to such a degree that their entire future was in doubt. Things finally came to a head in 1980, following the failure of Operation Eagle Claw (see Delta Force), which led to the formation of the joint counterterrorist task force and the Special Operations Advisory Panel.

Following many years of questions and internal re-education about the role of special forces within the US Armed Forces, the Department of

Defense activated USSOCOM. This consists of some 46,000 Army, Navy and Air Force SOF personnel, both active and reserve. These forces are organized as follows:

US Army Special Forces – 75th Ranger Regiment; 160th Special Operations Aviation Regiment (SOAR); and psychological and civil affairs units.
US Navy – sea-air-land forces (SEALS); special boat units; and

SEAL delivery units.
US Air Force – special operations squadrons (fixed and rotary wing); a foreign internal defence squadron; and a combat weather squadron.

US ARMY SPECIAL OPERATIONS COMMAND (USASOC)

USSOCOM's function is to provide highly trained, rapidly deployable and regionally focused SOF personnel in support of global requirements from the national command authorities, the geographic commanders in chief and the US ambassadors and their country teams. The Geographic Commander in Chief's area of responsibility is divided into various commands. In 1999, SOF had units deployed in 152 countries and territories (not including classified missions and special access programmes). On any given day, some 5000 SOF are deployed in 60 countries. The characteristics of SOF personnel are shaped by the requirements of their missions and include foreign-language capabilities; regional orientation; specialized equipment, training and tactics; flexible force structure; and an understanding of the political context of the mission.

Activated on 1 December 1989 and commanded by a lieutenant general, USASOC is the Army component of USSOCOM and controls:

Five active and two Army National Guard (ARNG) special forces groups, totalling fifteen active and six ARNG battalions.
One active Ranger Regiment (the 75th) consisting of three battalions.

Left: A US special forces tactical air control operator trains for operations in Afghanistan at Pope Air Force Base, North Carolina. The role of forward air controllers is growing rapidly in the special operations world as you cannot beat having a set of eyes on the ground.

Above: A heavily armed LSV (light strike vehicle) shows off its impressive range of weaponry.

An active special operations aviation regiment (160th SOAR) with a detachment in Puerto Rico.

Four reserve civil affairs (CA) commands, seven reserve CA brigades, and one active and 24 reserve CA battalions.

One active and two reserve PSYOP groups, totalling five active and eight reserve PSYOP battalions.

One active special operations support command composed of one special operations signal battalion (the 112th), one special operations support battalion (the 528th) and six special operations theatre support elements.

Right: A US special forces soldier makes good use of his track bike during Operation Desert Storm.

Two active and two reserve chemical reconnaissance detachments (CRD). The John F Kennedy Special Warfare Center and School, which is responsible for developing doctrine, running training courses for Army special forces in civil affairs, psychological operations, escape and evasion, survival, and resistance to interrogation.

75TH RANGER REGIMENT

The 75th Ranger Regiment is one of the finest light infantry units in the world and is a key component of the US Army's Special Operations Command (USASOC). Based in Fort Benning, Georgia, the Ranger Regiment comprises 2300 highly trained and well motivated soldiers divided between three battalions.

Within each battalion, there are three combat companies, each containing three platoons, all of which are supported by a weapons platoon.

According to its mission statement:

The mission of the Ranger Regiment is to plan and conduct special operations and light infantry operations in any operational environment. The primary special operations mission of the Regiment is Direct Action, or DA. DA operations conducted by the Rangers may support or be supported by other special operations forces. They can conduct these missions alone or in conjunction with conventional military operations. Rangers can also operate as special light infantry when conventional

Above: US special forces demonstrate to Filipino soldiers how to storm a house during a close-quarter battle.

light infantry or airborne forces are unsuited for or unable to perform a specific mission. In fact, modern-day Rangers conduct basically the same types of missions their forebears conducted three hundred years earlier.

The Ranger Regiment is well supported by the US Army and has priority over other units when it deploys. Its budget alone is that of an entire Infantry Division. The Rangers work very closely with other US special forces units, such as Delta Force and the 160th Special Operations Aviation Regiment (SOAR) – also known as the 'Night Stalkers'. The Rangers can deploy anywhere in the world within a few hours, as they maintain a company at a high level of operational readiness. They are trained to infiltrate enemy territory by land, sea or air and can operate independently without outside support for up to five days. To ensure that maximum firepower and tactical flexibility is maintained at all times, every weapon used by the Rangers must be man-portable. Although the Rangers can undertake many different types of missions, they specialize in rescue and evacuation, snatch and grab, light strike, and tactical reconnaissance. They are also experts in urban combat, operating primarily at night, and are well equipped for such operations, as ably demonstrated in Mogadishu, Somalia.

Training requirements within the Ranger Regiment are extremely demanding: soldiers train for 11 months of the year with only two blocks of leave to break the rigorous programme. The Regiment trains all over the world in various environments, including jungle, desert, arctic and mountain terrain, ensuring that its soldiers are physically conditioned for different climates. At present, the main training focus within the Rangers is on the 'Big Four' fundamental skills that each Ranger should possess – marksmanship, battle drills, medical training and physical training.

With a fearsome reputation to protect, not to mention high standards, the Rangers are extremely selective. In theory, every soldier in the US Army is guaranteed a Ranger enlistment option, but the reality is somewhat different. Candidates must first pass the three-week Ranger Indoctrination Phase

(RIP). This assesses and prepares soldiers for their eight-month stint with a Ranger battalion, prior to attending Ranger School. Before attending RIP, soldiers must first pass through basic training and infantry school, followed by a three-week parachuting course at the Airborne School in Fort Benning, Georgia.

Soldiers who pass RIP remain with the battalion and work up their skills and physical strength in preparation for Ranger school, which will either make or break them.

Ranger School has three phases, which are held at different locations within southeastern United States – and all three are hard. The first phase of the course commences at the 4th Ranger Training Brigade at Fort Benning, where the soldiers face a series of long marches in realistic combat conditions. Throughout this phase, they are allowed little food or

sleep, and are driven to the edge of exhaustion by having to carry full kit at all times. Next they move on to the 5th RTB in Dahlonega, Georgia, where they undergo mountain training, while the final phase – jungle/swamp training – takes place at the 6th RTB, located at Eglin Air Force Base. Throughout this course, no rank slides are worn, as all Ranger soldiers are expected to show leadership skills.

Those who pass Ranger School can look forward to an exciting career that is diverse and demanding, yet highly rewarding. Once qualified, Rangers can undertake further courses in covert reconnaissance, demolitions, communications, combat medicine, sniping, vehicle operations, watermanship, scuba diving, and HALO/HAHO parachute infiltration. Service with the Rangers is also seen as a logical career stepping stone between

Right: A US Ranger with M16A1 at the ready. These soldiers are the finest light infantry in the world and have never let their nation down.

The Ranger Creed

Recognizing that I volunteered as a Ranger, fully knowing the hazards of my chosen profession, I will always endeavor to uphold the prestige, honor, and high 'Esprit de Corps' of my Ranger Regiment.

Acknowledging the fact that a Ranger is a more elite soldier who arrives at the cutting edge of battle by land, sea or air, I accept the fact that as a Ranger my country expects me to move further, faster and fight harder than any other soldier.

Never shall I fail my comrades. I will always keep myself mentally alert, physically strong, and morally straight, and I will always shoulder more than my share of the task, whatever it may be, one hundred per cent and then some.

Gallantly will I show the world that I am a specially selected and well trained soldier. My courtesy to superior officers, neatness of dress and care of equipment shall set the example for others to follow.

Energetically will I meet the enemies of my country. I shall defeat them on the field of battle for I am better trained and will fight with all my might. Surrender is not a Ranger word. I will never leave a fallen comrade to fall into the hands of the enemy, and under no circumstances will I ever embarrass my country.

Readily will I display the intestinal fortitude required to fight on to the Ranger objective and complete the mission. Though I be the lone survivor. 'Rangers lead the way.'

conventional infantry and special forces, as many Rangers go on to serve with Delta Force.

THE 75TH RANGER REGIMENT'S OPERATIONAL HISTORY

The Ranger Regiment has a long and proud history dating back some 300 years, and it is the oldest regiment in the US Army. The name Ranger dates back to the 17th century, when American colonists used the word to describe how far they had travelled in a day over rough terrain – for example, 'We ranged eight miles this day.'

1754–63

First formed by Major Robert Rogers of Connecticut, who fights for the British against the French and Red Indians. His most famous operation is

Below: Rangers from the 1st Ranger Battalion being deployed to Panama during Operations Just Cause board a C-141 aircraft at Hunter Army Airfield, Georgia, on December 1989.

against the Abenaki Indians, who are based in St Francis, 64km (40 miles) south of Montreal.

Travelling by canoe and by foot, Rogers and his force of 200 Rangers cover 644km (400 miles) in 60 days without the enemy being alerted to their presence. On 29 September 1759, the Rangers attack the Abernaki's camp and kill hundreds before withdrawing to their base. It is a spectacular victory and leads to Rogers being commissioned into the 60th Foot (The Royal Americans), where he writes his famous 19 standing orders for the Rangers, many of which are valid today.

1774–6

Rangers fight on the side of the British during the American War of Independence.

1861–5

Rangers fight on both the Union and Confederate side during the American Civil War, and later for America in the Mexican War.

1942–5

The Ranger title is revived again for World War II, six battalions being deployed in Europe and the Far East. The first unit was in fact formed at Carrickfergus, Northern Ireland, in 1942, under the command of Major William Derby, and fought at Dieppe alongside British Commandos.

Other actions fought include North Africa; Sicily; and Salerno, Italy, where the 1st and 3rd Ranger Battalions were virtually wiped out in the battle for Cisterna. Their finest hour, however, is during the D-Day landings of June 1944, when Ranger

Above: US special forces secure an airfield during an arctic warfare exercise, hence their snowsuits.

Force A from the 2nd Battalion assaulted the well-defended concrete fortifications on the cliffs of the Point du Hoc. For two days, they hold the position and fight off the German 914th Infantry Regiment in an action that costs them 135 killed and wounded out of a force of 225.

At Dog White beach on Omaha, soldiers of Ranger Force C, 2nd Ranger Battalion, are pinned down by heavy enemy gunfire and unable to move. Near to the Ranger Force is Brigadier General Norman Cota, assistant divisional commander of the 29th Infantry Division, who shouts the famous words 'Rangers lead the way', motivating them to break out of the

Above: A US special forces soldier mans a 40mm (1.57in) grenade launcher mounted on a HMMWV during Desert Storm.

deadly killing zone. After that, 'Rangers lead the way' becomes the force motto.

Although most of the Rangers' better known actions are fought in Europe, they also fight in the Pacific, where they carry out a daring raid on a prisoner-of-war camp at Cabanatuan on Luzon, liberating 500 American prisoners. After World War II, the Ranger units are disbanded, though Ranger training continues, eventually becoming a qualification that is highly valued in the same way as a parachuting or diving qualification.

1950

During the Korean War, Ranger companies are attached to every Army Division that fights there and carry out

missions such as reconnaissance, hit and run, and sabotage.

1969

After the Korean War, all Ranger units are disbanded and their soldiers sent to other Army units that have Long Range Reconnaissance Patrols, or 'Lurps', as they are called. The Lurps carry out more or less the same function as Rangers and perform superbly during the Vietnam War, where their skills are highly valued.

At the height of the war, the US Army redesignates the LRRPs as specific companies of the 75th Infantry Regiment (which later became the 75th Ranger Regiment): O Company Rangers is attached to the 82nd Airborne, and L Company Rangers goes to the 101st Airborne. In Vietnam, the Rangers are used primarily for reconnaissance and

intelligence-gathering missions, but on several occasions they make attempts to rescue American prisoners of war.

1980

A small team of Rangers is sent to Iran, as part of the ill-fated Operation Eagle Claw, led by Delta Force. It is mounted after Iranian terrorists took over the American Embassy in Tehran and seized 53 hostages. During the operation, Rangers secure the Desert One rendezvous site (from where the rescue mission is to be mounted) and also capture a bus containing civilians (which happened to drive through the site) before the operation is aborted.

1983

Rangers from both the 1-75th and 2-75th are deployed to Grenada for Operation Urgent Fury and are involved in numerous actions.

1989

During Operation Just Cause, two battalions of Rangers are parachuted into Rio Hato airfield, 80km (50 miles) west of Panama City, and ordered to seize and hold the airfield.

1991

During Operation Desert Storm, Rangers patrol behind Iraqi lines in heavily armed vehicles and destroy a communications centre located near the Jordanian border.

1993

While performing snatch-and-grab operations in Mogadishu, against Somali warlords, Rangers suddenly find themselves under attack from hundreds of Somali gunmen. A fierce firefight follows, and this is to become the most intense action fought by American soldiers since Vietnam. Lasting for less than 10 hours, it costs the lives of 18 American servicemen and leaves 70 others wounded, while the Somalis lose over 500 killed and over 1000 wounded. This action calls on all aspects of Rangers' training, for it involves urban combat, night fighting, combat rescue, snatch and grab, sniping, firefights, and evacuation of wounded while under fire.

1995

Elements of the Ranger Regiment deploy to the Balkans for operations against the Serbs.

1999

Rangers deploy to Kosovo in support of US forces engaged in operations against Serbian fielded forces.

2001

Rangers deploy to Afghanistan and neighbouring countries as part of Operation Enduring Freedom and help in the search for Al Qaeda terrorists, in particular their leader Osama bin Laden.

Uniforms worn by the Rangers include standard US Army combat fatigues, Lizard suits and Ghillie sniper suits. The Rangers also make extensive use of body armour and night-vision devices, such as the AN /PVS-7 night vision goggles. For additional protection while operating in open areas, they wear Bolle T800 ballistic goggles.

Weapons and equipment used by the Rangers include the · Colt M4 assault rifle; M16A2 assault rifle Mini 14 assault rifle; Steyr AUG assault rifle; HK G3 assault rifle; SOPMOD (Special Operations Peculiar Modification) M4A1 assault rifle; CAR 15 assault rifle; Stoner SR-25 self-loading rifle; Colt Model 733 assault rifle; Walther MP-K submachine gun; HK MP5SD submachine gun; MAC 10 submachine gun; UZI submachine gun; M249 SAW light machine gun; HK13E light

Below: US special forces carry out a recce patrol during a work-up exercise prior to deployment.

Right: The shoulder flash worn by Rangers of the 2nd Ranger Battalion.

machine gun; M60 medium machine gun; M240B medium machine gun; Browning M2 .50 heavy machine gun; Remington 870 combat shotgun; Mossberg Cruiser 500 combat shotgun; HK PSG-sniper rifle; M40A1 sniper rifle; M24 sniper rifle; and Barret M82A1 .50 heavy sniper rifle,

Support weapons include the M203 grenade launcher; M79 'Blooper' 40mm (1.57in) grenade launcher; 81mm (3.19in) mortar; Carl Gustav 84mm (3.3in) recoilless rifle; 66mm (2.6in) LAW and Mk-19 40mm (1.57in) automatic grenade launcher; Stinger MANPAD and M136 AT-4 anti-tank rocket; Beretta 92F handgun; and SIG Sauer P-228 handgun.

Specialist weapon sights include the Aimpoint Comp M close-quarter battle sight; M68 Aimpoint; the M28 Aimpoint sight; and the AN/PEQ2 Infrared Target Pointer/Illuminator/Aiming laser (IPITAL) dual beam aiming device.

The Rangers also operate an extensive fleet of vehicles, which includes the Land Rover Defender 110 SOV (Special Operations Vehicle); Humvee; Quad ATV (All Terrain Vehicle); Harley-Davidson Track Bike. Vehicle-mounted weapons include the Mk-19 40mm automatic grenade launchers; M60 medium machine guns; M240B medium machine gun; and Browning M2 .50 heavy machine gun. Other specialist Ranger equipment includes Zodiac boats and rigid raiders. Rangers also use heavily modified parachutes for HALO and HAHO parachute operations.

The Rangers also make use of helicopters, including the MH-47 D/E Chinook, MH-60 K/L Blackhawk and MH-6 Little Bird, which are operated by the US Army's 160th Special Operations Aviation Regiment.

Major Robert Rogers, 19 Standing Orders

Although Major Robert Rogers wrote these standing orders during the 17th century, many of his tactics are relevant today:

1. Don't forget anything.
2. Have your musket clean as a whistle, hatchet scoured, sixty rounds powder and ball, and be ready to march at a minute's warning.
3. When you're on the march, act the way you would if you was sneaking up on a deer. See the enemy first.
4. Tell the truth about what you see and what you do. There is an army depending on us for correct information. You can lie all you please when you tell other folks about the Rangers, but don't never lie to a Ranger or officer.
5. Don't ever take a chance you don't have to.
6. When we're on the march we march single file, far enough apart so no one shot can't go through two men.
7. If we strike swamps, or soft ground, we spread out abreast, so it's hard to track us.
8. When we march, we keep moving till dark, so as to give the enemy the least possible chance at us.
9. When we camp, half the party stays awake while the other half sleeps.
10. If we take prisoners, we keep 'em separate till we have had time to examine them, so they can't cook up a story between 'em.
11. Don't ever march home the same way. Take a different route so you won't be ambushed.
12. No matter whether we travel in big parties or little ones, each party has to keep a scout 20 yards ahead.
13. Every night you'll be told where to meet if surrounded by a superior force.
14. Don't sit down to eat without posting sentries.
15. Don't sleep beyond dawn. Dawn's when the French and Indians attack.
16. Don't cross a river at a regular ford.
17. If somebody's trailing you, make a circle, come back onto your own tracks, and ambush the folks that aim to ambush you.
18. Don't stand up when the enemy's coming against you. Kneel down, lie down, hide behind a tree.
19. Let the enemy come till he's almost close enough to touch. Then let him have it and jump out and finish him up with your hatchet.

Left: A Green Berets trooper wearing the famous beret. The Green Berets were created by John F. Kennedy and distinguished themselves in the war in Vietnam through their unconventional warfare methods.

Below: A captain of the 5th Special Forces Group in South Vietnam in 1965 displaying the classic look of the Green Berets. He is wearing standard US Army green jungle fatigues and carries a .30 M2 Carbine automatic rifle.

GREEN BERETS

The main role of the Green Berets is, when directed, to deploy and conduct unconventional warfare, foreign internal defence, special reconnaissance, and direct-action missions in support of US national policy objectives within the designated areas of responsibility. The Green Berets are organized in a formation known as the 12-man Operations Detachment 'A', usually known as an 'A Team'. This unit is the key operating element of the force, and five of these A Teams make up a B Team, which comprises six officers (including the major commanding the unit) and 18 men. There are 12 A Teams per company, five companies per battalion, and three battalions per group. At present, there are seven groups, three regular, two National Guard and two reserve.

All members of the Green Berets are volunteers, who must be parachute-qualified, either before joining or after. Once accepted for training, candidates participate in a a rigorous training programme that lasts for some 60 weeks. Those that qualify undergo a further period of training in advanced skills, including demolitions, signals, engineering, languages, communications, and intelligence gathering. All Green Berets must be specialists in at least two skills and can volunteer for advanced parachute courses, such as HALO and HAHO.

The famous motto of the Green Berets is 'De oppresso liber' ('Freedom from Oppression').

Uniforms worn by the Green Berets include standard US Army combat fatigues, Lizard suits, Ghillie sniper suits, and jungle tiger suits. The Green Berets also make extensive use of body armour and night-vision devices, such as the AN/PVS-7 night vision goggles. For additional protection while operating in open areas, they wear Bolle T800 ballistic goggles.

Weapons and equipment used by the Green Berets include the Colt M4 assault rifle; M16A2 assault rifle Mini 14 assault rifle; SOPMOD (Special Operations Peculiar Modification) M4A1 assault rifle; CAR 15 assault rifle; Stoner SR-25 self-loading rifle;

Colt Model 733 assault rifle; Walther MPK submachine gun; HK MP5SD submachine gun; MAC 10 submachine gun; UZI submachine gun; M249 SAW light machine gun; HK13E light machine gun; M60 medium machine gun; M240B medium machine gun; Browning M2 .50 heavy machine gun; Remington 870 combat shotgun; Mossberg Cruiser 500 combat shotgun; HK PSG sniper rifle; M40A1 sniper rifle; M24 sniper rifle; and Barret M82A1 .50 heavy sniper rifle.

Support weapons include the M203 40mm (1.57in) grenade launcher; M79 'Blooper' 40mm (1.57in) grenade launcher; 81mm (3.19in) mortar; Carl Gustav 84mm (3.31in) recoilless rifle; 66mm LAW and Mk-19 40mm (1.57in) automatic grenade launcher;

Stinger MANPAD; M136 AT-4 anti-tank rocket; Beretta 92F handgun; and SIG Sauer P-228 handgun.

Specialist weapon sights include the Aimpoint Comp M close-quarter battle sight; M68 Aimpoint; M28 Aimpoint sight; and AN/PEQ2 Infrared Target Pointer/Illuminator/Aiming laser (IPITAL) dual beam aiming device.

The Green Berets also operate an extensive fleet of vehicles, which includes the Land Rover Defender 110 SOV (Special Operations Vehicle); Humvee; Quad ATV (All Terrain Vehicle); and Harley-Davidson Track Bike. Weapons mounted on vehicles

Below: Heavily armed US special forces carry out a recce patrol during a training exercise. Note the variety of weapons.

include the Mk-19 40mm (1.57in) automatic grenade launcher; M60 medium machine gun; M240B medium machine gun; General Electric 7.62 (0.3in) mini gun; 20mm (0.79in) cannon; and Browning M2 .50 heavy machine gun.

Other specialist Green Beret equipment includes Zodiac boats, high-speed patrol boats and rigid raiders. They also use heavily modified parachutes for its HALO and HAHO parachute operations. The most common means of transport for the Green Berets is the helicopter. Types used include the MH-47 D/E Chinook, MH-60 K/L Blackhawk, and MH-6 Little Bird operated by the US Army's 160th Special Operations Aviation Regiments. For long-range missions, they use the MH-53J, which is operated by the USAF's Special Operations Group (SOG).

Below: US special forces troops, displaying their versatile skills, ride on horseback alongside members of the Northern Alliance in Afghanistan during Operation Enduring Freedom.

The US Special Forces Creed

I am an American Special Forces soldier. A professional!

I will do all that my nation requires of me.

I am a volunteer, knowing well the hazards of my profession.

I serve with the memory of those who have gone before me: Roger's Rangers, Francis Marion, Mosby's Rangers, the first Special Service Forces and Ranger Battalions of World War II, the Airborne Ranger Companies of Korea.

I pledge to uphold the honor and integrity of all I am – in all I do.

I am a professional soldier.

I will teach and fight wherever my nation requires.

I will strive always to excel in every art and artifice of war.

I know that I will be called upon to perform tasks in isolation, far from familiar faces and voices, with the help and guidance of my God.

I will keep my mind and body clean, alert and strong, for this is my debt to those who depend on me.

I will not fail those with whom I serve.

I will not bring shame upon myself or the faces.

I will maintain myself, my arms, and my equipment in an immaculate state as befits a Special Forces soldier.

I will never surrender though I be the last. If I am taken, I pray that I may have the strength to spit upon my enemy.

My goal is to succeed in any mission – and live to succeed again.

I am a member of my nation's chosen soldiery. God grant that I may not be found wanting, that I will not fail this sacred trust.

COUNTER-REVOLUTIONARY WARFARE

The 1970s inaugurated the era of modern terrorism. Hijackings, hostage-taking, bombings and assassinations became common global events. By the 1980s, around 1000 terrorist actions were being committed each year. Governments quickly saw the need for a strong corrective, and so the counter-revolutionary warfare (CRW) unit was born. CRW operatives are usually selected from elite military or police backgrounds. Training is rigorous and ruthless, with an average 80 per cent failure rate amongst applicants. Those that make the grade are placed on a 24-hour alert status, ready to respond to any terrorist threat. Their talents range from hostage rescue and sniping to lock picking and covert surveillance. Units such as the SAS, Delta Force and GSG-9 are powerful resources against irregular enemies. Whether executing an urban hostage rescue or assaulting a terrorist camp in the mountains of Afghanistan, their lethal professionalism makes the world much less safe for terrorist operatives.

Left: The 9mm (0.35in) Heckler & Koch MP5 is a popular CRW weapon, with a controllable 800rpm full-automatic burst.

COUNTER-REVOLUTIONARY WARFARE

The massacre of Israeli athletes at the Munich Olympics in 1972 revealed the international deficit of anti-terrorism skills. Dedicated counter-revolutionary warfare (CRW) units provided the solution.

Western democracies suddenly found themselves under threat of attack in the early 1970s from a plethora of terrorist organizations hellbent on making their extremist opinions heard. Not content with breeding a culture of violence and intimidation in their own countries, many of these extremist groups wanted to take their grudges to the West and attack its values, too. They often had sponsors in the Middle East and Communist Eastern Europe, who were doing everything possible to undermine the West. In September 1972, they showed the world just what they could do.

The event chosen by the terrorists to achieve maximum publicity for their cause was the Munich Olympic Games. On 5 September 1972, armed members of the Palestinian group Black September took advantage of the low security at the Olympic village in Munich and seized 11 Israeli athletes. They demanded the release of 234 fellow members of their group and a safe passage to Egypt – if their demands were not met, they would begin executing the hostages. The German Police had never dealt with a situation like this before and decided apparently to accept the terrorists' demands, taking them to the airport by helicopter. Once the airport was reached, however, hidden snipers opened fire, killing two and wounding several others, including the helicopter pilots. In response, the remaining terrorists took shelter in the helicopters, coming under further attack from German troops with armoured

cars. A fierce firefight erupted between the terrorists and the troops, in which a helicopter exploded, killing several people. Shortly after, the terrorists executed five other hostages, who were being held in another helicopter, before it, too, was blown up.

THE BIRTH OF CRW UNITS

The rescue operation had been a complete disaster for the German security forces: eleven Israeli athletes and five terrorists had been killed. But even in death, the terrorists had achieved a victory, for the story dominated world headlines for weeks after. In response, Germany set up a dedicated anti-terrorist organization, Grenzschutzgruppe 9, or GSG-9 as it was more commonly known.

After witnessing the Munich events, virtually every country in the world was prompted to examine its ability to deal with a similar situation. Although many countries within Europe possessed special forces, none was trained for counterterrorism. Munich was a painful wake-up call for many governments

around the world: terrorism was now recognized to be a growing problem, and the next targets were likely to be those countries least prepared for it.

In response, numerous CRW (counter-revolutionary warfare) units were set up around the world. As they worked hard to develop new tactics, techniques and procedures relevant to counterterrorism, several CRW teams stood out from the rest as being highly adept at this new type of warfare. In effect, these teams, including the British SAS and German GSG-9, became an elite within an elite.

By the early 1980s, the standard of training within most CRW teams was generally good, regardless of whether they were regular Army, special forces, para-military or police units. Essentially, most Western units are the same in their composition, structure, discipline, and weaponry, with many modelling themselves on the British SAS and US Delta Force. The days of the ad hoc CRW team are long gone – no modern country can afford to be without some form of dedicated counterterrorist unit.

Right: Today's anti-terrorist units are imposing figures usually clad in black to add to their intimidating presence.

Terrorist Organizations

Terrorism is currently on the increase throughout the world, hence the growing need for more counterterrorist units. Listed below are some of the known active terrorist organizations around the world.

TERRORIST ORGANIZATION	NATIONAL AFFILIATION	TERRORIST ORGANIZATION	NATIONAL AFFILIATION
Abu Sayyaf Group (ASG)	Philippines	Manuel Rodriquez Patriotic Front (FPMR)	Chile
Al Gama'a al Islamiyya (The Islamic Group, IG)	Egypt	Moranzanist Patriotic Front (FPM)	Honduras
Al Qaeda (The Base)	Afghanistan	Mujahedin-e Khalq Organization (MEK or MKO)	Iran
Armata Corsa	France	National Liberation Army (ELN) Colombia	Colombia
Armed Islamic Group (GIA)	Algeria	National Liberation Front of Corsica (FLNC)	France
Aum Shiri Kyo	Japan	Nestor Paz Zamora Commission (CNPZ)	Bolivia
Basque Homeland and Freedom (ETA)	Spain	New People's Army (NPA)	Philippines
Chukaku-Ha (Nucleus or Middle Core Faction)	Japan	Palestine Liberation Front (PLF)	Iraq
Democratic Front for the Liberation of Palestine (DFLP)	Palestinian	Palestinian Islamic Jihad (PIJ)	Palestinian
Fatah Revolutionary Council (Abu Nidal Organization)	Lebanon	Party of Democratic Kampuchea (Khmer Rouge)	Cambodia
Fatah Tanzim	Palestinian	Popular Front for the Liberation of Palestine (PFLP)	Palestinian
Force 17	Palestinian	Popular Struggle Front (PSF)	Syria
Hamas (Islamic Resistance Movement)	Palestinian	Qibla and People against Gangsterism and Drugs (PAGAD)	South Africa
Harakat ul-Mujahedin (HUM)	Pakistan	Real IRA	Northern Ireland
Hizbollah (Party of God)	Lebanon		
Hizb-ul Mujehideen	Pakistan	Red Army Faction (RAF)	Germany
Irish Republican Army (IRA)	Northern Ireland	Red Brigades (BR)	Italy
Jamaat ul-Fuqra	Pakistan	Revolutionary Armed Forces of Colombia (FARC)	Colombia
Japanese Red Army (JRA)	Japan	Revolutionary Organization 17 November	Greece
Jihad Group	Egypt	Revolutionary People's Liberation Party/Front (DHCP/F)	Turkey
Kach and Kahane Chai	Israel	Revolutionary People's Struggle (ELA)	Greece
Kurdistan Worker,s Party (PKK)	Turkey	Sendero Luminoso (Shining Path)	Peru
Lashkar-e-Toiba	Pakistan	Sipah-e-Sahaba Pakistan (SSP)	Pakistan
Lautaro Youth Movement (MJL)	Chile	Tupac Amaru Revolutionary Movement (MRTA)	Peru
Liberation Tigers of Tamil Eelam (LTTE)	Sri Lanka		
Loyalist Volunteer Force (LVF)	Northern Ireland		

ARGENTINA

Brigada Especial Operativa Halcon

The Brigada Halcon is a small CRW squad manned by former special forces soldiers.
Although based in Argentina, its operations take it throughout Latin America.

The Brigada Especial Operativa Halcon is a tactical unit trained to carry out a variety of tasks that are beyond the scope of the police force, including hostage rescue from aircraft or buildings, operations against narco-terrorists, VIP escorts and special support missions for the security forces. The unit, formed in 1986, consists of 75 commandos divided into five 15-man teams. It reports to the Ministry of Justice and Security for Buenos Aires Province and is based at 601 Battalion, Campo de Mayo.

The 15-man teams are made up of two snipers, one medic, one negotiator, an explosive ordnance demolition (EOD) expert, a communications specialist and eight assault experts. Membership of the the brigade is voluntary and is subject to a rigorous physical and psychological examination. About 40 per cent of candidates make it through the first phase, after which they receive intensive training in different kinds of weapons, explosives and self-defence. Roughly 10 per cent of the candidates make it through this

phase. These then enter an 18-month consolidation phase with the main unit.

Equipment used by the Brigada Halcon includes infrared reflective goggles; radio; combat suit; Kevlar helmet; nomex headcover; bulletproof vest; Nomex gloves; tactical boots; handcuffs; and torch.

Weapons used include the Glock Model 8 knife; Glock 18 9mm (0.35in) automatic pistol; Browning HP 35 cal. 9mm (0.35in) pistol; Barrett 82 sniper rifle with bipod; and HK 33E cal. 5.56mm (0.22in) rifle.

AUSTRALIA

Tactical Assault Group and Offshore Assault Team (TAG & OAT)

Australian CRW units derive from the national SAS force. The units train regularly
with foreign CRW squads such as the British SAS and the US Delta Force.

The Tactical Assault Group and the Offshore Assault Team (OAT) were developed from the Australian Special Air Service Regiment (SASR), which was formed in 1957. The TAG was created to allow for more specialist training in counterterrorist activities, and training in the High Range Training Area outside Townsville includes fighting in built-up areas and

Right: A three-man squad of the Tactical Assault Group (TAG) demonstrates urban room-clearing procedures in full assault gear using MP5 submachine guns.

Above: A TAG assault team abseils from two hovering Blackhawk helicopters onto a rooftop during an exercise in Sydney prior to the 2000 Olympic Games.

Right: A four-man TAG team shown here in typical assault dress, including fire-retardant overalls, Kevlar assault helmets and chest-mounted ammunition pouches.

aircraft assaults. The unit has close links with the British SAS, as well as with the New Zealand SAS and Germany's GSG-9. It comprises 200 men. The TAG would have been on stand-by for large international events such as the Sydney Olympics, but in general the internal terrorist threat in Australia is not perceived to be very high. In the field of anti-terrorism, however, there is no room for complacency.

AUSTRIA ▬▬
Gendarmerieeinsatzkommando 'Cobra'

Despite attracting little terrorist activity, Austria boasts a world-class anti-terrorist unit, the Gendarmerieeinsatzkommando 'Cobra'. It currently has a force of around 200 operatives and is unrivalled in many aspects of urban assault technique.

This unit was formed in 1978 after the Gendarmeriekommando Bad Voslau was reorganized in the wake of rising terrorist attacks. Members of the unit are recruited from the Austrian Gendarmerie. The 'Cobra' unit has close contacts with GSG-9 in Germany and with GIGN in France, including joint training arrangements. Primarily trained for anti-terrorist duties, the 'Cobra' unit is adaptable enough to take on a wide range of specialist roles, including close-protection work. The unit is renowned for its ropework skills.

Typical weapons include the MR73 .357 magnum revolver; and the Glock 17, Steyr 5.56mm (0.22in) AUG, or Steyr 7.62 (0.3in) rifles, for sniping.

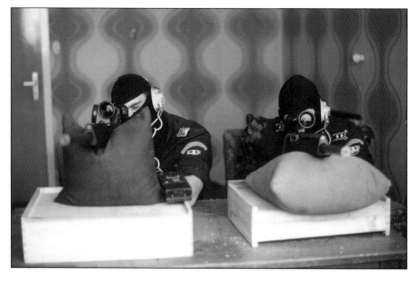

Above: Two snipers from the 'Cobra' unit hone their skill during a target practice.

BELGIUM
Esquadron Speciale d'Intervention (ESI)

The Esquadron Speciale d'Intervention (ESI) is an active CRW unit at national and international levels. Missions have included raiding an IRA safe house in Antwerp prior to a visit to Belgium from Diana, Princess of Wales, and neutralizing gangs of armed bank robbers.

The ESI is also sometimes known as SIE (Speciaal Interventie Eskadron), reflecting Belgium's two official languages, French and Flemish (Dutch). Previously the group was named 'Diane', after the Greek goddess of hunting, and Diana is featured on the unit's emblem.

It was originally created in the wake of the infamous 1972 Olympics as a unit within the Empire Guard, which came under military authority, and the ESI/Diane is trained to carry out a range of both military and civil duties. It sometimes work in conjunction with the plainclothes Grope de Repression du Terrorisme (GRT) or the Securité de L'État.

The unit comprises 200 men and women divided into an assault group, an observation and arrest group, and a medium-sized logistical unit. There is a rigorous two-week preselection course, followed by three months of intensive training.

Like many of the world's anti-terrorist units, the ESI/Diane can call on a range of unmarked vehicles as well as its range of weapons and other equipment. Typical ESI/Diane assignments include the interception of narcotics traffickers, fighting organized crime, and counterterrorism.

BRAZIL

1st Special Forces Battalion and Counterterrorist Detachment

Brazil's 1st Special Forces Battalion and Counterterrorist Detachment has to master combat environments ranging from the urban landscape of Brazil's major cities to vast areas of tropical rainforest. Training for the unit is so tough that up to 90 per cent of candidates fail the course.

In 1983, this unit was formed for counterterrorist duties, as a development from a previous unit that had been trained for jungle infiltration and rescue work. Although there are other elite units in the Brazilian forces which perform similar roles, the 1st Special Forces Battalion is the primary special operations force.

Its training is based on the United States Delta Force, and volunteers to the unit undergo a tough two-week preselection course. The few survivors of this graduate to a 13-week counterterrorist course at a secret location. The training covers a range of activities, from parachuting through heliborne insertion to long-range patrols, reconnaissance and sabotage. The unit is trained to operate in jungle areas, such as the Amazon basin.

Weapons

The 1st Special Forces Battalion weapons include the Colt 45 revolver; Beretta pistol, Imbel M-976 pistol; Belgian FN FAL rifles; US M4 carbine; HK53 rifles; Franchi shotgun; Remington shotgun; Mossburg shotgun; Heckler & Koch MP5 series submachine gun; Uzi submachine gun; PSG-1 sniper rifle; US M79 40mm (1.57in) grenade launcher; Imbel 60mm (2.36in) light mortar; and Hydroar 11M1 flame thrower.

FN FAL

The 1st Special Forces Battalion is organized into five companies, comprising a command and services company, two special forces companies, one commando company and a counterterrorism company.

CANADA

Joint Task Force 2 (JTF2)

Joint Task Force 2 is a secretive unit built on the CRW traditions of the Royal Canadian Mounted Police's Special Emergency Response Team (SERT). The SERT operatives were never deployed in seven years of existence; however, the JTF2 is likely to be more active.

Joint Task Force 2 was formed in 1993, when the unit took over antiterrorist duties from the Royal Canadian Mounted Police. Although few details of the unit have been officially released, it is believed to comprise about 200 men drawn from all three services, and it is based in an unknown location near the Canadian capital, Ottawa.

The unit is trained to carry out forceful anti-terrorist operations within national territory, and there has also been unconfirmed speculation regarding the deployment of Joint Task Force 2 in Kosovo for SAS-style target identification duties.

The unit is also said to have been put on alert for a possible mission to rescue Canadian soldiers taken captive by Serb forces.

CHILE

Unidad Anti-Terrorista

Chile has experienced more terrorism within its borders than most countries in the western hemisphere. Its Unidad Anti-Terrorista force sits at the cutting edge of CRW skills and liaises with US special forces units.

This is the leading anti-terrorist unit in Chile and consists of 120 operators divided up into seven-man teams. Entrants to the unit are required to have completed the Chilean Army Commando course.

The Commando course was first begun in 1962, with advice from the US Rangers. It lasts for five months and is designed to equip soldiers to operate in a wide variety of terrain and weather conditions. The course is

conducted at the Chilean Paratroop and Special Forces school, which trains recruits for special roles in the Navy, Army and Air Force. These specializations may include sea-air-land operations or sniping.

CHINA

Special Operations Unit

Many question marks remain over the capabilities of China's CRW forces. Although highly trained, their equipment is often outdated or even substandard. To date, there is no information about whether they have been committed to action or not.

The SOU was formed in the mid-1980s and operates from out of a base in the Beijing Military Region of China. The SOU is very similar to the US Delta Force in structure and composition, and is tasked with conducting similar missions – namely counterterrorism, light strike, hostage rescue, POW rescue, hit-and-run, CSAR and anti-piracy.

Although the SOU has a greater autonomy over its selection of weapons and equipment compared to that of other special forces units within the People's Liberation Army (PLA), there is still has some way to go before its equipment matches that bestowed on Western special forces.

Selection and training standards for the SOU are comparable to those of Western special forces units and indeed have a very similar drop-out rate, reportedly 50–90 per cent. Recruits are generally selected from the best

units within the PLA and undergo training in parachuting (static-line, free-fall and use of powered chutes); heliborne insertion and extraction; sniping; rappelling; scuba diving; boat

Above: Chinese soldiers demonstrate their martial arts skill.

skills; martial arts; reconnaissance; and foreign languages.

COLOMBIA
Lanceros

Colombian CRW forces are amongst the best in the world and receive frequent operational experience through counternarcotics operations. These operations are often conducted with the assistance or training of US Army special forces units.

Faced with La Violencia, a period of organized violence that followed the outbreak of civil war in 1955, Colombia created the Escuela de Lanceros to train paratroop counter-insurgency operators. The school's training staff were themselves trained at the US Army's Ranger School.

Consisting of a highly trained mobile force, the Lanceros are taught a range of skills over a 10-week period, including mountain climbing, jungle warfare, martial arts and airborne operations. An important part of the course is the planning and conduct of operations against guerrilla insurgents.

The reputation of the Lanceros school is such that trainees from a number of countries in the Americas and Europe are sent there.

Right: An anti-terrorist policeman on patrol armed with an Israeli 5.56mm (0.22in) Galil assault rifle.

DENMARK
Aktions-Styrken (Action Force)

Danish special forces units train heavily with US and European CRW teams to produce an expert force. They are especially talented in maritime and amphibious operations, protecting Denmark's long and complex coastline from terrorist intrusion.

This force comes under the jurisdiction of the National Police and is primarily trained for anti-terrorist hostage rescue, although it is most likely to be called upon to deal with dangerous criminals. The unit consists of about 70 men and is broken down into eight-man assault units, including snipers and fire-fighters. The unit trains alongside the elite army unit Jaegerkorpset, which may be used in police SWAT roles.

The Jaegerkorpset was founded in 1961 and modelled on the British SAS and US Rangers. It is trained for long-range reconnaissance, sabotage and counterterrorism, in cooperation with the Police Aktions-Styrken.

107

ESTONIA ▬
Special Operations Group (SOG)

Estonia's fledgling CRW team – the Special Operations Group (SOG) – benefits like many other CRW teams worldwide from US Army special forces training. The unit is currently small in number, but boasts excellent standards.

Estonia's Special Operations Group (SOG) is based in Tallinn and comprises some 30 operators. Formed only in the mid-1990s, its lacks in operational experience is made up for by the enthusiasm of its members.

Most of the unit's current training is provided by US special forces (usually Green Berets) under America's military assistance programme. Candidates wishing to join the SOG must be extremely fit and speak at least one foreign language. Before being considered for entry, they must first complete a one-year conscription period. This is followed by nine months of rigorous training in disciplines such as marksmanship; rappelling; climbing; parachuting; scuba diving; unarmed combat; and close protection. Parachute training commences with the Soviet static line D-5 and advances to free-fall, and

some candidates even go on to attend courses in the United States to become HALO/HAHO qualified. Candidates can volunteer to undertake further specialized training in sniping, explosives and hostage rescue.

Weapons used include the HK MP5 and Uzi submachine guns; Steyr

Above: Estonian soldiers crouch by an M923 truck during a joint international exercise in the US in 1998.

AUG Assault rifle; SIG Sauer Sniper rifle; Remington 870 Shotgun; and the entire range of Makarov and Tokarev combat pistols.

FINLAND ✚
Osasto Karhu (Bear Force)

Hailing from the icy landscape of Finland, the operatives of the Osastu Karhu (Bear Force) are experts in subzero warfare. Combat skiing, skating and swimming skills are heightened to professional levels alongside more regular combat training.

Osasto Karhu force, which translates from Finish as Bear Force, was developed from a previous unit known as ETY, which in turn was created in the aftermath of the massacre at the Munich Olympics in 1972 along with several other

Europeand counterterrorist units. The unit consists of 40 police officers, who are trained in a range of skills, including winter survival skills, martial arts and marksmanship.

The unit can call upon a fleet of unmanned vehicles, including Saab

900s, Volkswagen vans and a Bell Huey helicopter.

Weapons used include the Smith & Wesson .357 magnum; Glock 17 9mm (0.35in); Heckler & Koch MP5 assault weapon; and Heckler & Koch PSG-1 7.62mm (0.3in) rifle.

FRANCE ▉ ▉
GIGN
EPIGN
RAID

French counterterrorist units – particularly the elite GIGN – have proved themselves in several high-profile aircraft hijackings and hostage-taking situations. Most were formed to counter pro-Arab anti-French terrorism in the 1970s.

Formed in 1974, GIGN consists of 82 NCOs and five officers, divided into four operational groups of 15 members each, along with a four-man negotiation cell. Within these groups there are specialists in free-fall parachuting and diving. The area for which GIGN is renowned, however, is marksmanship, and the GIGN shooting school is admired and used by foreign counterterrorist organizations. The members of the squad are trained to neutralize rather than kill the target where possible, which requires a remarkable level of accuracy. GIGN trains with a variety of weapons, the intention being that members become thoroughly familiar not only with their own weapons, but also with those likely to be used by an enemy.

Above: Members of a RAID unit jump from a helicopter during a rapid-response exercise in a Paris soccer stadium during security preparations for the 1998 World Cup.

Right: A GIGN operative equipped with fast-roping kit, night-vision goggles and a Giat 0.3in FR-F2 sniper rifle fitted with a precision sniper scope.

Above: French special forces perform crowd control during the arrest of a Corsican nationalist leader found with arms in his home.

To join the squad, an applicant must have spent at least five years in the Gendarmerie and also have a first-class record. Once the initial rigorous selection process has taken place, the applicants embark on a 10-month training course.

GIGN has been involved in a variety of incidents, including the rescue of children on a bus at Djibouti in 1976 and the rescue of hostages in the hijacking of Air France Flight 8969 at Marseilles/Magnane Airport in 1994. GIGN members are on constant stand-by against terrorists, drug traffickers and bank robbers.

Weapons used by GIGN include SIG P-228; Heckler & Koch P7 and MR-73 .357 handguns; Uzi 9mm

EPIGN

Consisting of about 140 men, divided into four platoons, EPIGN was formed in 1984 and often works in conjunction with GIGN. For example, the unit supported GIGN in the rescue of hostages from the hijacked Air France Flight 8969 at Marseille/Magnane airport. The unit is also trained to carry out security and protection tasks, and thus often works alongside the French Secret Service, GS PR.

Other aspects of training include surveillance and intelligence gathering, as well as combat swimming, mountaineering, defensive driving and advanced weapons handling.

The EPIGN has operated in a number of crisis areas around the world, including Beirut, Chad, the Congo and Rwanda. It has also carried out a number of operations against the Basque terrorist group ETA.

Weapons used by EPIGN include the Heckler & Koch MP5 series machine guns; Matra-Manurhin MR-73 .357 revolver; Smith & Wesson Chief 60 .38 revolver; Glock 19 and 26 semi-automatic pistols; Remington 870 shotgun; FAMAS rifle; 7.62mm PGM commando sniper rifle; Barret L82A1 and PGM Hecate .50 cal. rifles; Minimi 5.56 (US M29) grenade launcher; and HK69 40mm grenade launcher

(0.35in); HK MP5 SD; SIG 551 and FAMAS 5.56mm (0.22in) sub-machine guns; Ruger HB 308; 7.62mm (0.3in) carbine; Remington 870 12 gauge; Benelli 12 gauge; FR-F1 and Barrett or McMillan 12.7mm (0.5in) sniping rifle; and HK 40mm (1.57in) grenade launchers.

RAID

The RAID unit was formed in 1985 by the French Police Nationale. Consisting of 60 operators divided into four 10-man assault groups, one 10-man group of specialists and another group of commanders, the RAID unit is designed to carry out incisive action against terrorism and serious crime.

Recruits to the unit must have at least five years' experience in the police force. Those who pass the rigorous selection process go on to a nine-month training course. This

Right: French CRW operatives display a typical range of equipment for operations in an urban environment, including a fast-roping kit for abseil assaults.

Left: A man flees for safety with his children as French CRW police exchange gunfire with a criminal gang in Roubaix, northern France.

includes assaults on aircraft and other vehicles, parachuting, combat diving and surveillance. A high level of physical fitness is required.

RAID operations have included the rescue of schoolchildren from a terrorist in 1993 and the rounding-up of Islamic terrorist organizations in France in 1994.

Weapons used by the RAID unit include HK MP5 submachine guns; SIG SG551 5.56mm (0.22in) rifle; Matra-Manurhin MR-73 .357 revolver; Beretta 92FS pistol; and Glock 19 semi-automatic pistol.

GERMANY ▬

Grenzschutzgruppe 9 (GSG-9)

*Germany's GSG-9 ranks alongside the United Kingdom's SAS in terms of its CRW skills.
Like the SAS, it was brought to public attention through a single action, the breaking of a hijack
situation aboard a Lufthansa airliner in 1977.*

GSG-9 was brought into operational use six months after the massacre at the 1972 Munich Olympic Games. Applicants must be volunteers already serving in the Bundesgrenschutz, or Federal Border Police Force. Once accepted, new entrants embark on a 22-week initial training course in which they learn counterterrorist tactics. The unit is divided into three groups: GSG-9/1, for counter-terrorism; GSG-9/2, for maritime counterterrorism; and GSG-9/3, for airborne counterterrorism.

The unit was used to storm a Lufthansa 707 airliner in 1977 in Mogadishu, Somalia. The operation was successful, resulting in the release of the hostages, while three terrorists were killed. The unit was employed in various operations against the Red Army Faction, one of which resulted in a controversial incident in 1993, when Wolfgang Grams was killed after he had shot dead a member of GSG-9 and wounded another.

Above: Freed hostages from the Lufthansa 707 airliner in Mogadishu are helped to safety by GSG-9 operatives.

Right: GSG-9 troopers fast-rope from a helicopter during a training exercise and adopt defensive positions.

The unit has a number of vehicles at its disposal, including unmarked cars, minibuses and trucks. A specially designed aviation group is also used to transport the unit to more distant locations when necessary.

Weapons used by GSG-9 include the MP5 family of weapons; Steyr rifle; PSG-1 sniper rifle; Heckler & Koch G3, P7 and P9; and the Glock and .357 magnum.

Left: Marksmanship is a highly valued skill. GSG-9 sniper training aims to give the operative a first-round kill capability at ranges of up to 600m (1968ft).

INDIA

National Security Guards 'Black Cats'

India's first CRW team was the 12,000-strong Special Frontier Force (SFF) formed in the 1970s. While the SFF had many operational problems, the later Indian National Security Guards (NSG) has performed several successful high-risk operations.

Formed in 1985 by the Indian Government, the NSG is a large force comprising about 7500 members. Its duties are largely concentrated on anti-terrorism and hostage rescue, and it also carries out close-protection work and bomb disposal. The NSG is divided into two groups: the Special Action Group (SAG) and the Special Rangers Group (SRG). There is an introductory basic training course of 90 days, survivors of which pass into the NSG for further intensive training.

Operations involving the NSG include the storming of the Golden Temple at Amritsar in 1986 and 1988. The unit also stormed a hijacked Indian Airlines Boeing 737 in 1994, killing the hijacker and releasing the hostages unharmed. The unit is said to be operating deep-penetration missions in Kashmir. NSG teams are on permanent stand-by at certain key airports.

Weapons used by the 'Black Cats' include the Heckler & Koch 9mm (0.35in) submachine guns, PSG-1 sniper weapon; and Heckler & Koch 512 12-gauge shotgun.

Right: Less well funded than many Western CRW teams, National Security Guards can be seen with basic assault weapons such as these Soviet-made Kalashnikov AKMs.

INDONESIA
Detachment 81

Detachment 81 no longer exists as a unit, but its elite personnel still operate within Indonesian Special Forces. Indonesia contains many extremist religious and political groups, and the Special Forces are frequently called into action.

The Indonesian authorities created Detachment 81 in 1981, following the rescue of hostages held by Muslim fundamentalists aboard an Indonesian Garuda aircraft at a Thai airport.

The unit was based on similar units in the United Kingdom and the United States and consisted of 300 men. Due to the high level of ethnic tension in a country that is made up of 13,000 islands and has a variety of cultures and religions, Det 81 was on constant stand-by for operations against rebel action. This may have included actions in areas such as East Timor, where the Indonesian military maintained a controversial presence. Indonesia reorganized its counter-terrorist forces in the 1990s, and Det 81 has been subsumed into a larger Army Special Forces organization.

Below: Indonesian commandos during a demonstration. Note the undesirable inconsistency in the weapons displayed – two men have AK-series rifles, while the third (centre) has an Israeli Galil.

ISRAEL
Sayeret Golani
Sayeret Mat'kal
Caesarea

Israeli special forces receive more actual combat experience than any other CRW unit. They have perfected the full range of CRW techniques and use them against highly organized terrorist networks throughout Israel and the Arab world.

Since its creation, the state of Israel has been plagued with the curse of terrorism and associated violence. In response, it has developed a robust political and military counter-terrorism policy that is the result of many years of bitter experience.

To combat terrorism, Israel has developed a number of counter-terrorist measures, including:

Operative Measures – proactive activity by the army and security forces against known terrorist targets. Typical measures include precision air strikes, naval bombardments and ground incursions.

Defensive Operations – carrying out disruptive activities to prevent terrorist attacks. Typical measures include the use of road blocks, electric

Right: A female soldier during a sniper training course for an anti-terror unit. Female operatives provide special forces with enhanced tactical options for covert surveillance or insertion.

Left: Israeli Sayeret Mat'kal operatives lead freed hostages away following Operation Isotope, 9 May 1972. Ehud Barak, later to be Israeli prime minister, stands over the body of a terrorist.

fencing, and stop-and-search tactics; and the building of fortified villages.

Punitive Measures – legal activity against terrorist planners, activists, financiers and supporters. Typical measures include the arrest of suspects; the seizure of assets; restriction of movement; assassination; and the sealing and destroying of houses belonging to proven terrorists.

Operation Defensive Shield

March 2002 saw an upsurge in terrorist attacks by Palestinian gunmen and suicide bombers, and these left 80 Israeli citizens dead and hundreds injured. The Israeli government, led by Prime Minister Ariel Sharon, decided to launch a series of decisive attacks against key Palestinian strongholds on the West Bank. The operation was named 'Defensive Shield', and its focal point was the Palestinian refugee camp at Jenin, for years a hotbed of violent resistance to Israeli occupation and a major stronghold for Islamic terrorists.

On 2 April 2002, under the cover of darkness, Israel's elite Golani Brigade began an assault on Jenin. At first, everything went to plan because the Israeli soldiers leading the advance had extensive night-vision devices and the support of both APCs (armoured personnel carriers) and tanks. Then dawn broke. Suddenly, and

from just about every rooftop and back alley, Palestinian gunmen opened fire. It was a highly coordinated movement, and within seconds several of the exposed Israeli soldiers had either been killed or wounded. As the Israelis recovered from the attack, they began to advance, only to discover that all around them lay numerous booby-traps that had not been identified by their intelligence units.

What then followed can only be described as a series of short, vicious and bloody contacts, as the soldiers of the Golani Brigade fought for each house, street by street, until they had cleared a way for the advancing armour. Just as the Israelis seemed to be gaining the upper hand, disaster struck: a Palestinian suicide bomber emerged from the doorway of a wrecked building and ran into the midst of a group of Israeli soldiers before detonating the device. At the same time, a number of smaller devices, which were hidden in nearby rubbish bins and wrecked cars, exploded. While Israeli medics tried in vain to save their fallen comrades, Palestinian snipers, who were hidden among the damaged buildings, opened fire, killing or wounding every soldier in the vicinity.

For the Israelis, enough was enough. Until this point, they had been careful to avoid civilian casualties, declining the use of air support because the risks were too high. Now, though, the soldiers of the Golani Brigade were determined to avenge their dead and wounded comrades. While they regrouped and recommenced their attack, Apache and Cobra helicopter gunships raked the buildings in front of the advance to flush the Palestinians out from their defensive positions.

Following several more days of intense fighting, the Palestinians eventually surrendered, leaving what was left of Jenin firmly in Israeli hands. The cost was heavy: in four days of fighting, 23 Israeli soldiers were dead (mostly reservists) and 75 wounded, while Palestinian losses were put at 50 dead and 130 wounded.

Left: Palestinian gunmen patrol the Jenin refugee camp in the West Bank just before Israeli troops entered and took hold of the town. Long regarded as a militant stronghold, Israel was keen to gain control of the town following an increase in terrorist attacks and suicide bombers since March 2002.

Above: Sheik Ahmad Yassin, former leader of the Islamic 'Hamas', is pictured being brought to court in January 1991.

Most of these activities are carried out by specially trained units of the IDF, such as the Golani Brigade, Matkal Brigade and Caesarea (see also Special Forces on Land section).

CAESAREA

Israel's Caesarea is a special operations hit squad tasked with the elimination of the commanders, controllers and financiers of Israel's enemies abroad. Some years ago, it was disbanded after a failed assassination attempt on Hamas leader Khaled Masha'al, but in September 2002 the unit was reactivated, following almost two years of continual violence against Israeli citizens and members of the armed forces by Palestinian terrorists from the groups Islamic Jihad and Hamas. The Israeli government and its security advisers felt that they had no choice but to take drastic action against the terrorists and their supporters.

Caesarea is currently headed up by Meir Degan, a former army commando and agent. He operates under the command and control of the Israeli intelligence service, Mossad. According to Mossad, Islamic extremists living abroad will now be as vulnerable to attack as those killed by the IDF in the West Bank and Gaza – and Mossad's reputation is such that this promise is likely to be kept.

Caesarea comprises some 30 highly trained fighters – the elite of the elite within the Israeli security services. The squad is generally made up of former commandos, who are fluent in at least one foreign language and have the ability to blend into new environ-ments. For security reasons, their faces are never shown, even to other Mossad agents, and many live as 'sleepers' in foreign countries. Indeed, years can pass before operatives receive a mission; however, once activated, their reactions are immediate and precise.

The selection criteria to join Mossad itself is extremely demanding, and only one in every 1000 applicants receives is successful. From this already elite group, only one candidate in 100 is accepted as a Caesarea operative. Once deployed on operations and regardless of the numbers involved, only the best Caesarea agent within a hit squad will be allowed to carry out the hit.

Much of Caesarea's operational history is highly classified, but its members are known to have killed the Palestinian terrorists responsible for the murder of 11 Israeli athletes during the 1972 Munich Olympics.

ITALY ▰ ▮

Gruppo Intervento Speciale (GIS)
Nucleo Operativo Centrale di Sicurezza (NOCS)

*Italy has experienced many terrorist threats within its borders, mainly from
radical left-wing revolutionary groups. Both GIS and NOCS were formed in 1978 and have
become world-class CRW units with a limiting effect on terrorist activity.*

The Gruppo Intervento Speciale (GIS) was formed by the Italian Carabinieri in 1978 to deal with a growing terrorist threat. The unit consists of 100 men divided into four sections, including a sniper/reconnaissance unit.

All prospective candidates are drawn from the 1st Carabinieri Parachute Battalion, Tuscania, and attend a two-week selection course, after which the successful candidates pass on to a 10-month training course to become qualified operators, which includes combat shooting, explosives and martial arts.

Weapons used by GIS include the Beretta 92F; Heckler & Koch MP5; Beretta M12; Steyr TMP; Smith & Wesson Patrolman .357 magnum; SPAS 12 and 15 shotguns; Beretta SCP 70/90; Steyr AUG; Mauser 86SR

Below: The Heckler & Koch PSG-1 is favoured by Italian counter-revolutionary warfare snipers. It is accurate to 8cm (3.1in) at 300m (984ft).

sniper rifle; Barret M82 .50 calibre sniper rifle; and the Franchi SPAS 12 and 15 12-gauge shotgun.

NOCS

The Nucleo Operativo Centrale di Sicurezza (NOCS) is the counter-terrorist and hostage rescue unit of Italy's Polizia di Stato – the Italian State Police. The NOCS consists of about 100 men who are divided into various sections, including operational interventions, a protection squad and a support group.

Below: An Italian Nucleo Operativo Central di Sicurezza (NOCS) CRW team usually contains one shotgun, which is employed to blast away locks and hinges during forced entries.

Candidates for the unit must have at least four years' service in the police force. Those who pass the preselection tests go on to a six-month basic training course, which includes shooting, climbing, unarmed combat and defensive driving.

Beyond this stage, members of the unit may then go on to more specialized training in areas for which they display a particular aptitude, such as combat driving.

The NOCS unit retains close associations and cooperation with

Right: A NOCS operative wearing standard urban special forces clothing and protective helmet with visor, and carrying a 9mm (0.35in) Beretta Model 12S submachine gun.

compatible units in other European countries, such as the Belgian ESI (Diane) and the German GSG-9.

Weapons favoured by by NOCS operatives include the 9mm (0.35in) Heckler & Koch submachine gun; 9mm (0.35in) Beretta 92FS semi-automatic pistol; Colt Python .357 Magnum .38 special revolver; Beretta AR 70/90 rifle; Galil SAR rifle; Heckler & Koch G41 rifle; and Barrett M82 sniper rifle.

Right: An Italian police sniper positions himself at an open window. As trained, he has placed himself inside the shadows of the room, rather than framing himself within the window itself.

JAPAN •
Special Assault Team (SAT)

Japanese society contains over 50,000 individuals who are potentially or actually involved with terrorist activity. The job of combating these elements falls to the Police Special Assault Team.

The Special Assault Team (SAT) was formed in April 1996, largely as a result of the Sarin gas attack carried out in the Tokyo subway in 1993 by the Aum Shiri Kyo religious sect. The SAT consists of 200 personnel divided between 10 platoons, which in turn are split between separate police prefectures. SAT members have extensive training in counterterrorism work, with particular expertise in hostage rescues from aircraft, buildings or vehicles. The unit is believed to have received joint training with the British Special Air Service (SAS), the German GSG9 and the French GIGN.

Right: Japanese anti-terrorist police practise apprehending a subject during training for the 2002 FIFA World Cup security operations.

JORDAN
Special Operations Unit

*The Jordanian Special Operations Unit is an elite force trained along similar
lines to the US Delta Force unit and the British SAS CRW units. It is a battle-tested force
frequently called to deal with radical Palestinian factions.*

Jordan has suffered a host of terrorist incidents, including hijackings and the murder of diplomats. It is also a nation at the centre of Middle East tensions. To provide an adequate response to these threats, the Jordanian Army developed a Special Operations Unit, which was evolved from its 101st Special Forces Battalion.

The unit consists of an elite body of men selected from amongst the best of Jordan's military personnel. It has earned a reputation for proficiency in martial arts and close-quarter battle skills. Its 150 operators are divided into teams of about 40. Training covers a range of skills, from explosive ordnance disposal to sniping, climbing, rappelling and heliborne insertion. The unit is trained to assault and rescue hostages from buildings, aircraft and other vehicles.

MEXICO
Force F – 'Zorros'

*Mexico's Force F is comprised entirely of volunteers from police or military backgrounds,
and it trains extensively with US security and military units across the border.*

Based north of Mexico City is Mexico's counterterrorist unit, Force F – or the 'Zorros', as they are more commonly known. It is a police unit, but models itself on military units and is equipped accordingly. The unit comprises some 350 well-trained commandos who are expert in a specific discipline such as weapons handling, close-quarter battle, hostage rescue, sniping, bomb disposal or communications. Typical missions include hostage rescue, bomb disposal, counterterrorism and anti-narcotics.

Weapons used by Force F include the HK MP5 submachine gun; M16 A2 assault rifle; CAR-15 assault rifle; Smith and Wesson 12-gauge shotgun; and Beretta 9mm (0.35in) pistols.

Right: Members of the 'Zorros', or the Foxes, with faces covered by sky masks form a picket line in November 1997.

NETHERLANDS ☰
Korps Commandotroepen (KCT)
Bijzondere Bijstands Eenheid (BBE)

Dutch CRW units employ some of the harshest selection procedures of any elite force in the world.

Holland, like many countries in Europe, lives under the constant threat of terrorism. However, unlike many of its neighbours, it has a very capable and highly trained deterrent, the Korps Commandotroepen (KCT). This comprises three commando companies – 104, 105 and 108, which is a dedicated special forces company tasked with the planning and execution of special operations during times of crisis. One unusual aspect of the KCT is the fact that all three companies have their own counterterrorism teams as part of their ORBAT, along with other specialists who are expert in all aspects of infiltration.

This system works extremely well, giving the Dutch Government and its Armed Forces a greater flexibility in the planning and conducting of both proactive and reactive missions against terrorist cells operating in Holland and indeed overseas. The KCT is well placed to respond quickly to a crisis

and works very closely with the 11th Air Mobile Brigade and other units within the Dutch Armed Forces. The skill levels within each team are extremely high: each of the teams

Above: An assault team from the Royal Netherlands Marine Corps BBE unit prepare for action in a dockyard.

contains two demolition experts, two snipers, two communication specialists and two medics.

BIJZONDERE BIJSTANDS EENHEID (BBE)

The Bijzondere Bijstands Eenheid is part of the Royal Dutch Marines and consists of about 90 highly trained volunteers, divided into three platoons. Training is a 48-week course in which members learn about demolitions, weapons and other counterterrorist skills, such as assaults on buildings, aircraft, ships and trains. The successful freeing by the BBE

KCT Training

Training requirements for the KCT are very demanding. Each recruit has to go through either 12 months (for soldiers already serving) or 14 months (for those who volunteer from civilian life) of commando training. This is split into preparatory training, of either 4 or 12 weeks, depending on experience; 14 weeks of basic commando training; and 26 weeks of advanced commando training. Those that make it as far as phase two receive the coveted green beret and go on to complete the final 26-week phase of operational training, which includes free-fall parachuting, combat driving, sniping, demolitions, medicine and communications.

operatives of more than 200 hostages captured by South Moluccan extremists from a train and a school in May 1977 – killing six terrorists in the process – stands as a textbook example of innovative CRW methods.

The BBE works in collaboration with the Dutch police, especially in the area of riot control, and also has close links with other counterterrorist units, including the Belgium ESI (Diane), German GSG-9 and French GIGN.

NEW ZEALAND
1st Special Air Service Squadron (SAS)

Although New Zealand is a small country militarily, its 1st Special Air Service Squadron (SAS) has an international reputation for excellence.

The 1st Special Air Service Squadron (SAS) is New Zealand's counterterrorist unit. Although not as large as its British and Australian SAS cousins, the 1st SAS Squadron is nonetheless a very professional and well trained unit. Details of the squadron are extremely difficult to come by, as the unit puts a close guard over its secrecy. It is believed to comprise some 120 personnel, plus support units, and is structured on the principle of four-man teams. Typical missions include counterterrorism, hostage rescue, tactical reconnaissance, hit and run, and light strike. The unit has seen action in Brunei, Borneo, Indonesia and Vietnam, and was deployed to the Gulf in 1991 as part of the Australian SAS contingent.

Weapons used include the HK MP5 submachine gun; M16A2 assault rifle; Remington 870 shotgun; and HK PSG-1 sniper rifle.

NORWAY
Beredskaptrop
Forsvarets Spesialkommando (FSK)

Norway has remained remarkably free of terrorism throughout its postwar history. Norwegian CRW operatives place a high emphasis on amphibious and arctic warfare.

Beredskaptrop was created in 1975 to provide Norway with a rapid response to potential terrorist or hostage incidents. The unit falls under the control of the Oslo Police Department, but is on call to all parts of the Norwegian National Police system.

Comprising about 50 operators, the Beredskaptrop function on a needs-must basis and spend most of their time working as regular police officers in various roles. They must undergo, however, a considerable amount of annual training in order to maintain their skills at the level necessary to respond effectively should an incident arise. Training takes in aspects as varied as parachuting, combat diving, and a variety of weapons work. Due to the nature of the Norwegian coastline and the importance of its offshore oilfields, the Beredskaptrop maintains a high level of seamanship, as well as the ability to board ships and oil rigs.

The Beredskaptrop has close associations with similar units, such as the British SO19 and German GSG-9.

FSK

The Forsvarets Spesialkommando (FSK) was formed in 1952 and comes under Norwegian Army Command. Although trained for military special operations roles, such as long-range reconnaissance, the FSK is tasked primarily in peacetime with counterterrorism. Members of the unit are drawn from the Army Jægerkommand and the Marinejægertropp.

The unit spends a large proportion of its time training for assaults on oil rigs because of their strategic value to Norway. The FSK is also trained for hostage-rescue operations on aircraft and buildings, and provides protection for members of the Norwegian royal family and government.

The unit maintains strong links with the British SAS and trains with other foreign units as well.

POLAND ▬
Grupa Reagowania Operacyjino Mobilnego (GROM)

Poland is a relative newcomer to the world of modern CRW units. Yet its Grupa Reagowania Operacyjino Mobilnego (GROM) unit, founded in 1991 by the passionate special forces officer Colonel Slawomir Petelicki, is just as capable as any Western force.

Poland's GROM counterterrorist unit may have been formed only in 1991, but it has already gained an excellent reputation within the world's special forces communities. GROM operators are recruited from other Polish special forces units, including the Army's 1st Commando Regiment and the Navy's 7th Lujcka Naval Assault Brigade. Much of GROM's success is down to its commander, Colonel Slawomir Petelicki, a man who is greatly admired and respected for his dedication and high standards.

GROM is secretive about its size and order of battle, but its combat force is believed to number some 250 operatives plus support personnel. As well as receiving standard military training, operatives within GROM must speak at least two languages and have good medical skills.

Indeed, almost 75 per cent of GROM's personnel are qualified as either paramedics or nurses, and as such they provide excellent support for the unit's doctors.

GROM also has female operatives to carry out intelligence-gathering and surveillance operations, both in Poland and overseas.

Below: GROM operators practise storming an aircraft during a routine hostage rescue exercise. This type of training is known as tubular work.

Generally, GROM operates in four-man assault teams in the same manner as the British SAS, with specialized support teams available for tasks such explosive ordnance demolition (EOD). These teams are often run by former operators who either have been injured or are too old for operational service, but want to continue serving with the unit.

All members of GROM must have high standards in weapons handling, as all training is carried out using live ammunition. Training is made as realistic as possible to ensure sharp reactions and realism, and often involves mock assaults on ships, aircraft and buildings.

In 1994, GROM was selected to participate in Operation Restore Democracy, the American-led invasion of Haiti. Prior to this operation, 55 members of the unit were sent to Puerto Rico to train with members of the US 3rd Special Forces Group. While there, they were briefed in Haitian politics and social systems to help them understand the need for this important operation.

On arrival in Haiti, GROM operators were tasked with providing security for several important VIPs, including UN General Secretary Buthros Buthros Ghali and the US Secretary of Defense William Perry.

While in Haiti, GROM took part in a hostage-rescue operation which involved storming a building, putting out a blaze and rescuing a young boy who had been taken hostage by a group of heavily armed gunmen. The boy was freed without any need for bloodshed, and GROM received enormous praise for its actions, which

Above: Two GROM operators provide fire support to a hostage rescue team during an anti-terrorist exercise near Warsaw on 22 November 2001.

earned its creator and commander, Colonel Petelicki, the US Army Commendation Medal — the first time in American history that a foreign unit has been commended in this way.

Further operations that involved GROM include protecting Pope John Paul II during his visit to Poland in 1995, as well as a tour in Bosnia during 1998, in which the unit apprehended a suspected Bosnian war criminal.

Weapons used by GROM include the HK MP5 submachine gun; Tantal 5.45 mm (0.21in) assault rifle; HK PSG-1; and Mauser 86 7.62mm (0.3in) sniper rifles. Personal sidearm selection is at each operator's discretion.

RUSSIA ▬
Alpha/Beta Groups

Russia has retained quality special forces in spite of a general structural and economic crisis in the Russian military since 1989. The Alpha/Beta Group was created for Cold War CRW, but has since found operational experience in places such as Chechnya and Georgia.

Alpha Group and Beta Group were formed in 1974, as part of the 7th (Surveillance) Directorate of the KGB, following an upsurge in terrorist activities within the Soviet Union. Essentially, Alpha Group is responsible for all anti-terrorist operations within Russia and its borders, while Beta Group, which models itself on the US Delta Force and has more or less the same role, operates abroad.

Both Alpha and Beta Group recruit their operators from specially selected Spetsnaz volunteers. Candidates for both groups are subjected to a lengthy selection process, as well as nine months of basic infantry training. Additional training for these Alpha

Below: Spetsnaz operatives conduct a search exercise during urban warfare training. The trooper in the foreground holds a 5.45mm (0.21in) AK74 assault rifle.

Above: Russian special forces training incurs a higher number of casualties than any other elite training regime. Most fatalities and injuries occur during live-firing or demolitions training.

Right: Russian Alpha Group soldiers after ending a three-day siege by Chechen rebels holding hostages in a theatre in Moscow in October 2002. Tragically 67 hostages were also killed in the assault.

and Beta Group operatives includes language skills; unarmed combat; high-speed driving; reconnaissance; intelligence-gathering techniques; sniping; tracking; heliborne insertion and extraction techniques; and airborne skills (both line and HALO).

Although most of Alpha and Beta Groups' operations are classified, it is known that Alpha Group has been involved in numerous operations within Russia, against organized criminal gangs and Chechen terrorists, while Beta Group has seen extensive action both in Afghanistan and Chechnya.

SINGAPORE
Special Operations Force

Singapore has a force of around 200 CRW personnel within its armed forces, in addition to a similar number of operatives within the Singaporean police service. Together they have provided national CRW protection since the early 1990s.

The Special Operations Force was created in 1992 and is trained to carry out a wide variety of anti-terrorist duties, including vehicle assaults, explosives techniques, defensive driving and heliborne operations. The unit comes under the operational control of the Singapore Armed Forces Commandos.

It was employed operationally in the rescue of 123 hostages from a hijacked Singapore Airlines Airbus A310 at Changi Airport. The hijackers were demanding the release of the husband of Benazir Bhutto in Pakistan and are believed to have been armed only with domestic cutlery. After a nine-hour period of negotiations and preparation, the Special Operations Force stormed the aircraft, killing all four hijackers and rescuing the hostages unharmed. The incident demonstrates the foolhardiness of taking on highly trained state counter-terrorism squads, especially in view of the relative unimportance of the political issue under dispute.

SOUTH AFRICA
SAPS Special Task Force

South Africa has one of the highest rates of armed crime in the world, and many of the criminals have received military training. Being a Special Task Force member is consequently a risky job, and fatality levels are high.

This force was established in 1976 and recruits directly from the South African Police Service (SAPS). All recruits are volunteers, and they have to pass a rigorous selection course before passing on to equally rigorous training.

Training is carried out at the Task Force training centre, which is about 230km (145 miles) from Pretoria. The pass rate is about 25 per cent.

The unit is on stand-by to tackle any hostage emergencies that may arise, which means learning to carry out assaults on buildings, vehicles, aircraft, ships and oil platforms. The unit is also trained to carry out sniper duties, often related to VIP protection. Members of the unit are trained in a wide range of skills, including maritime operations and mountaineering.

Above: SAPS policemen lay a wreath at a memorial for a murdered policeman in 1999. The previous year, 230 SAPS personnel were killed in the line of duty.

SOUTH KOREA
National Police 868 Unit

*The 868 Unit was created mainly to combat potential terrorism at the 1988 Seoul Olympics;
however, they have remained operational as a highly competent squad ever since.*

Formed in 1982, this unit is tasked with carrying out counterterrorism and hostage rescue operations. Consisting of about 90 members, the unit is divided into 12 teams. The unit receives training in urban assaults as well as hostage rescue from aircraft and other vehicles.

The 868 unit works in collaboration with the larger 707th Special Missions Battalion, which is the Army counterterrorism unit. The 707th is about 200-strong and includes combat diving and paratroop operations in its range of skills. The South Korean special forces have access to state-of-the-art training facilities, including mock-ups for realistic aircraft assaults.

Right: Troopers from 868 Unit preparing for the 2002 World Cup. The unit operates mainly against small-scale or localized threats. Major terrorist incidents are handled by the military.

SWEDEN
Ordningspolisens Nationella Insatsstyrka (ONI)

*Sweden is a peaceable country and has only a small CRW unit as part
of its national police force. Based in Stockholm, the ONI personnel usually spend half their
time with the unit and the other half serving in regular SWAT teams.*

Members of the Swedish ONI, or Ordningspolisens Nationella Insatsstyrka, are drawn from the Swedish police force. The 48 personnel in the unit are divided into five groups; two are designated for assault duties, while the other three groups are responsible for cover sniping, command and control, and intelligence gathering. The unit is highly trained in hostage rescue relating to a variety of scenarios, ranging from urban assaults to civil aircraft rescue operations.

In keeping with generally high Scandinavian standards of using minimum force, the ONI is trained to use force only as a last resort, and authorization for the use of lethal force passes through a rigorous chain of command.

SWITZERLAND ✚
Stern Unit

'Stern Unit' is the popular name for the Kantonspolizei Bern CRW team. Along with the Stadtpolizei Bern 'Enzian Unit', it provides round-the-clock CRW cover within Swiss borders and specializes in non-lethal weapon technologies.

Like many counterterrorist units, the Stern Unit was formed to deal with the kind of terrorist threat that had shocked the world at the 1972 Munich Olympic Games. Formed in 1975, the Stern Unit draws its members from police forces across all the Swiss cantons.

The best recruits, who have at least five years' exemplary police service behind them, are put through a testing six-month training course. This includes mountaineering, scuba diving, defensive driving and weapons instruction, including sniper work.

National units such as the Stern Unit are backed up in Switzerland by local canton units, which have built up very formidable reputations in their own right. The Geneva anti-terrorist unit, for instance, was responsible for the rescue of hostages from a hijacked Air France jet.

Above: Swiss CRW snipers tend to use the 7.62mm (0.3in) SIG Sauer SSG 2000 or the 7.62mm (0.3in) SIG Sauer SG550 Sniper, both excellent precision weapons.

UNITED KINGDOM 🇬🇧
Special Air Service (SAS)
SO19 Firearms Unit (Metropolitan Police)

The United Kingdom relies on the SAS to handle major terrorist incidents and the police SO19 armed response teams to combat armed criminal threats or low-level terrorism.

Following the Munich Olympics in 1972, Britain decided to develop a counterterrorist capability and tasked 22 SAS with forming a Counter-Revolutionary Warfare (CRW) Wing. Within a short period of time, the SAS had formed a 20-man CRW team under the command of Lieutenant Colonel Anthony Pearson. This became known as 'Pagoda' Squadron, and essentially it had three roles: collecting intelligence on possible terrorist threats, pre-empting terrorist activity, and mounting direct operations against any terrorist threat.

The squadron was also tasked with developing specific tactics for likely terrorist targets – in other words, hostage rescue from aircraft, ships, buildings, oil rigs, nuclear power stations and even public entertainment centres. To enable the SAS to perform these tasks to a high standard, new communication systems and highly sensitive surveillance equipment were procured from various sources around the world. In addition to their internal training, crosstraining was also carried out with regional police forces throughout the United Kingdom, as well as counterterrorist forces overseas, including the German GSG-9, French GIGN and US Delta Force.

As 'Pagoda' Squadron continued to develop, it received notification in 1975 of a hijack at London's Stansted airport and was put on stand-by. However, the incident ended peacefully before the SAS could be deployed. Later that year, a four-man IRA Active Service Unit (ASU) was compromised by police during an anti-terrorist operation, and in response the

Below: Each SAS trooper is responsible for neutralizing threats in a specific sector of the room. Entry is either through the door or via a hole blasted in an adjoining wall.

Above: Respirators are usually worn to protect the wearer from the smoke generated by their stun grenades or CS gas canisters used to precede room entry.

men seized an elderly couple and held them hostage in a flat in London's Balcombe Street. With no means of escape, the terrorists remained in the flat for almost six days, until they heard a news report on the radio stating that the SAS had been brought in to end the crisis.

In part this was true: 'Pagoda' Squadron had indeed been deployed to London on stand-by, but it was quite prepared to wait for events to take their course, and the police were slowly bringing the situation to a peaceful conclusion. For the IRA, however, the mere mention of the SAS was enough to force a rethink: convinced that a spell in jail would be preferable to trying to survive an SAS assault, they surrendered.

MOGADISHU

In May 1977, the Dutch authorities requested SAS assistance after a train was hijacked by South Moluccan terrorists. The SAS responded by sending over a small advisory team, whose role was purely passive: they played no part in the assault phase of the hostage rescue operation.

This was to be in stark contrast to the next SAS operation, which took place in Mogadishu, Somalia. SAS assistance was requested by the

Below: Operation Nimrod – an SAS trooper is trapped over flames from the burning embassy by his tangled abseil rope.

German authorities after Palestinian terrorists hijacked one of their national carrier's planes en route from Majorca to Frankfurt. Following a refuelling stop in Rome, the Lufthansa Boeing 737 aircraft and its 86 passengers and five crew were subjected to a series of stopovers and diversions before eventually ending up in Mogadishu. Following close behind the hijacked aircraft was another Lufthansa aircraft, which contained German hostage negotiators and 30 members of the GSG-9 anti-terrorist unit. Upon arrival, they were met by two members of the SAS, Major Alastair Morrison and Sergeant Barry Davies, who had been sent in to assist with the rescue operation.

Without warning, one of the Lufthansa pilots was murdered, and the decision was taken to storm the aircraft. The SAS provided stun grenades, and GSG-9 created a diversion

by setting off a number of them around the aircraft before storming it. During the assault phase, three of the four terrorists were killed, and only four passengers were injured – a very successful operation.

The SAS later revealed that the surviving terrorist, a young female, remained alive because a member of its team shot to injure rather than kill. Some years later, the soldier and the terrorist met. Now happily married with children, she wanted to thank him for sparing her life.

PRINCES GATE

As for the rest of 'Pagoda' Squadron, the men continued to train, in readiness for any incident that might develop anywhere in the world. Month in and month out, the SAS practised their hostage rescue techniques until these had become second nature. All that was needed

now was a chance to show them off; on 5 May 1980, it came. Six days earlier, on the morning of 30 April 1980, six terrorists entered the front door of the Iranian Embassy in Princes Gate, London. Members of the little known Democratic Revolutionary Front for the Liberation of Arabistan, they were sponsored by Iraq. For PC Trevor Lock, the lone police officer standing guard outside the embassy, the approach of six Arab men was nothing out of the ordinary. As he went to open the door for them, one of the terrorists pulled a gun and attempted to rush the door. Acting instinctively, the officer pushed him back and slammed the door in his face. At this point, some of the terrorists pulled out a variety of small pistols and Skorpion submachine guns and opened fire on the embassy, while others forced the flimsy front door. As they burst into the embassy firing their guns, two female embassy staff managed to escape through a back door, while a third male member of staff made his way out through an adjacent office window. As for the remaining Embassy staff, the terrorists were too quick for them: one member of staff attempted to escape from an upstairs window, but injured himself during the process and was quickly dragged back into the building by one of the terrorists.

The terrorists now had 26 hostages within the Iranian Embassy, while police began to arrive outside, having been alerted by PC Lock before he, too, was captured. Within a short period of time, the entire area surrounding the embassy was alive with specialist units, including D11 police marksmen, C-13 anti-terrorist officers, the Special Patrol Group (SPG) and members of Scotland Yard's C7 technical support branch. In addition, SOP (standard operational procedure) meant that the SAS had been notified and was on its way.

At this point, the SAS had around 20 men on permanent stand-by as part of the Special Projects Team (SPT), their role being anti-terrorist operations. A second SPT rotated with the first to enable 24/7 cover. To ensure that the SAS could deploy at a moment's notice, an RAF C-130 Hercules was on permanent stand-by, along with a number of Army Air Corps (AAC) Augusta A-109 utility helicopters.

OPERATION NIMROD

The SAS had now codenamed the incident Operation Nimrod, and its men were based nearby in readiness for further orders. Meanwhile, the terrorists issued their demands to the British Government: the immediate release of 91 Arabs held in Iranian jails – Arabistan is a region of Iran populated by ethnic Arabs, rather than Iranians; all of the released prisoners were to be

Above: SAS troopers prepare to enter the Iranian embassy through the windows by using shaped cutting charges.

flown to Britain and given political asylum, and negotiations were to take place under the supervision of Arab ambassadors. A deadline was set for midday on 1 May for full compliance. Failure to meet these demands would mean death for the hostages. There was no question, however, that any of these demands would be met.

Even if the British Government had been prepared to negotiate, relations with Iran were very poor at this time, following the demise of the pro-Western Shah of Iran. Moreover, Prime Minister Margaret Thatcher was determined that Britain should be seen taking a tough stance against terrorism or situations like this would become commonplace.

By this time, police negotiators had persuaded the terrorists to drop their demands for the release of prisoners, but agreed that they could make a broadcast for mediators. Meanwhile, Prime Minister Margaret Thatcher summoned COBRA, the Cabinet Office Briefing Room, which included members of the SAS, MI5, MI6 and the Ministry of Defence (MOD). After discussing all the options, it passed on its recommendations to the Joint Operations Centre (JOC) at MOD HQ.

Around the same time that COBRA met, SAS planners were discussing methods of entry into the Embassy with their police colleagues in C7. A very sophisticated surveillance operation had already been put in place at the Iranian Embassy, including microphones in rooms and miniature cameras capable of providing highly detailed pictures. At one stage, extra noise had been needed outside the embassy to drown out the sound of drilling as the surveillance devices were put in place. When Margaret Thatcher heard of this problem, she immediately ordered the CAA (Civil Aviation Authority) to divert all flights over London so that they flew over the embassy at a far lower height then normal. In addition, she ordered British Gas to dig the road up outside the rear of the Iranian Embassy as cover for C7's operations.

PLAN OF ACTION

The SAS was now ready for an assault against the embassy; all the men needed now was the go-ahead. Their plan was simple: two four-man teams would abseil from the roof top down

Above: The Iranian Embassy operation turned the SAS into overnight heroes and brought them an unwanted publicity which threatened to compromise their secrecy.

the rear of the building, while another team would enter the building via the first-floor windows. As the windows were bulletproof, frame charges would be used to blast through them, then stun grenades and CS gas canisters would be tossed into the building to disorientate the terrorists as the SAS clearance teams made their entry.

For safety reasons, the SAS team members wore black one-piece overalls, which enabled the soldiers to be seen in smoke-filled rooms. For protection, they also wore fragmentation jackets and S6 respirators, and the effect of this clothing was extremely intimidating. Each man carried

Flame-proof
hooded overalls

Respirator

Abseil rope

Belay device

Submachine gun

Body armour

Hammer

Pistol

Gloves

Rope bag

Kevlar boots

Harness

Browning
magazine

Grenades

*Above: Illustration of the outfits worn by
the SAS troopers who successfully
stormed the Iranian embassy in London.*

Heckler and Koch MP5 submachine guns, as well as 9mm Browning Hi-Power pistols.

On Monday 5 May, the terrorists' leader, Awn Ali Mohammed, spoke to the police negotiators as normal, but sounded edgy. At 1850, three shots were heard from within the embassy, and the body of the embassy's chief press officer, Abbas Lavasani, was afterwards dumped on the steps outside the building. Responsibility for the embassy operation was now passed over to the Commanding Officer of the SAS, Lieutenant Colonel Michael Rose.

THE ASSAULT

It was time to bring this crisis to an end. At 1920, three four-man teams abseiled over the side of the building to gain entry via the second- and third-floor windows. At the same time, other members of the SAS climbed onto the first-floor balcony from an adjacent building and placed frame charges around the windows, and another team smashed its way into the embassy through the rear basement windows. Inside the building, the terrorists panicked as they heard the sound of breaking glass. In one office, there was a struggle between the terrorist leader and PC Lock, who now knew that help was on its way. Within seconds, an SAS soldier burst through the door and opened fire, killing the lead terrorist instantly. Another terrorist armed with a pistol rushed to the rear of the building and was gunned down by two SAS soldiers before he had a chance to fire.

Meanwhile, on the second floor, SAS members had entered the main office where most of the hostages had been held, only to find that the terrorists had moved them into the telex room at the front of the building, which was now locked. As the SAS tried to force the door, one member of the team left the room and climbed out onto the balcony with the idea of entering the locked room from the window. As he did so, he spotted a terrorist attempting to start a fire within the room, but could not do anything about it because his weapon had jammed. Within the telex room itself, two of the four remaining terrorists were now shooting the hostages with their handguns, and the SAS was powerless to stop them. Eventually they burst into the smoke-filled room, only to find that the terrorists were now posing as hostages. One of them was quickly spotted and pulled away from the genuine hostages. As he was being dragged away, he made a suspicious movement and was instantly shot dead. When his body was turned over, a grenade was seen in his hand, vindicating the SAS action and avoiding a later accusation of murder. A second terrorist armed with a gun was shot dead when he tried to mingle with hostages who were being evacuated from the burning building. As for the last living terrorist, he was found hiding among the hostages and was spared because he was unarmed.

MISSION ACCOMPLISHED

The entire operation, from the moment that the police handed over responsibility to the moment that the SAS returned it, lasted just 46 minutes. All in all, this was a remarkable achievement for the SAS, made all the more spectacular because it had been captured on live television and beamed across all of the world. As for the SAS men themselves, once the assault had finished they were bundled into waiting vans and driven away at high speed for a well-deserved celebration.

In total, around 50 members of the SAS had been involved in the operation, both directly and indirectly. The casualty figures for this day's work were two hostages murdered, two hostages wounded and one SAS soldier slightly injured by burns caused when his rope became entangled during the initial assault phase. As for the terrorists, six walked into the embassy, but only one came out alive.

SO19 Firearms Unit (Metropolitan Police)

This unit was formed in 1966 as a response to the growing threat of armed attacks on police officers. As the principle that policemen should be unarmed continues to be valued in the United Kingdom, the SO19 Firearms Unit is designed to provide firearms support only if and when it is considered necessary.

In 1991, Armed Response Vehicles (ARVs) were introduced to maximize the operational effectiveness of the SO19 Firearms Unit. These ARVs are on permanent patrol and are designated as the first response to hostage incidents. Depending on the nature of the crisis, the police may collaborate with and eventually hand over control to the Army. This is precisely what happened when the Special Air Service regiment was given clearance by the Home Secretary to assault the Iranian Embassy in London in 1980.

SO19 runs a number of firearms training courses at its centre at Lippitts Hill. These courses range from basic firearms training to full tactical building assaults.

UNITED STATES OF AMERICA 🇺🇸
Delta Force
Task Force 11

Despite some mission disasters, Delta Force is still rightly regarded as one
of the world's top counterterrorist units. Many Delta members now also serve with Task Force 11,
a truly elite force established in the wake of the September 11 attacks.

Delta Force is the best trained and equipped counterterrorist unit the world. Although formed only in 1977, it has grown rapidly since its inception and currently comprises some 800 trained operators. Delta Force is based at Fort Bragg, North Carolina, and has the Airborne and Green Berets as close neighbours. The compound which they occupy is protected by large razor wire fences and a series of armed checkpoints, which are covered with motion detectors and infrared cameras, thus making it virtually impregnable.

Delta Force was officially formed on 19 November 1977 by Colonel Charles A. Beckwith (known as 'Charging Charlie'), who was both founder and Commanding Officer of Delta. The inspiration to create a highly trained special forces unit came from Beckwith's service in the British SAS (Special Air Service Regiment) on an exchange posting in the early 1960s. Colonel Beckwith was fascinated by the SAS and its ability to fight in an unconventional manner, and he had seen at first hand what they could accomplish, for he deployed with them to Malaya during the Malayan Emergency of 1950–1960. Beckwith greatly admired the multiple skills that each SAS trooper possessed, which enabled small four-man teams to operate more effectively than a larger conventional force.

Beckwith was so impressed with the SAS that he decided to form an American version. This would be

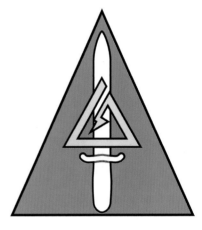

Above: The Delta Force insignia depicting a lightning flash superimposed over a dagger and set within a triangular frame.

virtually identical in terms of training and methods of operation, differing only in choice of weaponry, uniforms and operational accountability.

Getting Delta Force off the ground, though, was no easy task for Beckwith, who had to justify the need for another special forces unit at a time when those that already existed were performing poorly in Vietnam. Eventually, after much pleading and lobbying on his behalf, the Pentagon and Congress agreed to Beckwith's request, and the 1st Special Forces Operational Detachment Delta (SFOD-Delta) was born.

Below: Helicopters prepare to disembark for Operation Eagle Claw, 1980. Delta's first operation was a total disaster, with eight US soldiers dead and five injured.

Above: Sea Stallion helicopters taking off for Operation Eagle Claw. Two of the helicopters lost their way en route to a rendezvous with Delta operators.

ORIGINS

Delta Force was set up in great secrecy, initially as an overseas counterterrorist unit that specialized in hostage rescue. It soon became clear, however, that Delta could perform other missions, such as long-range covert reconnaissance and snatch-and-grab missions.

Delta's selection and training programmes were initially based on tried-and-tested methods used by the SAS; however, as Delta developed, the training programmes were refined to better reflect current American thinking on close-quarter battle (CQB) operations, placing a much greater emphasis on the use of firepower.

Delta's first operational deployment took place in April 1980, after the American Embassy in Tehran was attacked on 4 November 1979 by supporters of the Ayatollah Khomeini. Sixty-six Americans were taken hostage in a bid to force the United States to hand over the pro-Western deposed Shah of Iran.

EAGLE CLAW

Once all political avenues had been exhausted, US President Jimmy Carter gave Delta Force the go-ahead to enter Iran covertly and mount a rescue operation. Codenamed 'Eagle Claw', it was an extremely ambitious plan that required Delta to fly into a remote desert area by C-130 and rendezvous there with eight Sea Stallion helicopters that were to be used in the actual rescue attempt.

However, there were problems even before the operation commenced: two helicopters were lost on their way to the rendezvous point, while another developed mechanical problems on the ground. In addition, some of Beckwith's men were forced to stop a bus containing civilians as it attempted to drive past the parked aircraft.

If that were not enough, another group of his men had to open fire on a fuel truck that failed to stop at one of Delta's roadblocks. The truck exploded, lighting up the night sky for many miles around.

Delta's rescue plan depended on the use of at least six working helicopters. Beckwith now had only five, and his other problems meant that he had no choice but to abort Operation Eagle Claw. Even then, the problems continued. One of the hovering helicopters hit a C-130 that was about to take off. Despite valiant efforts by both the surviving aircrew and Delta operators to save those remaining trapped in the burning wreckage, eight American servicemen died and five were seriously injured.

Operation Eagle Claw had ended in failure; however, no blame was apportioned to Delta Force because mechanical failure and sheer bad luck were largely responsible. During the official Congress inquiry that took place to examine the issues surrounding Eagle Claw, no mention or reference was made to Delta Force, the existence of which is not officially recognized to this very day.

PANAMA

After Eagle Claw, Delta intensified its training and was deployed to Panama in 1989 as part of Operation Just Cause. Here, Delta performed to plan and was highly successful in a number of key operations, including the capture of General Manuel Noriega and the rescue of US citizen Kurt Muse, who was being held captive by the Panamanian Defence Force (PDF) in Carcel Modelo prison in Panama City. Prior to the invasion, Delta conducted a number of missions in Panama as part of an intelligence-gathering operation against General Noriega and the PDF.

On one occasion, Delta received a tip-off about Noriega and a number of his known associates, who were believed to be using the Island of Bocas del Toro as an operations base. A covert reconnaissance team was despatched to the island, but found nothing of interest apart from an old shack and a couple of squealing pigs.

Many of Delta's operations remain secret; however, they are known to have participated in a considerable number of missions in South America against the Colombian drug cartels, who are known to fund organized crime in the United States.

During the Gulf War in 1991, Delta played a key part in hunting down Iraq's mobile Scud missiles launchers, which were causing considerable problems for the Allied Coalition Force. Delta Force worked alongside the British SAS to resolve this problem, mounting patrols in the areas where Scud launchers were known to operate most frequently. Within weeks, the Iraqis had been forced to move out of this area because it had become impossible to operate without being attacked.

In 1999, Delta deployed a small number of detachments to Bosnia and Kosovo for operations against Serbian war criminals, who were proving difficult to capture. However, their biggest manhunt so far has been in Afghanistan, where they have been hunting down the world's number-one terrorist, Osama bin Laden, and his Al Qaeda supporters after the events of 11 September 2001.

ORGANIZATION

Delta is organized along the same lines as the British SAS and consists of three operating squadrons (A, B and C), which are subdivided into smaller units known as troops. Each troop specializes in a particular skill, such as mountaineering, HALO, scuba or land

Right: Delta Force operatives commonly use the 5.56mm (0.22in) M4 carbine, a short-barrel version of the standard M16A2 rifle fitted with a collapsible stock.

mobility. For greater operational efficiency, each troop can be divided into smaller four-man units which can either operate alone or join up to form a section.

Delta also has its own support squadron, which handles selection and training, logistics, finance, technical and medical issues. The technical unit is of particular interest because it provides Delta with highly sensitive equipment, such as human tracking devices and eavesdropping sensors, which are used during hostage rescue

operations. Delta operators also enjoy some of the best training facilities in world, and they have access to an Olympic-sized swimming pool, dive tank, three-storey climbing wall and numerous shooting ranges (including a close-quarter battle and sniping facility).

The vast majority of Delta's recruits come from the elite Ranger and Airborne battalions. That said, a significant number of candidates also come from conventional Army units, including the Army Reserve and National Guard. Selection and

Training for Delta Force is extremely demanding, and only the finest candidates are chosen. (See Selection and Training chapter for further information on Delta's recruiting criteria and selection process).

A NEW COMMAND

Following the events of 11 September 2001, elements of Delta Force were assigned to a new command known as Task Force 11. This force is responsible for all special forces activities connected with America's ongoing war against terrorism and is part of Operation Enduring Freedom. Task Force 11 comprises both Delta operators and Navy SEALS, and it is known in the United States as the Super Force, as it has two of the best special forces units in the world within its ranks.

Although most of Delta's missions within this force are classified, they are known to have participated in Operation Anaconda, a large-scale search-and-destroy mission mounted against Al Qaeda and the Taliban, in the mountain ranges of eastern Afghanistan. The mission lasted for 16 days and involved some 1200 US personnel, including 200 special forces, and was highly successful.

Prior to this mission, Delta are known to have been involved in a number of combined operations with the British SAS, including the searching of the Tora Bora mountain cave complexes, which were believed to have been occupied by Al Qaeda's leader, Osama bin Laden. Other missions involving Delta took place in both Afghanistan and Pakistan in September 2002.

In one of them, Delta operators foiled an assassination attempt against Afghanistan's President Hamid Karzai, shooting dead a lone gunman who had opened fired on the president's motorcade. On 14 September, Delta operators were despatched to Karachi,

Pakistan, to back up Pakistani security services, who had discovered the whereabouts of Ramzi Binalshibh, the mastermind behind the terrorist attacks of 11 September 2001.

As operations in Afghanistan were scaled down, elements of Delta Force were redeployed to the Gulf, following the threat of another war with Saddam Hussein and Iraq.

Weapons

Weapons and equipment used by Delta Force include the Colt M4 assault rifle; M16A2 assault rifle Mini 14 assault rifle; Steyr AUG assault rifle; HK G3 assault rifle; SOPMOD (Special Operations Peculiar Modification) M4A1 assault rifle; CAR-15 assault rifle; Stoner SR-25 self-loading rifle; Colt Model 733 assault rifle; Walther MPK submachine gun; HK MP5SD submachine gun; MAC 10 submachine gun; UZI submachine gun; M249 SAW light machine gun; HK13E light machine gun; M60 medium machine gun; M240B medium machine gun; Browning M2 .50 heavy machine gun; Remington 870 combat shotgun; Mossberg Cruiser 500 combat shotgun; HK PSG sniper rifle; M40A1 sniper rifle; M24 sniper rifle; and Barrett M82A1 .50 heavy sniper rifle.

Support weapons include the M203 40mm (1.57in) grenade launcher; M79 'Blooper' 40mm (1.57in) grenade launcher; 81mm (3.19in) mortar; Carl Gustav 84mm (3.3in) recoilless rifle; 66mm (2.6in) LAW and Mk 19 automatic grenade launcher; Stinger MANPAD; M136 AT-4 anti-tank rocket; Beretta 92F handgun; and SIG Sauer P-228 handgun

Specialist weapon sights include the Aimpoint Comp M close-quarter battle sight; M68 Aimpoint; M28 Aimpoint sight; AN/PEQ2 Infrared Target Pointer/Illuminator/Aiming laser (IPITAL) dual-beam aiming device.

Delta also operates an extensive fleet of vehicles that includes the Land Rover Defender 110 SOV (Special Operations Vehicle); Humvee; Quad ATV (All Terrain Vehicle); Harley-Davidson Track Bike; and LSV (light strike vehicle). Weapons mounted on vehicles include Mk-19 40mm automatic grenade launchers; M60 medium machine guns; M240B medium machine gun; General Electric 7.62mm (0.3in) mini gun; 20mm (0.79in) cannon; and Browning M2 .50 heavy machine gun.

Other specialist Delta equipment includes Zodiac boats, submersibles, high-speed patrol boats and rigid raiders. Delta also uses heavily modified parachutes for its HALO and HAHO parachute operations.

The most common means of transport for Delta Force is the helicopter. Types used include the MH-47 D/E Chinook, MH-60 K/L Blackhawk and MH-6 Little Bird, which are operated by the US Army's 160th Special Operations Aviation Regiments. For long-range missions, Delta uses the MH-53J, which is operated by the USAF's Special Operations Group (SOG).

Delta Force is extremely well funded and can buy almost any weapon or piece of equipment it wants without going through laborious purchasing procedures. It is probably the best equipped special forces unit in the world today.

DELTA FORCE OPERATIONAL HISTORY

1979

Works alongside the FBI during the Pan American Games in Puerto Rico as part of an anti-terrorist team that is set up in anticipation of a possible terrorist attack.

1980

Deploys to Iran to rescue American hostages who are being held by Iranian fundamentalists in Tehran. Shortly after a decision is taken to abort the mission, a helicopter collides with a transport aircraft on the ground, leaving eight American servicemen dead.

1983

Participates in Operation Urgent Fury in Grenada and carries out a helicopter assault on Richmond Hill Prison, where a number of local government officials are being held hostage. It also assists other units in seizing a key airfield during the initial assault phase of the operation.

1984

Sent to the Middle East after two Americans are killed during the hijacking of a Kuwaiti Airways airliner.

1985

Deployed to Cyprus in response to the hijacking of a TWA airliner.

1987

Deployed to Greece following a report that Vietnamese agents were going to kill US Army Colonel James Rowe.

1989

Participates in Operation Just Cause in Panama, where it successfully rescues an American citizen being held hostage in Panama City. It also helps to capture General Manuel Noriega.

1991

In Operation Desert Storm during the Gulf War, it provides protection for senior US officers and also helps to locate and destroy Iraq's mobile Scud missile launchers.

1993

Deployed to Mogadishu, Somalia, as part of Task Force Ranger and mounts numerous operations against Somali warlords. One ends in a major battle that leaves 18 Americans dead and 70 badly injured, but costs the Somalis more than 500 men.

Below: US special forces are pictured here training Filipino troops in counter-insurgency warfare tactics.

Task Force 11 Weapons and Equipment

Task Force 11 (TF-11) is extremely well funded and can buy almost any weapon or piece of equipment it wants without going through laborious purchasing procedures. For its size, Task Force 11 is the best armed and equipped unit in the world.

Weapons and equipment used by TF-11 include the Colt M4 assault rifle; M16A2 assault rifle; Mini 14 assault rifle; Steyr AUG assault rifle; HK G3 assault rifle; SOPMOD (Special Operations Peculiar Modification) M4A1 assault rifle; CAR-15 assault rifle; Stoner SR-25 self-loading rifle; Colt Model 733 assault rifle; Walther MPK submachine gun; HK MP5SD submachine gun; MAC 10 submachine gun; UZI submachine gun; M249 SAW light machine gun; HK13E light machine gun; M60 medium machine gun; M240B medium machine gun; Browning M2 .50 heavy machine gun; Remington 870 combat shotgun; Mossberg Cruiser 500 combat shotgun; HK PSG sniper rifle; M40A1 sniper rifle; M24 sniper rifle; Barrett M82A150 heavy sniper rifle; Beretta 92F handgun; and SIG Sauer P-228 handgun

Support weapons include the M203 40mm grenade launcher; 81mm (3.19in) mortar; 66mm (2.6in) LAW and Mk-19 40mm (1.57in) grenade launcher; Stinger MANPAD; and the M136 AT-4 anti-tank rocket.

Specialist weapon sights include the Aimpoint Comp M close-quarter battle sight; M68 Aimpoint; M28 Aimpoint sight; AN/PEQ2 Infrared Target Pointer/Illuminator/Aiming laser (IPITAL) dual beam aiming device.

Uniforms worn include standard US Army combat fatigues; Lizard suits; urban combat fatigues; Ghillie sniper suits; and black nomex overalls, which are worn during hostage rescue operations. TF-11 operators also make extensive use of body armour and night-vision devices, such as the AN/PVS-7 night-vision goggles. For additional protection, they wear Bolle T800 ballistic goggles while operating in open areas. During counter-terrorist operations, TF-11 operators wear British Avon S10 respirators, body armour, anti-lazer goggles and Nomex clothing.

TF-11 also operates an extensive fleet of vehicles, which includes the Land Rover Defender 110 SOV (Special Operations Vehicle); Humvee; Quad ATV (All Terrain Vehicle); Harley-Davidson Track Bike and LSV (light strike vehicle). Weapons mounted on vehicles include Mk-19 40mm automatic grenade launchers; M60 medium machine guns; M240B medium machine gun; General Electric 7.62 (0.3in) mini gun; 20mm (0.79in) cannon; and Browning M2 .50 heavy machine gun.

Other specialist equipment includes Zodiac boats, submersibles, high-speed patrol boats and rigid raiders. The unit also uses heavily modified parachutes for its HALO and HAHO parachute operations.

The most common means of transport is the helicopter, but the unit has been known to use horses during operations, as seen in Afghanistan. Helicopters used include the MH-47 D/E Chinook, MH-60 K/L Blackhawk and MH-6 Little Bird, which are operated by the US Army's 160th Special Operations Aviation Regiments. For long-range missions, TF-11 uses the MH-53J, operated by the USAF's Special Operations Group (SOG).

1995

Deployed to Bosnia as part of an international effort to locate Serbian war criminals.

1997

Sent to Lima, Peru, along with six members of the British SAS after the takeover of the Japanese Ambassador's residence in January 1997.

1999

Deployed to Kosovo in support of US forces operating against the Federal Republic of Yugoslavia.

2001

Following the events of September 11, Delta is deployed to Afghanistan in search of Al Qaeda forces, in particular their leader Osama bin Laden.

Uniforms worn by Delta Force include: Standard US Army combat fatigues, Lizard suits, Ghillie sniper suits and black nomex overalls, which are worn during counterterrorist operations. Delta operators also make extensive use of body armour and night-vision devices, such as the AN/PVS-7 night-vision goggles. For additional protection while operating in open areas, they wear Bolle T800 ballistic goggles. During counter-terrorist operations, Delta operators wear British Avon S10 respirators, body armour, anti-laser goggles and nomex clothing.

TASK FORCE 11

Task Force 11 is a super elite unit, comprising several hundred Navy SEALs, Army Delta Force soldiers and their respective support units from the Joint Special Operations Command in North Carolina. The unit was formed in late 2001, following the events of 11 September 2001, when terrorists belonging to the Al Qaeda (The Base) network attacked the United States.

In response, US President George W. Bush vowed to hunt down all terrorists who threatened the United States and its way of life, and launched Operation Enduring Freedom, a rolling campaign of military action that will fight terrorism around the world for decades to come. Task Force 11 has the prime mission of hunting down senior members of the Al Qaeda network and will continue to do so until it has been annihilated.

OPERATION ANACONDA

Although most of Task Force 11's operations are highly classified, the unit's members are known to have participated in Operation Anaconda, which was mounted during March 2002. This 16-day counterterrorist mission involved more than 1200 US personnel, including 200 special forces, who were deployed by the 101st Airborne Division (Air Assault) to the high mountain ranges of eastern Afghanistan. This dangerous and very difficult operation was successful, inflicting hundreds of casualties on the Al Qaeda/Taliban forces and driving them en masse from Afghanistan into neighbouring Pakistan. But it was also costly: eight Americans were killed and 73 wounded.

After Operation Anaconda ended, numerous follow-up operations were mounted by Task Force 11 throughout Afghanistan, mainly around villages and cave complexes. Some, however, involved hot pursuits over the border into Pakistan.

Task Force 11 tries to maintain a low profile and generally operates in small four-man teams; however, these can be increased in size if tactically

Right: US special forces stand guard for Afghan President Hamid Karzai. Acting as his bodyguards, they successfully foiled an assassination attempt on the President on 5 September 2002.

viable. As President Bush stated at the beginning of Operation Enduring Freedom, 'This will be a war that's going to go in various phases, some of which will be visible, some will not.'

RECENT OPERATIONS

In September 2002, Task Force 11 played a key part in two significant operations: one in Afghanistan, the other in Pakistan. On 5 September 2002, a small team of US special forces, acting as bodyguards for Afghanistan's President Hamid Karzai, foiled an assassination attempt after his motorcade was attacked by a lone gunman wearing the uniform of the new Afghan Army. During the short firefight, the gunman was killed, along with one of the president's Afghan bodyguards, and a plainclothes US special forces operator was slightly wounded as he attempted to protect the Afghan president.

The second significant incident involving Task Force 11 took place in Pakistan on 14 September 2002, and it involved other agencies, including the American CIA and the Pakistani ISI

(Inter-Services Intelligence). Ramzi Binalshibh, the mastermind behind the attacks on America, had earlier made a satellite telephone call. US intelligence agencies and Task Force 11 were able to trace the call to an apartment in Karachi, and they immediately launched an operation to apprehend Binalshibh. For political reasons, the arrest was made by members of the Pakistani security services; however, US special forces were on hand in the background, fully ready to take him out if called upon to do so.

Meanwhile, other members of Task Force 11 were training in preparation for operations against Iraq, following Saddam Hussein's refusal to comply with UN demands to hand over information about his nuclear and chemical warfare capabilities to Western weapons inspectors.

Although Task Force 11 was set up purely as a vehicle for carrying out specific missions during Operation Enduring Freedom, its success during this campaign has warranted an increase in both its operational responsibilities and its military capabilities.

SPECIAL FORCES AT SEA

There is nothing new about naval special forces: examples of combat swimmers can be traced back to classical warfare and in more recent centuries, a navy's infantry arm, the marines, have always been considered something of an elite. However, the modern concept of naval special warfare dates back to the World War I, when the Italian Navy's small fast attack boats and divers took the war into the supposedly secure harbours of the Austro-Hungarian Navy. The Italians continued to spearhead this method of warfare in World War II, and both the British and Germans took note. By the end of the war, naval warfare techniques such as maritime raiding, assaults on warships and merchant shipping by frogmen, sailors in mini-subs or kayaks were regularly employed by the fore-runners of today's special forces units. The need for naval special warfare units, such as the US Navy SEALs, the British SBS, the Israeli Flotilla 13 and the Russian Naval Spetsnatz has been further amplified by the modern scourge of maritime terrorism.

Left: A US Navy SEAL being extracted from the water by helicopter during an exercise.

ARGENTINA 🇦🇷
La Agrupacion de Commandos Anfibios
La Agrupacion de Buzos Tacticos

Argentina maintains both a marine commando unit and a combat diver group, both of which have seen service against neighbouring Chile and against Britain in the Falklands War.

La Agrupacion de Commandos Anfibios, or Amphibious Commando Group, is the Argentine Navy's elite marine infantry unit. It is the spearhead of the Argentine Marine Corps. While formation of the Argentine Marine Corps dates back to the Anglo-Argentine war of 1807, the lineage of the Commandos Anfibios can be traced to the building of the Mar del Plata submarine base in 1933. This large facility required specialized marine infantry to protect it, and the unit developed into the 7th Marine Infantry Company in 1955. This company took on the role of a quasi-special operations unit within the Marine Corps. By 1959, it had become the multiskilled special operations unit of the Argentine Marines that it remains to this day. The unit undertook operations in the 1978–9 border dispute with Chile and also in the Falklands War, most famously in the assault on the Governor's House in Port Stanley.

The Commandos Anfibios are part of the Fuerza Anfibia de la Flotas de Mar (the Fleet's Marine Landing Force), which also contains the 2nd Marine Infantry Battalion and a number of AMTRAC battalions. The Commandos Anfibios is responsible for raiding and amphibious reconnaissance, and also provides the vanguard for larger seaborne assaults by the Marine Infantry. Service within the unit is strictly voluntary, and only the best marines are allowed to attempt the year-long selection process. Standards are extremely high, which is reflected in the failure rate. All personnel are airborne- and scuba-qualified.

Left: An Argentine amphibious commando during the Falklands War of 1982. He is armed with a British-made silenced 9mm L34A1 submachine gun and Browning Hi-Power pistol in a leather holster. Members of this unit assaulted the Governor's House in Port Stanley during the initial assault.

BUZOS TACTICOS

La Agrupacion de Buzos Tacticos, or Combat Divers Group, is the Argentine Navy's special operations unit. It was formed in 1952 under the auspices of an Italian veteran of 20th MAS Flotilla and tasked with possible operations against naval rivals in the region – Paraguay, Uruguay and particularly Chile. Indeed, the unit saw service during the 1978–9 border clashes with Chile in the Tierra del Fuega.

With a strength of about 150 men, the unit is based at the Mar del Plata naval base. The selection process is rigorous, with a 70 per cent dropout rate. Primarily combat swimmers who undertake covert reconnaissance and demolitions operations, they are not intended as shock troops, but have recently begun counterguerrilla and urban, desert and mountain combat training. The unit is equipped with a variety of insertion craft, the mainstay being the Klepper canoe. All members are airborne-qualified.

Weapons used include the silenced 9mm (0.354in) L34A1 Sterling; PA3, Uzi and Mini-Uzi submachine guns; FN and Argentine Fara 83 5.56mm assault rifles; and FN MAG machine guns.

The Falklands War

Members of the Buzos Tacticos were part of the force that seized South Georgia, and large numbers of divers, deployed from the submarine *Santa Fe*, surveyed Yorke Bay beaches and Stanley Harbour. They also guided in the invasion fleet on 1 April 1982.

AUSTRALIA

Special Air Service Regiment (SASR)
Tactical Assault Group (TAG)
Offshore Assault Team (OAT)
Clearance Diver Branch (CDB)

Australia's naval special warfare capability rests with in the Army's Special Air Service Regiment, although the navy operates a combat diver unit established since 1951, the CDB, which has close links with the SASR.

Much of Australia's naval special warfare responsibility falls into the remit of the SASR. The unit traces it roots back to the 22 SAS Regiment and World War II, but the Australians did not form a specific maritime special forces unit. As a result, beach reconnaissance, seaborne raiding and underwater demolitions remained a SASR responsibility. Each of the unit's Sabre (combat) squadrons (A, B and C) therefore deploy a 'water operations troop'. This troop uses a variety of maritime craft, including Zodiacs, rigid inflatable boats (RIBs), Klepper canoes and swimmer delivery vehicles (SDVs). The troop's diving equipment includes Dräger LAR V and Oxymax rebreathing gear. All members have passed the rigorous SASR selection and are parachute-trained.

Above: CDB members in 1991 during Operation Desert Storm. Australian naval divers were heavily involved in 'clearing-up' operations around Kuwait's harbours in the aftermath of the Iraqi withdrawal.

Weapons

Weapons used by the SASR and TAG/OAT special forces include the CAR-15 and M16A2 assault rifles and the F-88, the locally produced version of the Steyr-Mannlicher AUG. Pistols used are the Browning HP; SIG Sauer P228; and Smith and Wesson .38 and .357 revolvers. The MP5 family is carried for close-quarter work, as is the Beretta RS 202 Shotgun. Favoured support weapons are the FN Minimi 5.56mm (0.22in) (M249 SAW) and M60 machine guns. SASR snipers use the Parker-Hale M82 7.62mm (0.3in) rifle. The CDB use much the same weapons as their collegues.

TAG AND OAT

Within the SASR is the specialist counterterrorism force, the Tactical Assault Group (TAG), which was formed in 1978. An offshoot of TAG is the Offshore Assault Group (later renamed the Offshore Assault Team), which was established two years later, initially to protect the oil rigs in the Bass Strait. This role soon expanded to cover all maritime counterterrorism, such as boarding hostile ships, retaking hijacked liners, ferries and oil rigs. OAT is analogous to the US Navy's DEVGRU. Membership of TAG/OAT requires at least two years' previous experience in a regular Sabre squadron as well as further specialist training.

CDB

Although the SASR undertakes the typical maritime special operations, the Royal Australian Navy (RAN) has its own elite unit of combat divers in its Clearance Diver Branch (CDB), which was formed in 1951. The members of the CDB are tasked with mine clearance and similar EOD tasks. However, they also undertake beach reconnaissance prior to any naval landing and raiding operations against enemy naval vessels and maritime installations. The CDB comes under the administrational command of the RAN's Commander Australian Mine Warfare and Clearance Diving Forces.

The unit saw service in Vietnam, clearing mines and other hazards and also conducting ship searches in the country's various rivers and inlets. The CDB also deployed to the Gulf during Desert Storm, where it was responsible for clearing both sea and land mines and other unexploded devices from Kuwait's harbours. Above water, the CDB teams use the Zodiac Hurricane RIB 630 O/B, which can be deployed from submarines, helicopters and aircraft. All CDB members are jump-qualified. Klepper canoes are also popular and the RAN maintains a fleet of SDVs, allowing the CDB teams a considerable covert capability.

The weaponry used by the CDB are similar to the SASRs, and there is a long history of CDB divers both training in and joining the regiment.

Above: Australian clearance divers disembark from their Hurricane RIB at Shuaiba pier after a mine/unexploded device clearance operation from one of Kuwait's harbours following the Gulf War. The CDB also undertook reconnaissance missions for the coalition during hostilities.

BELGIUM ▉▉▉
The 14th Para-Commando Engineer Company

The mainstay of Belgium's special warfare capability is the Para-Commando Brigade. The Brigade's 14th Para-Commando Engineer Company contains the unit's combat diving squad.

Given Belgium's maritime history and experience of warfare across the world, it is puzzling that the nation's special forces are so little geared to naval operations. Belgium's special forces capabilities are based around the Para-Commando Brigade, formed during World War II. In 1991, it expanded from a regiment of three battalions to a brigade with the addition of new support units. One of these is the 14th Para-Commando Engineer Company. The engineer company contains, within the staff element, a squad of combat divers, or 'frogmen'. Their primary task is to prepare for amphibious landings and river crossings, through reconnaissance and, if necessary, preparatory demolitions. All members of the engineer company are fully qualified para-commandos and the combat divers receive additional training in scuba and combat diving skills.

Above: A Belgium para-commando undertakes diver training at the Mine Warfare and Diving School at Oostende.

The unit's standard assault rifle is the FNC 5.56mm (0.22in). The P90 submachine gun is also used, and the FN 5.7mm (0.22in) special operations pistol is the handgun of choice.

The unit uses a wide variety of craft in addition to its normal diving equipment. The standard RIB is the Zodiac Mk VI HD with twin 70 HP outboard motors, although smaller Sillinger boats with 40 HP engines are also used. For more covert operations, kayaks are the preferred mode of transport for the unit.

BRAZIL 🔵

Grupo de Mergulhadores de Combate (GRUMEC)
GERR/MEC
Comandos Anfibios (COMANF) 'Tonelero'

Brazil has a wide ranging naval special warfare capability, provided by GRUMEC, the Navy's combat divers, GERR/MEC, the unit's specialist counterterrorist group and the Marine Corps' Comandos Anfibios 'Tonelero'.

Grupo de Mergulhadores de Combate (GRUMEC – Combat Divers Group) is the Brazilian Navy's special operations unit. GRUMEC was formed in 1970, when a large cadre of officers and NCOs was sent to Coronado to train with the US Navy SEALs and to Marseilles to learn from the French Jaubert Commandos. These men provided the nucleus of the new Brazil special maritime warfare group and set up the Brazilian

Combat Diver Course. Given the long and varied Brazilian coastal and riverine environment and the nature of guerrilla and drug organizations in the region, the formation of the unit made a lot sense. Furthermore, Brazil has the largest navy in the region, but has always been somewhat parsimonious with its resources. The unit provides a means to monitor and even harass neighbouring fleets without having to deploy major surface units.

GRUMEC's mission profile ranges from conventional naval special warfare operations – including beach and long-range maritime reconnaissance, underwater demolitions and clearance, and small-unit raiding – to combat missions in a wide variety of mountain, jungle or urban locations. During wartime, the unit would be tasked with missions such as oil rig destruction, intelligence gathering and anti-mine duties.

Weapons used by GRUMEC are similar to that used by the US Navy SEALS, with whom the unit maintains close links. The unit uses the CAR-15 and M16 5.56mm (0.22in) assault rifles, often with the M203 grenade launcher attachment. Submachine guns carried include the H&K MP5 family, MAC-10 and Mini-Uzi. The 9mm (0.35in) Taurus PT52S is the pistol of choice and heavier firepower is provided by the 7.62mm (0.3in) FN MAG machine gun.

GRUMEC uses a range of small surface craft, including the ubiquitous Zodiac CRRC. However, the Brazilian Navy can make a wide range of naval and aeronautical deployment platforms available, up to and including the BNS *Minas Gerais* (formerly HMS *Vengeance*), a light aircraft carrier. The submarine fleet is similarly impressive, and GRUMEC can deploy from its five attack boats. Indeed, the unit is officially part of Brazil's submarine command.

GRUMEC Training

GRUMEC is based on Moncanguê Island at Nitoroi, Rio Grande, where the gruelling six-month GRUMEC training course also takes place at the Brazilian Navy Diving and Submarine Centre (CIAMA). The training is divided into four sections: a preliminary five-week open-circuit SCUBA training and 'drown-proofing' stage; a five-week physical and stamina development and mental conditioning phase that culminates in 'Hell Week', where candidates are tested continuously for 100 hours with no sleep and minimal food; a third phase that teaches maritime combat tactics, particularly subaqua, sabotage and reconnaissance; and an advanced combat course, including raiding, riverine and jungle actions, survival training, hand-to-hand combat and military climbing. Airborne and parachutist instruction also takes place in this phase.

GERR/MEC

Within GRUMEC is the Brazilian Navy's specialist maritime anti-terrorist unit, GERR/MEC (Retake and Rescue Special Group). An elite within an elite, GERR/MEC consists of about 50 men, specially trained to rescue hostages from maritime and riverine craft or locations deep in Brazil's jungles, and the recapture of oil rigs, liners and the like.

COMANF 'Tonelero'

Formed in 1957 and part of the Brazilian Marine Corps, Patalhao de Operacoes Especiais de Fuzilieros Navais do Comandos Anfibios 'Tonelero' (COMANF – Tonelero Special Operations Battalion) is tasked with reconnaissance and commando actions, such as raiding, in support of Brazilian naval power. COMANF 'Tonelero' has gradually evolved into its current form as the Marines' special operations force and now also has the job of providing specialized training for the Marine Corps and other military units. A prospective member of COMANF is drawn from the best of the 15,000-strong Marine Corps and must complete the rigorous Amphibious Commando and Special Operations Course. Many undertake parachute training, and GRUMEC provides combat diving instruction. The Army provides courses in the many skills required to operate in Brazil's varied environments, such as mountaineering and jungle warfare.

The unit's strength is roughly 500 men. The battalion is made up of five companies, consisting of the headquarters and services company; two Amphibious Commando companies; the Amphibious Reconnaissance Company (RECONANF); and lastly the Ground Reconnaissance Company (RECONTER). The Amphibious Commando companies are tasked with raiding, ship assaults and similar muscular missions. RECONANF undertakes operations similar to those of the US Marine Recon Battalion, including beach reconnaissance and preparatory actions prior to large-scale seaborne assault. RECONTER, unsurprisingly, is tasked with ground reconnaissance and LRRP-type missions. COMANF 'Tonelero' also maintains a 120-man special unit, GERR (Special Rescue Group), which is closely linked with GRUMEC's GERR/MEC counter-terrorist team.

CHILE 🇨🇱
Buzos Tacticos

The Chilean Navy's special operations unit, the Buzos Tacticos, was established in 1958. The unit saw action during the border dispute with Argentina in 1979–80. It maintains close links with the US Navy SEALs and regional special forces groups.

Chile, with its extremely long coastline and history of border disputes with its neighbours, particularly Argentina, has long placed considerable emphasis on its navy. The Chilean Navy's amphibious warfare capability is provided by the 3000-strong Marine Infantry Corps. The spearhead of this particular capability is the Navy's special operations unit, the Buzos Tacticos.

The Buzos Tacticos was established in 1958 to provide the Navy with a force of combat divers specializing in beach reconnaissance, underwater demolition, maritime intelligence gathering, and small-unit raiding. The formation was deployed against Argentina during the bloody 1979–80 border dispute, and it reportedly performed extremely well.

The original unit was only 100-strong, but it has gradually expanded and today has about 200 members, who act as the Marine Infantry's vanguard. Somewhat inevitably, the Buzos Tacticos have also gained a counterinsurgency and anti-terrorism role. The unit comes under the control of Submarine Command and is based at Viña del Mar and Valparaíso. The basic Buzos Tacticos course is 16 months long and involves combat swimming, scuba operations, small-unit tactics, skiing, high-speed driving and parachute instruction. The drop-out rate for the course is over 70 per cent. Once in the unit, members are taught counterterrorism and espionage skills. There is a small maritime hostage rescue section.

Favoured weapons of the Buzos Tacticos includes the M16, CAR-15 and HK33E assault rifles; the locally produced 9mm (0.35in) Famae SAF submachine gun; and the Korean Ultimax 100 and Spanish version of the MG3 machine guns. The unit has close links with the US Navy SEALs and a number of other local special forces groups.

COLOMBIA
Grupo de Comandos Anfibious (GCA)

Colombia's marine and naval special forces are largely engaged in combating the country's narco-terrorist groups.

The role of Colombia's maritime special forces units, as with the entire Colombian military and law enforcement establishment, is dominated by the country's struggle with guerrilla and narcotics groups. Thus both the First Marine Infantry Brigade, based at Sincelejo on the Atlantic, and the Second Marine Infantry Brigade, based on the Pacific coast, at Buenaventura, deploy a battalion apiece in anti-guerrilla operations. The 8th Battalion tasked with providing security for naval headquarters at Bogota has elements that support the Army's counter-insurgency role.

GRUPO DE COMANDOS ANFIBIOUS (GCA)

The Navy has a SEAL-type unit, Grupo de Comandos Anfibious (GCA – Amphibious Commando Group), which was formed in the mid-1960s. The unit is based at the Cartagena Naval Base and is about 100 men strong. It is composed of 25-man platoons, as well as a Training Company and a Security Company. The Grupo de Comandos Anfibious reportedly received training soon after its inception from a Mobile Training Team from the US Navy's SEAL Team 2 Mobile Training Team. The unit was trained in, amongst other things, basic swimming, demolitions, SCUBA and land warfare.

The GCA is inevitably heavily involved in anti-drug trafficking work, as well as more traditional maritime counterterrorism and combat diving tasks.

151

CUBA 🇨🇺
Formacion Especial Naval (FEN)

Cuba's combat divers unit, the FEN, has operated across the Caribbean and saw service across the world in support of Cuba and the Soviet Union's allies during the Cold War.

Details of the Cuban Navy's combat divers unit, the Formacion Especial Naval (FEN – Special Naval Formation), are sketchy. However, the FEN is believed to be about 200-strong. Service in the unit is voluntary, but the candidates are drawn from naval conscripts who have completed their basic training at the Junior Specialist Training Centre at Playa de Solado. Only the best are selected for the year-long course at the Special Naval Formation School. The curriculum includes swimming and diving, military topography, hand-to-hand combat and marksmanship, NBC warfare and parachuting (although apparently all jumps are made over land). The failure rate is estimated to be over 50 per cent.

Despite being heavily influenced by its 30 years in the Soviet sphere, the FEN purchases much of its equipment, such as diving gear, from the West, on the open market. While the Zodiac is the rubber boat of choice, the FEN can deploy off the Cuban Navy's larger platforms, including three submarines, if preferred. A large number of specially prepared civilian craft, such as tugs, fishing boats and yachts, is also used. It is believed that the FEN has no mini-submarines or SDVs. Weapons used are a mixture of Soviet and Western designs.

Members of the FEN were amongst the personnel of the Cuban Revolutionary Armed Forces (FAR) that saw combat in politically sensitive 'special operations' in Africa (Angola and Eritrea) at the height of the Cold War. It has also deployed across the Caribbean. The unit maintains good contacts with the Vietnamese Navy. Since 1990, the Cubans have trained heavily in Vietnam, learning guerrilla and deep penetration skills from their Vietnamese counterparts.

DENMARK 🇩🇰
Frømandskorpset

Denmark's Frømandskorpset is considered by its allies to be amongst the most capable naval special forces units in NATO. During the Gulf War, the unit's expertise in close-quarter battle and ship boarding saw it tasked with boarding ships in search of contraband.

Denmark has a very highly regarded naval special forces unit, the Frømandskorpset, or Frogman Corps. The unit was a product of Denmark's strategic position in the Cold War, acting as it did as a choke point on the entrance to the Baltic. The country was also vulnerable to seaborne assault, so the formation of an aggressive naval special forces unit made considerable sense. In 1957, four naval officers were sent to train with the US Navy's Underwater Demolitions Teams. Further study of the British SBS and the Norwegian Froskemandskorps led to the establishment of the Frømandskorpset. Initially the unit was part of the Royal Danish Navy's Diving School, but in 1970 the Frømandskorpset became a separate entity under the direct control of the Søværnets Operative Kommando (SOK – Naval High Command). However, administrative control passes down through the Navy's 5th Flotilla (the submarine flotilla).

The unit is based at the Kongsore Torpedo Station and has a strength somewhere in the region of 200 men. It is divided into three squadrons: one of combat swimmers and a second responsible for the unit's boats and insertion craft, while the third is Denmark's maritime counterterrorism squadron. The Frømandskorpset range of tasks is an extensive one, including long-range reconnaissance, raiding and sabotage, guerrilla operations and underwater demolitions and clearance. Its operators have considerable close-quarter battle expertise, and ship-boarding is something of a Frømandskorpset speciality. Indeed, during the Gulf War (1990–91), the unit was tasked with enforcing the embargo on Iraq by boarding ships in search of contraband. During peacetime, it also helps the local police to search for people lost at sea.

Frømandskorpset training takes more than 15 months and includes advanced combat skills, scuba and combat swimming, demolitions, reconnaissance, hand-to-hand combat, marksmanship and parachuting. Shipboarding and seizure skills are honed on Denmark's corvettes, frigates and other craft. The unit has close ties with the British SBS, the US Navy SEALs, the German KSK, Norway's Marinejægers and Sweden's naval special forces in particular.

Weapons used by the unit are various: the main assault rifles carried are the Heckler and Koch G41 5.56mm (0.22in) and the incredibly rugged Swedish AK5; for close-quarter operations, the MP5SD 9mm (0.35in), MP53 5.56mm (0.22) and other H&K submachine guns are used, as is the Remington 870 12-gauge shotgun; a favoured sidearm is the Smith and Wesson .38 Detective Special; the primary support weapon is the H&K HK13E 5.56mm (0.22) light machine gun; and Frømandskorpset snipers carry the H&K PSG-1 7.62mm (0.3in) precision rifle.

Delivery crafts

The Frømandskorpset uses a variety of surface and subsurface delivery craft, particularly the Zodiac and Klepper canoes. The Danish Navy makes its Westland Super Lynx helicopters available, and the unit uses specially modified McDonnell Douglas 500 AN/MH-6 'Little Bird' helicopters to carry up to six heavily laden operators.

FRANCE ■ ■
Commandment des Fuilieriers Marins Commandos (COFUSCO)
Commando Hubert
Groupe de Combat en Milieu Clos (GCMC)
Détachment d'Intervention Opérationnelle Subaquatique (DINOPS)

France has several naval special forces assets available, ranging from the navy's four assault commandos, the Commando Hubert combat swimmer unit and the GCMC maritime counterterrorist unit, to the Foreign Legion's DINOPS.

In 1992, in the aftermath of the Gulf War, France drew on the practice of both US and British special forces to set up a joint special operations command, Commandement des Opérations Spéciales (COS). Prior to this, the Army, Navy and Air Force special forces lacked a joint command structure. So the five naval commando units and the Groupe de Combat en Milieu Clos (GCMC – Close Quarters Combat Group) counterterrorist team are part of the Commandment des Fuilieriers Marins Commandos (Marine Infantry and Special Forces Command – COFUSCO), which provides the COS with its marine special warfare assets.

COFUSCO's current incarnation dates from 1983. Three of the five commando units now active are based at Lorient and another in Djibouti, and they are rotated through these postings. Hubert is stationed at Toulon. Each unit takes a turn at being on immediate call and can move at six hours' notice. This offers France tremendous flexibility and speed in its military response. There are four assault commandos: Trepel, Jaubert, Monfort and Penfentenyo. François was converted to a reserve unit in 1953 and later deactivated.

Commando Units History

French marine special warfare units date from World War II, when the Free French troop of No 10 Inter-Allied Commando became the core of the 1er Bataillon Fusiliers Marine Commandos, which took part in the Normandy landings. After the war, six commando units were raised between 1945 and 1947, and named after wartime officers who had been killed in action: Trepel, Jaubert, Monfort, Penfentenyo, François and Hubert. These units immediately began to see action in France's numerous colonial wars. They operated along the coast, in the Mekong Delta and around Tonkin against the Viet Minh during the French Indo-China War. The commandos also saw service during the Suez Crisis and in Algeria, from where they were withdrawn to France in 1962. Since then, these units have taken part in every French deployment across the world, including France's various peacekeeping operations and interventions in its former colonies.

The commandos are about 80-strong and are divided into four platoons of 20 men. These further divide into two squads of 10 men. Each platoon has a specific task: command, assault, reconnaissance and fire support. The command section consists of the commander and his second in command, an intelligence officer, two communications specialists, two radio operators and supporting troops; the reconnaissance platoon reconnoitres the prospective landing beach and decides whether it can be held; the assault team's main task is to take and hold the beachhead with the support of the heavier weaponry of the support platoon. Teams from the various sections can be combined if circumstances require. Acting as the spearhead for France's amphibious forces, particularly the 9th Marine Division, the naval commandos also undertake ship assaults and conduct CSAR. All members are airborne-qualified and insertion methods can be

by air (parachute or helicopter) or from surface ships or submarines, via Zodiacs or rigid raider craft. A Puma helicopter can carry half a platoon complete with Zodiac, while a Super Frelon is capable of taking 12 men and two Zodiacs.

Prospective commandos are drawn from French naval and marine units. They undertake an exhaustive four-month training/selection process at Lorient. Successful candidates then

undertake airborne training. This is followed by a month of commando training, and the final stage is instruction in amphibious operations. Some men are selected to attend France's combat diver school.

Weapons used include the M16, Swiss SG-540, and French FAMAS assault rifles, often with the M203 grenade launcher attachment. For close work, the commandos use the MP5 family of submachine guns and Remington 870 shotguns. Heavier weaponry includes the FN Minimi 5.56mm (0.22in) light machine gun, and the support section will have access to FN MAGs, 60mm (2.36in) mortars and Milan anti-tank missiles.

COMMANDO HUBERT

Commando Hubert, or Commando D'Action Sous Marine (Underwater Action Commando), is COFUSCO's combat swimmer unit. Originally raised as an amphibious commando force, it converted to the combat swimmer role in 1953 during the war in Algeria. When the French withdrew, the unit moved to its current base in Toulon. Today Commando Hubert undertakes maritime special operations for the French Navy and the French

Right: A group of Commando Hubert combat divers prepare to deploy from an aircraft during an exercise.

Right: French naval commandos prepare to board a Super Frelon helicopter aboard the aircraft carrier Foch *off the coast of Albania during the Kosovo crisis of 1999.*

Foreign intelligence service, the DGSE (Direction General de la Securité Exterieure – General Directorate of External Security).

Commando Hubert is 80 men strong, and it is divided into two companies. The 1st Company is the unit's operational arm, which is made up of 50 combat swimmers and contains a further four sections which are designated A to D:

Section A – Commando Hubert's command section, which includes the unit's HQ. It is also responsible for the Hurricane Rigid Craft, which are built by Zodiac and are capable of carrying 10 men at a speed of up to 50 knots.

Section B – the maritime counterterrorist section, specializing in underwater approaches to terrorist-held targets. Its members work in cooperation with the GCMC and GIGN (Groupe d'Intervention de Gendarmerie Nationale – the police's counterterrorism unit), which also has a team of divers. B section divers probably act as guides for the other units.

Section C – the underwater operations unit, whose divers operate Hubert's SDVs (or PSMs – propulseurs sous-marin).

Section D – the reconnaissance and support unit, whose members are responsible for beach reconnaissance and underwater demolitions. They also provide the unit's heavy fire support and contain its snipers.

There are plans to form an E section, containing the Hurricanes. The 2nd Company is 30 men strong and provides Hubert's combat support. Its members specialize in logistics, communications and the maintenance

of the unit's SDVs and small boats. Hubert also has the French naval vessel *Poseidon* attached, which acts as a floating base for operations of both Hubert divers and their SDVs.

Candidates for Commando Hubert are selected from France's marine commando units. They must have done at least four years' naval service and six months with the commandos. They begin with basic diving instruction and undertake the advanced diving course, both held at the French Navy Dive School at Saint-Mandrier near Toulon. They then move on to small-boat handling and are introduced to the Klepper canoe. The final phase is dedicated to underwater demolitions and engineering and parachuting. Successful candidates are assigned to Hubert for an initial period of three years, where they will attend the advanced combat diver and master

parachutist courses. Hubert divers can go on to extend their tours after the initial three years.

Weapons used by Commando Hubert include the FAMAS 5.56mm assault rifle, often with the M203 40mm (1.57in) grenade launcher attachment; the Uzi and mini-Uzi; the Heckler and Koch MP5 family of submachine guns; and the FR-F2 7.5mm and PGM Hecate .50 calibre sniper rifles.

GROUPE DE COMBAT EN MILIEU CLOS (GCMC)

The French Navy's elite maritime counterterrorist unit is the Groupe de Combat en Milieu Clos (GCMC – Close Quarters Combat Group). Like the marine commandos, this unit is part of the French Navy's COFUSCO. Formed in 1994, the unit is extremely small, made up of only 17 men. It

divides into two eight-man sections and a unit commander, all of whom display a considerable range of skills, including marksmanship, combat medicine demolitions, small boat handling and combat diving. The GCMC specializes in ship take-downs and uses Zodiac and Hurricane rigid craft. Its members wear the distinctive navy blue uniforms of the GIGNs, and their body armour also acts as a flotation devices.

The GCMC usually operates in concert with other agencies, particularly Commando Hubert's Section B counterterrorist team.

Weapons used include G3 7.62mm assault rifle; M16 5.56mm assault rifle, often with M203 grenade launcher; MP5 submachine guns; .357 Smith and Wesson revolvers; FR-F2 7.5mm sniper rifles; and, for heavier firepower, the FN Minimi 5.56mm (0.219in) machine gun.

DÉTACHMENT D'INTERVENTION OPÉRATIONNELLE SUBAQUATIQUE (DINOPS)

Although not part of France's special forces or under COS command, the Légion étrangère (Foreign Legion) is

an undoubted elite, one which has undertaken special operations across the world for France. The Foreign Legion was formed in 1831 to control the French colonies in Africa, and has seen combat in just about every one of France's wars since then. After the French left Algeria in 1962, it moved to Corsica, where it is based today. In 1984, the Legion raised the 6ème Régiment étranger de génie (6th Foreign Engineer Regiment – 6 REG), based at Plain d'Albion. The 6 REG contains the Détachment d'Intervention Opérationnelle Sub-aquatique (DINOPS – Underwater Special Intervention Detachment). The section is attached to the regiment's Reconnaissance and Support Company and is tasked with conducting beach reconnaissance and hydrographic surveys and assisting in river crossings for the main body of the Legion's forces. DINOPS also provides the Legion's underwater EOD capability, and it is capable of conducting small-scale raiding and sabotage operations.

Since 1984, the unit has participated in most of France's military deployments. During the Gulf War

Above: French Naval Commandos chase Greenpeace environmental protestors who have entered the French military restricted area prior to the nuclear tests undertaken in French Polynesia in 1995.

(1990–91), DINOPS operated in support of the US 82nd Airborne Division in the Iraqi desert. After the ceasefire, they joined the Australian CDBs in mine-clearing operations.

Members of the unit undergo one of the most intensive training regimes in the French armed forces. They must pass both the French Navy's combat swimmers course and the Army's parachute course. They receive additional training in the Legion's and Army's various specialist schools. Thus successful candidates enter DINOPS both airborne- and diver-qualified. This means that these para-engineers can be inserted by parachute, helicopter, submarine, surface ship, Zodiac or Klepper canoe. All men can operate scuba and closed-circuit diving devices.

Weapons used include the FAMAS 5.56mm assault rifle; MP5 and Uzi submachine guns; and 5.56mm Paras, 9mm Beretta and .357 Smith and Wesson pistols.

GERMANY
Kampfschwimmerkompani (KSK)

*During the Cold War, Germany's Kampfschwimmerkompani was tasked with
operations against Warsaw Pact maritime assets. It has since operated in the Gulf
and in support of Germany's peacekeeping efforts in the Balkans.*

Germany has a long tradition of naval special operations. The K-Flotilla gained a formidable reputation operating against Allied shipping in the Baltic and North Sea during World War II. When West Germany rearmed in 1955, there was considerable suspicions of elite commando units. However, the newly reconstituted German Navy, the Bundesmarine, could see the need for such naval specialists to counter the threat of the Soviet special forces. A number of K-Flotilla veterans were recruited and sent to France to train with Commando Jaubert members, and this cadre established the Kampfschwimmerkompani (KSK – Combat Swimmer

Other Units

The German Navy also has the Minetaucherkompanie (MiTaKp – Mine Diver Company), which is tasked with traditional UDT tasks such as mine clearance and salvage, and also undertakes maritime CSAR. It is about 250-strong. Both the KSK and MiTaKp saw service during the Gulf War (1990–91).

The famous anti-terrorist unit GSG-9 also has a small combat swimmer unit within its Section 2, and this is trained by KSK operatives.

Company) in 1959. The unit became independent in 1964, gaining its own insignia in 1966.

The KSK is about company-sized (no more than 250-strong), and it is divided into three platoons, a support platoon and a training platoon. It is based at the Eckernförde Naval Academy on the German Baltic coast, the perfect location to counter the maritime threat posed by the signatories to the Warsaw Pact. Indeed, for the entire Cold War, the KSK's primary mission was the surveillance of the ports in East German and Polish waters. Had the war broken out, the KSK would have been tasked with securing the northern West German ports, evacuating strategic areas near Denmark, and taking more offensive actions against Warsaw Pact ports and ships. These operations would have been undertaken in cooperation with Allied units, and thus the KSK has close links to this day with the British SBS and a special relationship with the French. The unit has also trained with elite Belgian, Spanish, Italian and Israeli units. Indeed, the KSK is very

*Left: Two KSK members man a Milan
anti-tank missile system. These combat
swimmers are also well versed in
ground combat.*

Left: A KSK swimmer walks away from the drop zone carrying his parachute canopy over his shoulder. All KSK operatives are airborne-qualified.

in the region of 80 per cent. The first four months of training teach diving skills at Neustadt and Eckernförde. Candidates then learn to operate the unit's various craft – Zodiacs, RIBs, SDVs and Klepper canoes – and afterwards undertake a gruelling course in the skills of ground combat, such as weapon skills and airborne training, at Altenstadt. Finally, EOD and reconnaissance skills are learnt at Großenbrode. Only at this point is a candidate finally considered a *Kampf-schwimmer* (combat swimmer).

Weapons used by the KSK include the H&K MP5 and Uzi submachine guns; the G3 family of assault rifles; H&K 21A1 machine guns; and H&K PSG-1 sniper rifles. The unit also uses the H&K P11 underwater pistol, which can fire six 7.62mm (0.3in) darts up to 30m (98ft) above water and 15m (49ft) below the surface.

highly regarded in the naval special warfare community.

Prospective recruits to the unit must have least four years' service in the Bundesmarine; for officers, the requirement is eight years. They must

first go through a series of physical and mental tests, followed by a final 'aquatic test' of a 5km (3-mile) freestyle swim and 1km (3280ft) crawl swim, followed by a 25m (82ft) speed dive. Even at this stage, the dropout rate is

GREECE
Monas Ymourhon Katastpofon (MYK)

The Greek MYK naval special forces unit is based on the US Navy SEAL model and has been deployed across the Aegean, in the Gulf and in the Adriatic.

The Greek Navy maintains a naval special forces unit known as the Monas Ymourhon Katastpofon (MYK – Underwater Demolition Unit). Given Greece's long maritime tradition and similarly long hostility to neighbouring Turkey, such a unit must be considered a necessity. The MYK was formed in 1957 after two naval officers were sent to Little Creek, near Norfolk, Virginia. They undertook the UDT/R training course (the

forerunner to BUD/S) and returned home to establish a 12-strong unit of combat divers. The unit expanded and set up its headquarters at the Squaramanga Naval Base in 1959. The MYK comes under the control of the Greek Navy's Amphibious Operations Command.

Currently the MYK is divided into four sections, known as Omada Ymourhon Katastpofon (OYK – Underwater Demolition

Detachment). Basically these are 'teams' based on the US Navy SEAL model. The MYK is 110-strong, and each OYK section is made up of 25 men and has its own specialization: OYK-1 and OYK-2 are both unconventional warfare and intelligence-gathering teams; OKY-3 specializes in beach reconnaissance and hydrographic surveying; and OKY-4 has responsibility for maritime EOD operations. There is

Right: Two MYK commandos aim their CAR-15 assault rifles with M203 grenade launcher attachments during an exercise near the Greek capital. The unit is preparing for its role protecting the 2004 Athens Olympics.

a reserve team, OYK-5, which is inactive in peacetime.

The unit saw service during the Gulf War, was deployed to the island of Imia during the 1996 sovereignty dispute with Turkey, and in 1997 assisted in the evacuation of Greek nationals from Albania.

Recruits for the unit can be drawn from naval conscripts (who must sign on for an extra 23 months of service), but most are career sailors. The MYK training course lasts seven months and culminates in a five-day 'Hell Week'. On completion, prospective members must attend the Greek Airborne Course before joining the unit.

Favoured weaponry includes the M16A2 and the MP11 assault rifles; the MP5 submachine gun; and the MG3 light machine gun.

The MYK has a variety of delivery vehicles at its disposal, which includes Zodiacs, speedboats and ex-US Navy SEAL SDVs.

INDIA

Marine Commando Force (MCF)

India's Marine Commando Force has gained a fearsome reputation during its operations in the disputed territory of Kashmir.

Indian combat diving began in 1955, when a diving school, under British SBS instruction, was established at Cochin. However, the divers produced were in effect salvage and clearance specialists, and, when used for sabotage operations in the 1971 Indo-Pakistan War, they were largely unsuccessful. It was not until 1986 that steps were taken to form a proper naval commando element capable of undertaking a range of missions, from beach reconnaissance to maritime counterterrorism. Volunteers from the diving unit were sent to train with the US Navy SEALs

at Coronado, and a series of exchanges followed with the SBS. The result of this education in maritime special forces practice was the formation of the Indian Marine Special Forces in February 1987.

The unit was renamed the Marine Commando Force (MCF) in 1991. It is presently about 2000 men strong. The intention is to form 10 groups of 200. The MCF has three main bases around India: one in Bombay, to cover the west; in Cochin, covering the south; and in Vizag, to cover the east. Each group has a Quick Reaction Section, a platoon-sized team (30

men) of counterterrorist and hostage rescue specialists. The MCF has seen service in Sri Lanka against the Tamil Tigers, and it has gained a formidable reputation during ongoing operations in Kashmir.

Weapons favoured by the Marine Commando Force include the locally produced versions of the Sterling 9mm (0.354in) submachine gun and FN FAL 7.62mm (0.3in) assault rifle. The QRS favour the AK-47 family.

The MCF favours surface craft on operations, although the unit does deploy from the Comos CE-2F/X100 two-man mini-sub.

INDESIA ▬
Kommando intai Para Amphibi (KIPAM)

KIPAM is the Indonesian Marine Corps maritime special forces unit, which operates in and around the country's many islands.

The Indonesian Marine Corps contains the nation's maritime special forces unit, the Kommando intai Para Amphibi (KIPAM – Amphibious Recon Para-Commando). Given Indonesia's geography and terrain, such a capability is vital to the nation. In 1960, a cadre of Indonesian Marines was trained at the British Royal Marine Jungle Warfare Centre in Malaysia and subsequently attended Coronado and Camp Pendleton under US Marine tutelage. These men provided the basis of KIPAM, which was established in March 1961.

The unit is battalion-sized, with a strength of roughly 300 men. One detachment is stationed at Jakarta and the rest at their training centre at Surabaya. Training is believed to last seven months (or perhaps 10) and includes scuba, reconnaissance and airborne courses. KIPAM has seen some service on the Malaysian border and in East Timor.

The unit maintains contacts with the US Navy SEALs and US Marine Recon. KIPAM members have also trained with the SBS at Poole and the Dutch 7 NL SBS at Rotterdam. Although Indonesia is an Islamic nation, there are indications that its operators have also visited Israel.

For its underwater demolitions, clearance and salvage work, the

Above: A member of KIPAM carefully comes ashore near Jakarta during a naval exercise. He is armed with a AKS-74U, the shortened version of the AK-74.

Below: A rigid inflatable boat filled with KIPAM operatives bristling with weaponry. They carry a mixture of AKS-74U and AKS-74 assault rifles.

Indonesian Navy has PASKA, the Underwater Demolitions Team, based at Surabaya. There is also a specialist anti-terrorist team, made up of KIPAM members and Navy divers, known as 'Detachment Jala Mengkara'.

The unit's favoured submachine guns are the Uzi and Mini-Uzi. Although the standard weapon of the Indonesian Marines is the M16, KIPAM prefers the FNC 5.56mm and AK-47 7.62mm (0.3in) assault rifles.

ISRAEL
Shayetet 13

Israel's Shayetet 13 is one of the world's most highly regarded maritime special forces units. It has an almost unparalleled range of operational experience dating back to World War II and the pre-independence struggle against the British.

Israel possesses one of the most experienced and almost certainly one of the best naval special forces unit, Shayetet 13 (Flotilla 13), sometimes known as Kommando Yami (Naval Commandos).

The unit can trace its origins back to World War II, when the British Special Operations Executive sanctioned the creation of a naval commando unit, or Pal'mach (strike company), within the Haganah ('Defence' – Israel's pre-independence army) in 1940. Following the war, this force operated against the British, assisting illegal immigration and destroying several coastal craft. After Britain's withdrawal from Palestine, the sea section of the Pal'mach was integrated into the fledgling Israeli Defence Force (IDF) Navy. Thus it played a key role in the 1948 war, most spectacularly sinking the flag ship of the Egyptian Navy.

In the aftermath of 1948, Shayetet 13 was reorganized along the lines of the British SBS. Members underwent training with the British unit, and the French and Italian naval special operations teams provided further instruction. The unit acquired Klepper canoes and pioneered helicopter insertion techniques. However, Shayetet 13 performed poorly during the 1967 Six Day War, when a raid on

Alexandria Harbour went disastrously wrong. Indeed, it succeeded in none of the tasks set for it during the brief conflict. There was demand within the IDF for Shayetet 13 to be disbanded. However, its failure in the war brought a new era of professionalism to the unit, which established close ties with Sayeret Mat'kal. The new approach soon began to pay dividends. In 1969, the unit pulled off a spectacular raid on the Egyptian radar station at Ras al-Adabia, and this

Above: Naval commandos of Shayetet 13 in scuba gear check their weapons aboard a rigid inflatable boat.

was followed by the attack, in collaboration with Sayeret Mat'kal, on the Egyptian position on Green Island – still considered one of the classic naval special operations assaults in military history. Shayetet 13 performed well throughout the War of Attrition, also attacking Palestinian bases in Lebanon. The unit was equally

Above: Scuba-equipped Shayetet 13 operators move out into the Red Sea in preparation for an operation against the Egyptian Navy during the War of Attrition.

Right: An exhausted-looking Shayetet 13 candidate emerges from the sea during selection. The unit's selection process is the toughest in the Israeli military.

successful during the 1973 Yom Kippur War, causing the Egyptian Navy innumerable troubles. Shayetet 13 secured the beachheads for the IDF's largest ever amphibious operations: the 1982 landings in support of Operation Peace for Galilee, the invasion of Lebanon. In the 1980s, they raided Palestinian facilities along the Lebanese coast. The unit has also ensured that no seaborne attack has ever reached Israel's shores.

Shayetet 13 is about 300 men strong and is based at Atlit on Israel's Mediterranean coast. Selection and training is the most rigorous within the Israeli military. An initial selection phase tests the candidate's physical and mental suitability, and it includes a three-day 200km (124-mile) march. After this, candidates progress to the IDF's infantry school for advanced ground combat training, parachute instruction (both HAHO and HALO), and underwater and counterterrorism training at Atlit, where candidates learn seamanship, scuba, diving, and communication demolitions (both above and below water). The process takes 20 months before the operator enters Shayetet 13. The successful candidate then signs on for an additional 18 months' service.

Weapons

Shayetet 13 uses a variety of weaponry and is known to favour the AK-47 7.62mm (0.3in) assault rifle for its reliability, toughness and stopping power; the American CAR-15 is also used. The Mini-Uzi, particularly the silenced version, is the standard submachine gun. When heavier weapons are required, operators use the old Israeli standard, the FN MAG 7.62mm GPMG and the Soviet-built RPK light machine gun. Both the RPG-7 and LAW rocket launchers are available. Shayetet 13 snipers carry the Robar SR 60 .330 Win. Mag. and the Barrett Model 82A1/90 .50 BMG rifles.

Shayetet 13 uses a variety of insertion craft. The assets of the Israeli Navy are available, including various missile boats, patrol craft and submarines. The Navy is soon to receive three German-built Dolphin Class submarines, the first of which is reputed to be fitted with a dry deck shelter capable of launching SDVs and up to eight combat swimmers. The unit also uses Zodiacs and Snunit (Swallow) high-speed boats.

ITALY ▮▮
Commando Raggrupamento Subacquei e Incursori 'Teseo Tesei' (COMSUBIN)

*The Italian Navy is the originator of modern naval special forces, and this
fine tradition continues in COMSUBIN, which has seen a considerable variety of service
since its formation in the early 1950s.*

The Italians invented the modern concept of maritime special forces. During Word War II, on 18 December 1941, 12 men of 10th MAS Flotilla aboard Maiale midget submarines managed to penetrate the defences of Alexandria Harbour in Egypt and blew the bottoms out of two British battleships, subsequently opening a new chapter in naval special warfare tactics. The tradition continues on to this day in the Italian Navy's Commando Raggrupamento Subacquei e Incursori 'Teseo Tesei' (named after a legendary commander of 10th MAS), or COMSUBIN.

Banned initially from forming special forces units after World War II, the Italian Navy had to wait until the nation joined NATO before it could form a naval special warfare unit. COMSUBIN was established in 1954 with the amalgamation of a number of small diving units. It is based at the Varignano base near La Spezia and, in peacetime, answers to a rear admiral, thus coming under the direct control of the Navy Chief of Staff.

The unit has been deployed to Lebanon, Somalia, Rwanda, Albania and East Timor as part of Italian peacekeeping operations.

COMSUBIN is about 200 men strong, and the unit is divided into three groups:

Gruppo Operativo Incursori (GOI) – making up just over half of COMSUBIN's strength, the GOI is the unit's commando arm and divides further into three sections: Unita Interveni Speciali (Special Intervention Unit), the counterterrorist section; the Weapons Unit, which is responsible for

Below: During an amphibious assault training exercise, a COMSUBIN team comes ashore from its Zodiac.

Left: A mixture COMSUBIN operators and members of the elite San Marco Marine Battalion deploy from the Italian Navy's amphibious assault ship San Giusto near the port of Brindisi in 1997. Both units deployed to Albania soon after as part of the United Nations relief mission.

follows, during which time the recruit is assigned to the assault teams. Thus to become a fully qualified GOI operator takes in the region of three years.

The unit has close links with the British SBS, the US Navy SEALs and Marine Recon, Spain's UOE and Israel's Shayetet 13.

The unit uses a variety of weapons: its main assault rifle is the Beretta SC70 5.56mm, although the M16, CAR-15 and the G3 are used; the MP5 family of submachine guns is used for close work, but many COMSUBIN members prefer the Beretta PM 12S; pistols used include the Beretta 92CB 9mm and the H&K P11 underwater pistol; the Benelli M3 Super 90 Shotgun and SPAS 15 Mod B 12-gauge shotguns are used for ship boarding; and heavier firepower is provided by the FN Minimi 5.56mm (0.219in) and M3 7.62mm (0.3in) machine guns.

heavy weapons; and a Special Equipment Unit.

Gruppo Operativo Subacquei (GOS – Underwater Operations Group) – the combat divers force is charged with the protection of Italian naval vessels and carrying out the traditional UDT role. It is also tasked with ensuring that GOI teams are properly trained in scuba and diving operations, and has a maritime CSAR role.

Gruppo Navale Speciale (GNS – Special Naval Group) – the unit's special boat squadron also operates two naval support vessels for COMSUBIN.

Also part of the units is Ufficio Studi (Study and Research Centre), which evaluates new equipment and tactics.

Virtually all COMSUBIN personnel are drawn from the Navy's elite San Marco Marine Battalion. The basic training regime takes 10 months,

which is followed by an additional 42 weeks of airborne, light infantry and further specialized instruction. The candidates learn a whole raft of skills, including combat swimming, mine clearance, counterterrorism techniques and intelligence gathering. On completion, the new 'Incursori' attend six-month specialization courses. Finally, a 14-month probation period

Right: GOS combat divers in scuba gear make their way out to sea aboard their Zodiac inflatable craft.

KOREA, NORTH

North Korea has one the most active maritime special forces units in the world. These combat swimmers have been used extensively against South Korea, Japan and US assets in the region.

The Democratic People's Republic of Korea maintains a considerable maritime special warfare capability, which it uses against its southern neighbour on a regular basis. Indeed, it is estimated that the Korean Peninsula sees the greatest naval special forces activity in the world. The North Korean People's Army maintains three brigades of Amphibious Light Infantry, tasked with the seizure and destruction of coastal targets and the assistance of conventional forces, by mounting amphibious flank attacks and the reconnaissance and seizure of beachheads. They also have a covert special operations responsibility, such as intelligence gathering, assassination and small-unit sabotage and raiding.

These Army units come under control of the North Korean Naval Forces commander. One brigade of four battalions is based with the Army's III Corps at Hakkye; a second brigade of seven battalions is attached to the VII Corps at Wosnan; and the third of two battalions is with the VIII Corps at Tasa-ri. Each brigade has a specialist combat swimmer unit of an unspecified size (probably larger than a company) and a group using special operations craft, such as mini-subs and SDVs. North Korea also uses fishing boats and merchant vessels, as well its conventional submarines, to infiltrate its special warfare personnel. It is likely most North Korean operators are also airborne-qualified. The all-wooden (and thus virtually invisible on radar) Antonov An-2 Colt transport plane is also available.

The naval commando training, according to American estimates, lasts as long as two years and includes instruction in scuba and combat diving and all aspects of conventional and irregular warfare.

The North Korean special naval forces also gather intelligence, and it is clear that they have been extremely active against the South. A three-ton mini-sub was captured by the South Koreans in 1965, as was a high-speed agent infiltration boat in 1979. There have been other examples in the 1990s, most spectacularly in 1996, when 26 commandos went on the run in South Korea after their submarine ran aground.

The combat swimmers are equipped with local, Soviet and now Chinese scuba gear, wet and dry suits, and weaponry. However, captured equipment has shown that the North Koreans also use up-to-date Western rebreathers and other diving gear.

KOREA, SOUTH
Marine Corps SEALs

South Korea's naval special forces units, the Marine Corps Reconnaissance units and the Navy SEALs, have the difficult task of protecting the country from incursions carried out by its aggressive neighbour's combat swimmers.

Tasked with protecting South Korea against the naval special warfare incursions from the North are the Republic of Korea's Marine Corps and the Navy's SEALs. However, their task is not merely reactive. Apart from preparing for a full-scale invasion from the North, they are engaged in a constant covert struggle, gathering intelligence, conducting sabotage and undertaking coastal reconnaissance in the North for a possible retaliatory assault. Thus the South Korean naval special forces are regarded as amongst the best in the world.

The Marine Corps is the second largest such force in the world. It has a long and honourable tradition and an admirable combat record stretching back to the Korean War and through the Vietnam War. It consists of three divisions: the 1st, 2nd and 6th. Each division possesses an amphibious reconnaissance battalion. The example of the 1st Division illustrates the structure of the others: its recon battalion is split into two elements of two companies apiece. There are two Amphibious Reconnaissance Companies, to act as the spearhead of a larger invasion force; and two Special Reconnaissance Companies, which undertake sabotage, small-scale raiding and counterinsurgency tasks. They are manned solely by volunteers.

SEALS

The Navy has its own special warfare capability in its Navy SEALs, which are divided into three teams. SEAL Team One and SEAL Team Two undertake traditional naval special warfare tasks, such as intelligence gathering, beach reconnaissance and underwater demolitions. SEAL Team Three, like the US Navy's DEVGRU, deals with counterterrorism and hostage rescue. The unit has very close links with its American counterparts.

Weaponry includes the Daewoo K2 5.56mm (0.22in) assault rifle; H&K MP5 submachine guns; and Daewoo DP51 9mm and Beretta 92S 9mm (0.35in) pistols. The sniper rifle of choice is the H&K PSG-1 7.62mm (0.3in) precision rifle.

Unarmed Combat Techniques

The Marines have formed their own form of unarmed combat, based on the martial art of tae kwon do and known as 'mujeokdo', which means 'No enemy soldier can beat you'.

MALAYSIA
Paskal

Malaysia's maritime assets, particularly its oil rigs are protected by Paskal, the Navy's special forces group. Well armed and equipped, it has seen action against Filipino guerrillas.

Paskal, or Pasukan Khas Laut, is the Royal Malaysian Navy's special forces group. It traces back to 1975 when the Navy, recognizing the need for a security regiment, sent a team of officers and men to be trained by the Indonesian Navy's KIPAM-PASKA instructors. This cadre formed the basis of Paskal, which was formally established in 1980 as the Malaysian Government began to enforce the Exclusive Economic Zone in Malaysian waters and realized the need for more maritime 'muscle' in the Spratly Islands dispute. The unit is also responsible for the protection of Malaysia's 30 or so oil rigs. Apart from this counterterrorism brief, Paskal is also responsible for maritime reconnaissance, raiding, sabotage and demolitions in support of larger scale army landing operations.

Training is rigorous, including a three-month commando course, followed by the parachuting and diving courses at the Special Warfare Training Centre at Sungai Udang. The dropout rate is in the region of 90 per cent. The unit is highly influenced in structure and tactics by the British SBS and also has links with KIPAM/PASKA and the US Navy SEALs. Paskal is excellently equipped, thanks to contributions to the unit's finances made by the oil company consortium whose rigs the group protects.

An interesting mode of transport used by Paskal is the subskimmer, a submergible high-speed inflatable craft, in which the crew use closed-circuit breathing gear when below water.

Weapons used include the M16A2 and MP5 family of submachine guns.

Left: A Paskal member stands guard aboard a patrol boat during operations off the Sabah Coast in 2000.

NETHERLANDS
7 NL SBS

The Dutch Special Boat Section maintains a remarkably close relationship with its British counterpart. In wartime, this highly professional unit would provide support for British and Dutch amphibious forces.

The Netherlands is a maritime trading nation, whose empire once stretched across the world from South America and the Caribbean to Southeast Asia. To protect these interests, the Koninklijk Nederlands Korps Mariniers (Royal Dutch Marine Corps) operated across the world. An elite among the Dutch military, the Marine Corps also contains the nation's maritime special warfare unit, the 7 Troop Special Boat Section (NL) or 7 NL SBS (Amfibisch Verkennings Peloton). This unit has remarkably

close ties with its British equivalent, the Special Boat Service (SBS).

The Dutch began training combat swimmers in 1959, but changed their training in 1961, adopting US and French practices. The first combat swimmer or frogman section was formed two years later, consisting of 10 men. In 1973, the British and Dutch formed the joint United Kingdom/Netherlands Amphibious Force (UKNLAF), made up of the two nations' naval assets and Britain's Royal

Left: An SBS man hoists himself aboard a ship. Ship-boarding and vessel take-down are key skills for 7 NL SBS, which along with the BBE is tasked with Dutch maritime counterterrorism.

Above: Two 7 NL SBS members silently approach an oil refinery during an exercise. The man on the right is checking their position with a compass and depth-gauge board while he is covered by his MP5 armed partner.

Marine 3 Commando Brigade and the Dutch Group of Operational Units Marines (GOUM), which usually includes the 1st Marine Battalion. As part of this reform and the Marines' integration into this new formation, the structure of the frogman section was changed, and it was renamed 7 NL SBS. Thus 7 NL SBS is a subunit of GOUM's support battalion. However, in wartime or in other moments of international cooperation, the 7 NL

SBS would come under British command and act as part of the British SBS, becoming part of C Squadron, the reconnaissance element of 3 Commando Brigade.

The unit is only around 25–26 men strong. It is believed to be divided into four or five teams, and there is a small command element. Apart from its wartime role conducting operations in support of British and Dutch landing forces, 7 NL SBS is also responsible for long-range reconnaissance; small-scale raiding; training the Dutch Navy in anti-mine and security procedures; and

conducting, in concert with the BBE (the Dutch elite counterterrorist unit), maritime counterterrorist tasks, such as the protection of Dutch oil rigs in the North Sea and shipboard hostage rescue. It is worth noting that the BBE maintains a boat troop and is also technically part of the Royal Dutch Marine Corps, although it comes under the jurisdiction of the Ministry of Justice in a crisis.

Recruits must undergo a 22-week selection and training course, which has a failure rate somewhere in the region of 70 per cent. The process

starts with basic naval diving courses, and these are followed by an introduction to the Klepper canoe and inland diving operations. Also learned are reconnaissance, escape and evasion techniques, and counterterrorist skills. Finally comes an endurance test.

Weapons used include C-7 and C-8 5.56mm assault rifles (the Canadian-built version of the M16 and CAR-15, respectively); the MP5; the Glock 17 pistol; the FN MAG 7.65mm (0.3in) machine gun, to provide heavier firepower; and the Steyr SSG 7.62mm (0.3in), the unit's standard sniper rifle.

NORWAY 🇳🇴
Marinejægerkommando

As a member of NATO, Norway held a vital strategic location during the Cold War and was a prime target for Soviet special forces. The Marinejægerkommando was tasked with countering this threat.

Norway, with its long and rugged coastline and its vital strategic position during the Cold War, has a long tradition of naval special warfare units. Its commandos, both of Kompani Linge and from 10 Inter-Allied Commando, did fine service along the German-occupied Norwegian coast during World War II. In 1953, the Norwegian Navy established the Dykker and Froskemannskolen (Diving and Frogman School) to train

Norwegian divers in UDT techniques. The original tasks for the Norwegian frogmen was underwater demolitions and salvage and beach reconnaissance. However, in 1968, the growing threat of Soviet special forces meant that the frogmen were divided into units, an EOD/UDT section and the Marinejægerkommando, or Marine Ranger/Hunter Commando. This is a specialized naval commando unit in the pattern of the British SBS and US

Navy SEALs, and it is tasked with reconnaissance, raiding and intelligence gathering; during the Cold War, it was to stay behind in the event of a Soviet invasion.

The Marinejægerkommando is about 200-strong and has its headquarters at Ramsund Naval Station. Elements of the unit are based at the Navy's diving school and submarine base at Haakonsvern. Training/selection is a hard 22 weeks, during which candidates are taught combat diving, survival skills, mountaineering, small-unit skills and parachuting. Recruits can be drawn from Norway's conscripts, but most, if they join the Marinejægerkommando, sign on for professional service.

The unit has strong links with the US Navy SEALs, the British and Dutch SBS, and the Danish Frømandskorpset.

Weapons

Weapons used include the AG3 7.62mm assault rifle (the Norwegian version of the G3), often with a 40mm (1.57in) grenade launcher; H&K MP5A3 and MP5SD5 9mm submachine guns; the FN Minimi 5.56mm (0.22in) machine gun, for squad support; the H&K P7 9mm (0.35in) and .357 Smith and Wesson pistols; H&K USP 9mm special operations and Glock 17 pistols (both recently purchased); and the locally produced NM149S 7.62mm precision rifle, used by the unit's snipers.

PAKISTAN
Special Services Group – Navy (SSGN)

*Given the vulnerability of Pakistan's coastline and the country's long hostility
with her neighbour India, a well-trained naval special forces capability, such as is provided
by the SSGN, must be considered a necessity.*

The Naval Special Services Group (SSGN) is the Pakistani Navy's special forces unit. This commando force is tasked with special operations below the water line. The unit was created in 1966 from the Pakistani Army's Special Services Group, as the Navy had little tradition of combat diving, although it did have some scuba expertise in the shape of the Musa Company.

Initial training took place at the bases at Cherat, Peshawar and Karachi. Subsequently, the SSGN took responsibility for coastal and deep-water operations, while Musa remained responsible for inland waterways. The SSGN has over the following years gained considerable experience, particularly as it has undertaken widespread reconnaissance of the Indian coastline.

The SSGN has the strength of about one company, divided into a number of squadrons. The unit has its headquarters in Karachi. The training centre, PNS Iqbal, is also in the capital, and training takes 10 months. All SSGN members are parachute-trained, both HAHO and HALO. The unit has trained extensively with the US Navy SEALs, although the main influence in structure and ethos remains the British SBS. The unit has a wide variety of delivery vehicles available to it, including Zodiacs and Klepper canoes. The Pakistani Navy also uses the SX404 midget submarine and has large fleet of helicopters.

Weapons used by the SSGN include the Heckler & Koch G3 7.62mm assault rifle and the MP5 family of submachine guns.

Below: Pakistani Naval Special Services Group personnel march by during the National Day military parade in Islamabad, sporting a formidable array of weaponry.

PERU

Fuerza de Operaciones Especiales (FOES)

The Peruvian FOES undertakes the role of a traditional UDT role, but also has a considerable anti-terrorism and counterterrorist capability, which is something of necessity given the range of guerrilla groups faced by the government.

The Navy's maritime special warfare unit is Fuerza de Operaciones Especiales (FOES – Navy Special Operations Forces). Peru maintains one of the largest navies in South America and has the largest submarine arm (10 boats) in the Americas after Canada and the United States. Most of the surface fleet, including two cruisers, six destroyers and four frigates, is based at Callao, near Lima, while the submarines are at San Lorenzo Island. Thus the FOES has a good range of platforms for operations in the Pacific, although it often also goes into action in the Amazonian jungles against insurgents and drugs gangs. The FOES was formed in 1969 as an underwater demolitions unit. Since then it has developed into a naval commando group, which, as well as the traditional combat diver role, undertakes anti-terrorist and counterinsurgency operations, reconnaissance and marine hostage rescue. The FOES was involved in the rescue of 72 hostages from the Japanese ambassador's residence in Lima on 22 April 1997.

Members of the unit are recruited from the personnel of the Fuerza de Infantria de Marina (Marine Infantry Force). Training for the FOES involves combat swimming, scuba operations, underwater demolitions, jungle survival, hostage rescue and parachuting.

Weapons used include the M16A2; AK-47; Heckler and Koch MP5s; the locally produced 9mm (0.35in) MGP-79A and MGP-87 submachine guns; and the ultra-compact MGP-84 (sometimes called the MGP-15), which can be fitted with a suppressor and is manufactured at the Callao Naval Base near Lima.

Left: A member of the Peruvian special forces, carrying a heavily customized MP5, deploys prior to the storming of the Japanese ambassador's residence in April 1997. FOES personnel were involved in this operation.

PHILIPPINES
Special Warfare Group (SWAG)

The Philippine Navy special forces unit, SWAG, is heavily influenced and maintains close ties with the US Navy SEALs. SWAG has seen extensive service against guerrilla groups in the southern Philippines.

The Philippine Navy has long been an ally of the United States, and its special forces unit is therefore heavily influenced by American practices. The Navy decided to create a special warfare group in 1972 and turned to the United States for guidance. The result, the Underwater Operations Unit (UOU) of combat divers, was therefore very much a copy of the US

Below: The US 'War on Terrorism' has extended to support for the Philippine struggle with the Abu Sayyaf group. Here US Navy SEAL and Philippine Navy and SWAG personnel prepare for a joint training mission in June 2002.

Navy SEAL teams. It changed its name in 1983 to the Special Warfare Group (SWAG), when it took on a maritime anti-terrorism and hostage rescue role in addition to its traditional naval special forces work, such as underwater demolitions and clearance, and beach reconnaissance. SWAG's main unit is the Philippine Navy SEALs Brigade. This brigade is divided into 30 SEAL teams. The similarities with the US Navy SEALs, with whom they also regularly train, go further. The prospective Philippine SEALs undergo their own BUD/S and, when they pass, gain a trident similar to the US 'Budweiser'. It takes six months and

the dropout rate for the course is between 75 and 90 per cent. SWAG has gained considerable operational experience against guerrillas, particularly in the southern Philippines. It was behind the killing of the Al Qaeda-linked Muslim rebel leader, Abu Sayyaf, in the seas off Sibuco.

The Philippine Marine Corps also has a Force Recon Battalion (see US Marine Recon), which also undertakes a ship-boarding role. There is a joint Force Recon/SEAL Special Reaction Group under Naval Intelligence Control, and it is very much the Philippine counterpart of the US Navy SEALs DEVGRU.

POLAND ▬
GROM's Special Boat Unit

*In 1991, Poland's numerous special forces units of the communist era were reorganized
to bring them more in line with Western practices. The result of this was the formation of GROM,
an elite commando unit, which has already gained a formidable reputation. GROM's boat
troop provides Poland's maritime special warfare capability.*

Although the elite 7th Luzycka Naval Assault Division is tasked with the defence of Poland's Baltic Sea coast, Poland's maritime counter-terrorist force is the special boat unit of Grupa Reagowania Operacyjino Mobilnego (GROM). About 270 men strong, GROM was founded in 1991. One year later, realizing that the lack of a maritime counterterrorist capability left Poland's large ferry fleet and Baltic oil-drilling operations vulnerable, GROM's commander, Colonel Salwomir Petelicki, established a special boat unit (SBU).

GROM members who had scuba and diving experience, as well as those wishing to gain new skills, were recruited and instruction began under British SBS and US Navy SEALs tutelage. Today the unit's capabilities go far beyond its original remit; as well as counterterrorist tasks, the SBU is also responsible for maritime reconnaissance and small-scale raiding of maritime and coastal targets. Training for the unit begins during standard GROM selection: those with naval skills or a particular maritime bent are sought out by the SBU's commander, and these then undertake additional training in underwater and naval operations. All GROM members are airborne-qualified.

Weapons used include the MP5 submachine gun, the mainstay of the SBU; Tantal 5.45mm (0.21in) and PMK-DGN-60 submachine guns (Polish copies of the AKS-74U and AK-47, respectively); and the H&K

PSG-1 and Mauser 86 precision rifles, used by the unit's snipers.

The unit uses a range of RIBs and high-speed boats and can be deployed from PZL W-3 Sokol helicopters.

Above: Heavily armed and armoured GROM operatives take down a 'terrorist cell' during exercises in November 2001. GROM's Special Boat Unit are tasked with maritime counter-terrorism operations.

PORTUGAL
Destacamento do Acções Epeciais (DAE)

*The DAE provides the Portuguese Marine Corps, one of the oldest in the world, with
an elite cadre and a formidable special operations capability.*

**Left: Here an exhausted Portuguese marine
aboard a Zodiac takes a break during a
harrowing search-and-rescue operation in
2001. All DAE candidates are drawn from
the Portuguese Marine Corps.**

The Portuguese Navy's special warfare capability rests in the hands of the Destacamento do Acções Epeciais do Corpo de Fuzileiros Navais (DAE – the Special Actions Department of the Marine Infantry Corps). The Marine Corps has a long tradition dating back to 1618, although the DAE itself is a relatively new addition to the Corps, being formed only in 1985. The unit is tasked with amphibious raiding; the reconnaissance and removal of beach obstacles prior to larger Marine Corps operations; EOD tasks; maritime sabotage; and naval counterterrorism. The DAE is small, currently only about 28 men strong. Led by a commander, it is divided into a command cell and four combat teams of four. The unit is equipped with Zodiacs and the Skua assault craft, and the divers use LAR V closed-circuit breathing gear.

Weapons used include M16A2, CAR-15 and H&K G3 assault rifles; Walther MPK and MPL 9mm submachine guns; Walther PP 7.62mm and P-1 9mm (0.35in) pistols; and M3 light machine guns. Snipers use the Steyr-Mannlicher SSG-69 rifle.

Training and Selection

The DAE recruits experienced marines only, and they must undergo a rigorous 10-month selection and training process. The first phase takes place at the Navy's Combat Diver School, where lessons include combat swimming and EOD. The second phase involves advanced ground combat skills and English-language instruction. On completion, the candidate is assigned to the detachment.

RUSSIA
Spetsnaz

*Once intended to prepare the way for the main Soviet effort during the Cold War, the Spetsnaz
has evolved into something more akin to Western special forces since the collapse of the USSR.*

The Voyska Spetsial' Nogo Nazrachenniya (Forces of Special Designation), or Spetsnaz, were amongst the most feared Soviet units during the Cold War. With no direct equivalent within the Western military, these troops were tasked with *diversiya rezvedka* (diversionary reconnaissance). They would target

173

not just enemy leaders, but also command, control and communications installations, as well as nuclear weapons and other vital installations in preparation for the much larger Soviet follow-up effort. Although such operations never took place in Europe, Spetsnaz forces were deployed around the globe in support of Soviet interests throughout the Cold War. The driving force behind Soviet Naval special forces was Georgi Zhukov, who began the process of their establishment as Defence Minister in 1957. All the four Soviet fleets (Northern, Baltic, Black Sea and Pacific) deployed a Naval Spetsnaz brigade to undertake their naval special warfare tasks.

Above: Russian naval special forces in full dress uniform, the distinctive blue and white striped T-shirt of the Naval Infantry clearly evident. Spetsnaz troops wear the uniform of their corresponding service, in this case the Naval Infantry.

This remains the case today. The four fleets maintain their Spetsnaz capability, although there are indications that the units have undergone a transformation into a role more analogous to the US Navy SEALs and Israel's Shayetet 13 than to the traditional Soviet-era commandos. The Naval Spetsnaz remain outside the Russian Naval Infantry command structure, being subordinate rather to the GRU (Chief Intelligence Directorate of the General Staff) at Naval Headquarters. The Brigade (about 1000–1300 men strong) is divided into an intelligence company

PDSS

The Soviet Navy's equivalent to UDT teams, the PDSS (*protivodiversionniye sili i srredtava*), was established in 1967. Each unit (there is one with every fleet) is roughly 100 men strong and is recruited from volunteers among the Naval Infantry conscripts, but based round a cadre of career officers and NCOs. The candidates undergo a strenuous training/selection regime, during which they learn diving, reconnaissance and land and water combat skills. They have been deployed across the world and have occasionally been deployed to protect the Russian President when he is aboard ship.

and a number of specialist battalions: the midget submarine group, three combat swimmer battalions and an airborne battalion, a signals company and a support company. These battalions break down further into *spetzgruppi* (platoon-sized), which are made up of *spetsotedelyi*, or teams. (This is not dissimilar to the structure of a US Navy SEAL team.) The Naval Spetsnaz has operated widely – in Europe and Lebanon, off Japan, and against US bases worldwide; there are also reports of operations against Israel. During the Cold War, a favourite target for Spetsnaz reconnaissance via mini-submarines was Sweden.

Weapons used include the AK-74 5.56mm assault rifle, in its standard, shortened and silenced versions.

Operators also deploy an exotic array of underwater weaponry; the Under Water Assault Rifle (UAR) is a 5.56mm weapon that can be fired underwater and has a 26-round magazine and a range of some 100m (33ft) – presumably above the surface. Another Russian innovation is the SSP-1 underwater pistol, with an underwater range of 5–17m (16–56ft) below the surface.

A variety of SDVs and mini-submarines is used.

Left: A Naval Spetsnaz operative demonstrates his hand-to-hand combat skills. He wears a one-piece camouflage combat uniform and the traditional black beret of the Naval Infantry and is armed with the standard bayonet of the AK assault rifle family.

SPAIN
Unidad de Operaciones Especiales (UOE)

Spearhead of the Spanish Marine Corps, the marine special forces unit, the UOE, has evolved from an amphibious climbing company into a unit similar to the US Navy SEALs and the British SBS.

The Spanish Infanteria de Marina (Marine Corps) is the oldest in the world. Its special forces unit, Unidad de Operaciones Especiales (UOE – Special Operations Unit) is somewhat younger, but continues the long tradition of Spanish marine combat expertise. The UOE is part of the Tercio de La Armada (TEAR), which is roughly equivalent to the US Marine Corps Fleet Marine Force. TEAR is situated at the San Fernando base at Cadiz and is under the direct control of the Spanish Admiralty. UOE's role is to provide reconnaissance and offensive operations for the Marine Corps.

The unit was founded in 1952 as the Amphibious Climbing Company, a formation capable of spearheading a coastal assault, whatever the defences and conditions. Beachhead assault remained its primary mission. After studying similar NATO units, the Spanish Navy concluded that the unit's capability needed to be expanded, making the unit roughly equivalent to the British SBS and the US Navy SEALs. Thus in 1967 the formation was renamed Unidad de Operaciones Especiales (UOE) and took on responsibility for combat swimming, airborne insertions, small-unit raiding and sabotage. Counterterrorism was soon added to its remit. The unit was briefly renamed Comando Anfibio Especial in 1985, but reverted to its old name in the 1989.

The unit is about 170-strong and is commanded by a lieutenant colonel. It is made up of a small headquarters section; a command and services platoon responsible for logistical and medical support; two special operations platoons; and a combat diver platoon. Each special operations platoon is 34 men strong, and is divided into two 16-man divisions with a two-man command element; these divisions are then further divided into four four-man teams. Recruits are drawn from TEAR, and they must have served at least one year in the unit.

Training involves basic commando skills, advanced combat courses and mountaineering. The dropout rate during selection is in the region of 90 per cent. The prospective members then undertake jump training and

Unit Operations

The UOE first saw action in 1969, when it spearheaded the evacuation of Spanish citizens from the former colony of Equatorial Guinea. The UOE has operated extensively against the Basque terrorist group ETA, both at home and abroad. The unit also deployed to the former Yugoslavia as part of the Spanish contingent of IFOR and SFOR.

begin to specialize in a specific skill, such as combat diving, demolitions or sniping. The UOE has close links with the British SBS and the Portuguese DAE, as well as Italian, French and some South American special forces units.

Weapons used by the UOE include the CETME Model L 5.56mm assault rifle, although this is being phased out in favour of the H&K G36 5.56mm; the silenced 9mm Patchett/Sterling Mk 5 submachine gun; the Llama 82B 9mm pistol; the Ameli 5.56 (0.22in) and the M60 7.62mm (0.3in) machine guns, to provide heavy support; and the Mauser SP 66 7.62mm (0.3in), the unit's sniper rifle.

The UOE has access to the full range of the Spanish Navy's surface craft, submarines and aircraft. The unit itself uses Zodiacs and Klepper two-man canoes.

SWEDEN
Kustjägare, Attack Dykarna Bassäk

Sweden's naval special warfare developed to counter Soviet maritime special forces operations during the Cold War. The Kustjägare and Bassäk were developed specifically to meet this threat.

Sweden's extensive coastline was constantly probed by Soviet submarines and Spetsnaz during the Cold War. To protect the country, the Norwegian Navy established an elite commando force in 1959. Known as the Kustjägare, or Coastal Rangers, these men are tasked with conducting raiding, coastal reconnaissance, retaking lost territory and acting as the spearhead of any Swedish amphibious landing. Coastal Rangers are drawn from the top 10 per cent of the country's conscripts and must pass a rigorous six-month training programme. There are six Coastal Amphibious battalions, and each contains two Coastal Ranger companies. They are armed with standard Swedish weaponry, including the AK5 5.56mm assault rifle, the KSP-90 5.56mm light machine gun (Minimi); and the KSP-58 (FN MAG) 7.62mm machine gun and Carl Gustav 84mm recoilless rifle, used by support troops.

Attached to Coastal Ranger reconnaissance platoon is an Attack Dykarna (Attack Diver) section. These men are drawn from the Coastal Ranger units and are subjected to 10 months training in diving, underwater demolitions and small-unit tactics. The 18-man section is broken down into three six-man squads. They use standard Swedish weaponry, and for transport use Combat Boat 90H small patrol craft, Klepper canoes and Swedish naval aircraft.

Bassäk

A further Swedish naval special forces unit, the Bassäkerhetskompaniet (Base Security Company), or Bassäk, was formed in 1992 with the specific task of protecting Sweden's naval installations and ships from enemy special forces. The 134 company (HQ and support platoon, two ranger platoons and two guard platoons) is expert in security, tracking and hunting enemy infiltrators, and its members are considered amongst the best dog-handlers in Europe. Weaponry used is similar to the Kustjägare.

THAILAND ≡
Marine Recon Battalion and SEALs

The Thai government has invested heavily in its special forces and consequently the Thai SEALs and Marine Recon Battalion, with experience of numerous operations along the Cambodian border, are considered amongst the best special warfare units in Southeast Asia.

The Thai military's special forces units come under the control of the Royal Thai Special Warfare Command. The two naval units under this umbrella are the Royal Thai Navy's SEALs and the Marine Recon Battalion. The Royal Thai Marine Corps formed an amphibious reconnaissance company in 1965, and this expanded to battalion size in 1978. It is currently based at the Sattaship Naval Base. It consists of an HQ Company, two Motorized Recon companies and the Amphibious Recon Company, which is made up of the battalion's combat divers. All

Above: A group of Thai Marine Recon candidates sit up to their waist in mud and dirty water during the 13-week Reconnaissance Amphibious Course at the Sattaship Naval Base near Bangkok.

members of this latter company are scuba-trained and airborne-qualified. There is also a small counterterrorism detachment. The unit saw combat against the Pathet Lao guerrillas in the 1970s, and it has been involved in numerous operations on the Cambodian border.

In 1956, the Royal Thai Navy formed a small combat diver unit, along the lines of the US UDT. In 1965, the unit was reorganized to resemble a US Navy SEAL team, although a UDT section remained. The UDT continue to undertake salvage and underwater clearance operations, while the SEALs have responsibility for reconnaissance and maritime counterterrorism.

Training for both units takes place at Sattaship and lasts six months. This is followed by an airborne course. The SEALs' strength is in the region of 150, and they are divided into SEAL Teams One and Two. Each team is four platoons strong. The unit has been involved in skirmishes along the Cambodian border and in anti-piracy operations in the Gulf of Thailand.

Weapons are primarily of US origin, although H&K and Uzi submachine guns are also used.

Above: Further suffering for a prospective member of Marine Recon as he leaps through burning ground during training. He is carrying an M16 assault rifle.

TURKEY ☪

Su Alti Savunma (SAS) and Su Alti Taaruz (SAT)

Turkey maintains two naval special forces units: the SAS, a combat swimmer/UDT force, and the SAT, whose role and complexion is more analogous to that of the US Navy SEALs and British SBS.

Turkey's strategic position linking Asia and Europe, the Black Sea and the Mediterranean meant that the country played a key role during the Cold War. Today the country retains a large navy, but the scale of its naval special forces is small. There are two maritime special operations units, Su Alti Savunma (SAS – Underwater Defence) and Su Alti Taaruz (SAT – Underwater Attack).

SAS's main missions are roughly those of UDT and EOD groups, such as salvage operations and, more pertinently, the clearance of mines and other underwater explosives and obstacles for the Turkish Navy. It would undertake similar missions to prepare landing grounds for large Turkish Marine and Army operations.

SAT is similar in composition and mission profile to the US Navy SEALs

Above: Under the watchful eye of a naval officer, an SAT operator abseils down onto deck of the frigate Oruc Reis during a ship take-down exercise in 2000.

Left: An SAT commando 'dispatches' an 'enemy' sentry at Uzunkum Beach in Saros Bay, Northwest Turkey. This was part of NATO's 2000 'Destined Glory' exercise.

and the British SBS, and it has close links with Israel's Shayetet 13. The unit is responsible for reconnaissance, small-unit raiding, covert infiltration and maritime counterterrorism. All SAT operators are jump-qualified (both HAHO and HALO).

Both units have seen considerable combat in Cyprus and in operations against Kurdish guerrillas.

SAS/SAT weaponry is largely American or German, such as the M16 and CAR-15, often with the M203 grenade launcher attachment. The Heckler and Koch MP5 family is used, as is the G3 assault rifle. Squad support weapons include the MG3 machine gun. The PSG-1 sniper rifle is also carried.

The Turkish Navy's surface and submarine fleet is available as SAS/SAT platforms, although there is no dedicated special operations aircraft. No doubt, however, Turkey's UH-60 Blackhawks and AS 90 helicopter fleet is available to them.

Left: Turkish naval special forces rescue an illegal immigrant from the Mediterranean who had been adrift for 30 hours after the ship carrying him broke up and sank.

UNITED KINGDOM 🇬🇧
Special Boat Service (SBS)

The United Kingdom's Special Boat Service (SBS) may have received somewhat less publicity than its army counterpart, the SAS, but it is arguably the best maritime special forces unit in the world, with a long tradition and operational experience to match.

The United Kingdom's Special Boat Service (SBS) is undoubtedly the naval special forces unit against which all others are measured. The SBS, part of the Royal Marines, has a complicated history. It can trace its ancestry back to the bewildering number of small special operations groups that were set up by the British during World War II. Its lineage includes the Special Boats Sections of the Army Commandos and SAS; Combined Operations Pilotage Parties

Right: An RAF C-130 Hercules flies low over the west coast of Scotland, as SBS members launch their inflatable boat prior to parachuting into the sea after it.

of the Royal Navy; and, most importantly, the Royal Marine Boom Patrol Detachment (RMBPD), which famously launched Operation Frankton against the Bordeaux Docks in December 1942. The end of the war closed down many of these units, but a Royal Marine special warfare capability survived in the School of Combined Operations Beach and Boats, established in 1946. This merged with the RMBPD the following year and by 1948 was known as the Small Raids Wing of the Royal Marines, seeing limited service in Palestine. In 1950, it became the Special Boat Wing made up of Special

Above: A group of SBS frogmen come ashore on South Georgia during the Falklands War in 1982. Both SBS and SAS members were heavily involved in the recapture of the island.

Left: The SBS has also played a role in more recent conflicts. Here an SBS trooper, carrying a heavily laden Bergen rucksack and modified CAR-15 assault rifle, moves through the Tora Bora area of Afghanistan in December 2001.

Boat Sections, which revived the acronym 'SBS'. Members of the unit fought in Korea as part of 41 Independent Commando RM.

By 1950, the SBS was taking recognizable shape. Based in Britain was 1 SBS; with the Soviet threat growing, 2 and 3 SB sections were established in Germany for service with the Royal Navy's Rhine Squadron; 4 and 5 SBS were made up of members of the Royal Marine Forces Volunteer Reserve; 6 SBS was formed in the mid-1950s for use in the Mediterranean in support of 3 Commando Brigade, then based at Malta. The re-establishment of the SAS in this period led to the SBS's responsibilities being defined to include operations against ships and

Operational History

The SBS saw service in just about all Britain's postwar conflicts. It was activated for the Suez Crisis and fought in the Indonesia Confrontation, with elements of the SBS remaining in Malaysia until 1972. The growing threat of terrorism in the 1970s meant that the SBS began to take on responsibilities for maritime counterterrorism. In 1972, an SBS team was dropped into the mid-Atlantic to deal with a bomb threat to the cruise liner *Queen Elizabeth II*. In 1975, 1 SBS took on a dedicated counterterrorism remit, in part necessitated by the growing number of oil rigs in the North Sea. At the same time, the unit was renamed the Special Boat Squadron. In 1979, the Admiralty expanded Britain's maritime counterterrorist capability by the establishment of the 300-strong Commachino Company RM. Commachino was tasked with protection of Britain's nuclear installations as well as oil rigs. This unit was joined by 5 SBS, with 4 SBS taking the responsibility for the unit's reservists. The SBS was also deployed to Northern Ireland and provided support for the police in anti-drug operations.

Three SBS sections played a key role in the Falklands War in 1982. SBS teams carried out vital reconnaissance of suitable landing sites, and 2 SBS was part of the force that recaptured South Georgia. Following the Falklands War, Britain's special forces were reorganized, and the SBS (now the Special Boat Service) and the SAS were both brought under the umbrella of the Special Forces Group in 1987. The Special Forces Group is headed by the Director SAS, an Army brigadier; his deputy is a Royal Marine colonel.

An SBS squadron was deployed to the Gulf in 1990–91. It undertook at least one mission deep behind Iraqi lines. The SBS also secured the British embassy in Kuwait City at the end of the war. Since then, the SBS has continued its anti-drug operations with the Police and Customs and Excise. Elements of the unit have seen service in Bosnia (1993–6), and a small team was attached to 42 Commando RM during the 1999 Kosovo Crisis. The SBS was also deployed in East Timor in 1999 and was part of the Royal Marine presence in Afghanistan in 2002.

Above: Transport for the SBS is often provided by 539 Assault Squadron Royal Marines. Here a coxswain from the squadron mans a Rigid Raider in support of the SBS during Arctic operations off the coast of Norway.

coastal targets, waterborne raids, beach reconnaissance, landing preparation and agent infiltration and extraction. These tasks remain part of the SBS remit today.

The SBS was about 150 men strong until its reorganization in 1987. It has since expanded to perhaps 250. The unit is based at Poole in Dorset. The SBS's primary role remains that of beach reconnaissance, intelligence gathering, underwater demolitions and small-scale raiding. Its secondary responsibility is maritime counter-terrorism. It is made up of four squadrons (which replaced the sections 1–6):

C Squadron – apparently specializes in swimmer–canoeist operations.

S Squadron – has expertise in small craft, mini-submarines, SDVs (the British pioneered the use of these craft in the 1960s) and long-range insertion boats.

(It is worth noting that these divisions should not be overstated because swimmer–canoeist and small boat skills are uniform across the unit.)

M Squadron – formed from the old 1 and 5 sections, this is the counterterrorist troop. It is made up of three troops: Black, Gold and Purple. The operational troop is 16 men strong and can be split into a number of smaller divisions: two eight-man sections (or two RIB boatloads), four four-man patrols, or eight canoe or swim pairs. As is clear from the above, there is no equivalent to the SEALs Special Boat Units and SDV teams; the SBS undertakes these specialist roles within the unit.

The fourth troop is the reservist formation.

Above: Heavily laden Royal Marine Commandos on exercise in Egypt in 1999 prepare to board a Chinook HC.2 helicopter. SBS operators are recruited exclusively from the Royal Marines.

Support would be provided by the surface ships and submarines of the Royal Navy, the 539 Assault Squadron RM and from RAF Special Forces Flights and RN's Naval Air Commando squadrons.

The SBS is recruited from Royal Marines who have at least three years' service. The candidate must then pass a two-week aptitude test. Those who are successful go on to the Joint SAS/SBS selection course. Continuation training in ground combat and demolitions takes place at Hereford, followed by parachute

Left: An SBS trooper equipped for land operations during the 1982 Falklands War. SBS members usually wear standard Royal Marine uniforms, and this one is no exception, as he is dressed in the DPM camouflage-patterned Arctic smock.

training for those candidates who are not airborne-qualified. SBS candidates then go on the SBS boating and diving course. Fewer than 30 per cent pass and become Swimmer Canoeists Class Three. If they do, they then pass to an operational troop. The SBS conducts numerous joint exercises with friendly nations, although it has closest relations with the US Navy SEALs and Dutch SBS.

Weapons used include the M16, the standard SBS assault rifle, often used with the M203 grenade launcher; the H&K 53 was seen in SBS hands in East Timor. Submachine guns are drawn from the MP5 family; the Browning HP 35 remains the standard sidearm; heavier weaponry includes the L7A2 (FN MAG) General Purpose Machine gun, 66mm (2.6in) LAWs and the 51mm (2in) mortar. The main sniping weapons is the Accuracy International L96A1.

The current canoe in service is the Klepper Aeres Mark 13. The Gemini Inflatable and the Avon Searider RIB are the standard small craft, and a range of SDVs, both American and British-built, are used.

UNITED STATES OF AMERICA 🇺🇸
US Navy SEALs
SBS and SDV teams
Marine Recon

The United States Navy's special warfare capability is provided by its SEAL teams, which are supported by the SBS and SDV teams. Outside the US Special Warfare Command, the US Marine Corps also has an elite unit, Marine Recon.

Although the US tradition of special operations forces can be traced back to the seventeenth century, they were formalized only in the second half of the twentieth century. The youngest of the special forces are the US Navy's Sea-Air-Land (SEAL) teams, their SEAL Delivery Vehicle Teams (SDV) and the Special Boat Squadrons (SBS), which together make up the three branches of the Navy Special Warfare Command (NAVSPECWARCOM).

The SEALs specialize in unconventional warfare operations in a maritime setting. This includes not just the seashore, but also lakes, rivers and swamps, and they operate up to 20 miles (32km) inland. Inevitably, both their role and capability sometimes cross over those of their colleagues – for example, US Army Rangers use similar craft for their beach operations, and the US Army Special Forces may also undertake dive operations. The difference is in scale. To quote a SEAL team commander:

We in the SEALs are the United States military's small-unit maritime special operations force ... We don't belong in anything that involves multi-platoon operations – we've never been successful at it ... We keep our units small and separate from large force operations. We have a niche here to be very good in units often less than eight men. That makes us harder to detect, easier to command and control, and better at the small unique operations we train for. A further difference is the environment... We

Below: Two Navy SEALs undertake a reconnaissance mission during Operation Enduring Freedom in Afghanistan in January 2002.

keep one foot in the water. That means if we must do inland operations it is because they are attached to maritime reason… Keeping one foot in the water means that we don't get into areas that properly belong to other operators.

And so, despite 'traditionalist' resistance within the Navy, the SEALs have expanded, establishing a formidable combat reputation and developing a distinct ethos.

It was World War II that produced the forerunners of the SEALs. On 20 November 1942, the US Marine Corps attacked the Japanese-held island of Tarawa. The Americans possessed little intelligence about the island, its surrounding shores and tides, and they had conducted little reconnaissance. The Marines' landing craft grounded on a reef 500 yards (547m) from the beach, and the soldiers were forced to wade ashore in

the face of concentrated Japanese fire. Although eventually victorious, they suffered terrible losses, and the Navy decided that an amphibious assault would never again be made without adequate preparation. This led to the establishment of the Naval Combat Divers Unit (NCDU) of specialist swimmers trained in reconnaissance and demolition. The NCDU surveyed the beaches and attempted to clear the obstacles on the beaches prior to the Allied invasion of Italy in 1943 and the Normandy landings of June 1944.

When these techniques were applied to the Pacific, the NCDU teams were rechristened Underwater Demolition Teams (UDT). Their job, however, was identical to their colleagues in the European theatre – either reconnaissance or beach clearance. The end of hostilities meant that the UDTs were closed down, only to be hastily revived for the UN's

Above: A Navy SEAL provides cover for his colleagues during operations in Afghanistan in 2002. He is armed with a heavily modified CAR-15 assault rifle.

amphibious landing at Inchon in Korea in 1950. After Inchon, the role of the UDTs expanded to include more traditional commando operations away from the beaches, very much foreshadowing the mission profile of today's Navy SEALs.

Then came Vietnam. President John F. Kennedy, something of a student of unconventional warfare, was determined to expand the United States' special operations capability, convinced that low-intensity warfare would be the hallmark of many future conflicts. On 1 January 1962, he commissioned Navy SEAL Teams One and Two to conduct maritime special warfare and clandestine operations. The SEALs saw brief service in support of the Navy during the Cuban Missile Crisis in 1962 and US intervention in the Dominican Republic in 1965; however, it was in Vietnam that the unit made its reputation.

In 1962, the first SEALs were deployed to Vietnam in an advisory role, training the South Vietnamese Navy. Specific combat operations began when two platoons from SEAL Team One were deployed to Rung Sat Special Zone near Saigon in 1965.

Through a policy of careful reconnaissance and ambush, they quickly broke the Viet Cong hold on this area. Such was their success that the SEAL presence in Vietnam was expanded by the addition of four platoons. SEAL Team Two arrived in 1967. The teams surveyed the beaches, infiltrated deep inland using small boats or often swimming in from submarines, and conducted ambushes. The SEALs were particularly effective

during operations in the waters of the Mekong Delta. They also ran the Provincial Reconnaissance Units as part of the Phoenix programme. They played a key role in Operation Brightlight, which between 1970 and 1972 raided deep into enemy territory in an effort to free US prisoners of war held in the Mekong Delta. As SEAL Captain Richard Couch notes: 'POW rescues are perhaps the most difficult missions.' To an extent, Brightlight was successful: many ARVN (Army of the Republic of Vietnam) POWs were released and Vietcong compounds successfully raided, but no American prisoners were ever found. Couch, who led a Brightlight operation, recalled of his raid: 'Ours was a success. I only wish we could have found a few GIs in those cages.' The SEALs were finally withdrawn from operations in Vietnam along with the rest of the US forces in 1972.

Their success in Vietnam meant that the SEALS did not face the pressure placed on Army special forces

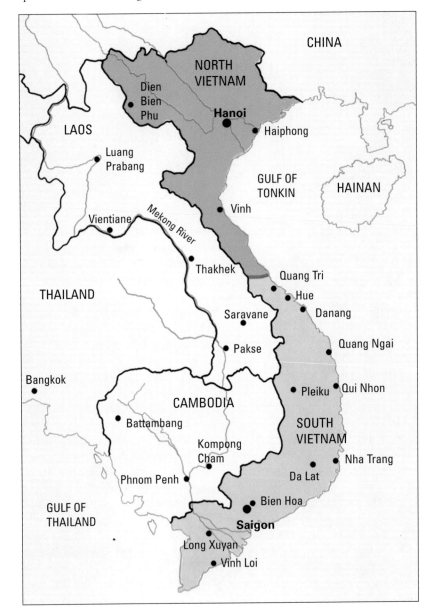

Left and above: The first SEAL unit, SEAL Team One, deployed to the Rung Sat Special Zone near Saigon in 1962. Other detachments were subsequently based at Nha Be, Binh Thuy, My tho and Da Nang. In 1966, SEALs operated around Saigon and later in the Mekong Delta. They withdrew with the rest of US forces in 1972.

Above: A SEAL unit leaps from a river patrol boat during operations against the Viet Cong southwest of Saigon in January 1968 in the midst of the Vietnam War.

in the aftermath of the conflict. The unit itself also recognized where the core role of Navy special forces lay. As one veteran recalled, 'A select group of senior SEALs realized we needed to return as quickly as possible to the mainstream of fleet priorities after Vietnam.' Mission emphasis shifted to the new submersible dive vehicle programme, and the number of SEAL teams expanded to five.

After the failed Delta Force rescue attempt of the American hostages held in Iran in 1980, the Navy established SEAL Team Six, specifically for maritime counterterrorism and hostage rescue operations. During the 1980s, Team Six was placed on alert on numerous occasions, such as the hijack of the SS *Achille Lauro* in 1985 and the Beirut hostage crisis. However, the hastily mounted US invasion of Grenada in 1983 proved disastrous for

Recent SEAL Operations

SEAL teams operated in the Persian Gulf during the Iran–Iraq War, keeping the sea lanes clear and securing the passage of oil tankers through the region. However, the largest test of the US Navy's special forces was Operation Desert Shield/Storm in 1990–91. During the coalition prepared to counter Saddam Hussein's invasion of Kuwait, the SEALs, supported by the SBS, cleared mines, supported combat search and rescue (CSAR) missions, raided Iraqi oil platforms, captured Qaruh Island and aggressively reconnoitred Kuwait's beaches in preparation for a possible Marine landing. When an amphibious assault was rejected, the SEALs were tasked with convincing the Iraqis that such an operation was in fact imminent.

On the night of 23 February 1991, a few hours before the main coalition ground assault began, the SEALs and their Zodiacs were taken in close to the shore by the SBS. The teams swam into two beaches, marked apparent landing zones, planted explosive charges, then returned to the SBS's high-speed boats (HSBs). At a given time, they exploded the charges and shot up the Iraqi beach defences, while coalition aircraft made air strikes in support. According to American sources, at least two Iraqi armoured divisions were diverted to the area. There is little doubt that, in the Gulf, the SEALs put the sorry experiences of Grenada and Panama well behind them.

After the war, SEALs operated in Somalia in 1993, evacuated US civilians from Liberia, participated in anti-drugs actions in South America and were part of the US deployment to Bosnia.

the SEALs. Although SEAL Team Four was successful in determining the unsuitability of a beach near Pearls Airfield for amphibious assault, four men of SEAL Team Six, which was tasked to perform reconnaissance, were drowned in two separate incidents off Point Salines. Members of SEAL Team Six also attempted to rescue the island's governor, Sir Paul Scoon, and had problems identifying suitable landing sites. When two platoons of SEALs fast-roped into the compound where the governor was held, they were pinned down by Grenadan and Cuban troops. Despite the intervention of an AC-130 Spectre gunship, the 'rescuers' had to hold out for 24 hours before they were reached by US Marines.

The operation in Grenada highlighted a range of problems within the US special forces community, perhaps most importantly the lack of coordination between the various Army, Air Force and Naval units. The special forces had gone in without adequate intelligence and preparation, and they had often been improperly used. An obvious example of this was the incident at the governor's compound, where SEAL Team Six, a counter-terrorist force, was used in a light infantry role. A number of reforms were instituted, the most important being the formation of the US Special Operations Command (USSOCOM) in 1986. This unified all special forces under a single command with its own budget, essentially creating a fifth arm of the US military.

As the tensions of the Cold War eased, funding was increased while the American military focus shifted towards the threats posed by small, low-intensity wars and terrorism. The results of these reforms became clear over the following years.

For Operation Just Cause against the Panamanian leader Manuel Noriega in 1989, the SEALs had two major assignments: the seizure of the Panama Defence Force (PDF) patrol boat *Presidente Porras* and the capture of Noriega's private jet. The first task was achieved smoothly. However, although the SEALs succeeded in disabling the aircraft, they ran into large-scale and competent PDF resistance at Paitilla airfield, and four Americans were killed and eight

Below: A member of the US Marine Corps 1st Recon Battalion on jungle training. Marine Recon has a lower profile than its SEAL counterpart, but is no less elite.

Above: A classic SEAL four-man formation fire team emerges from the water during an exercise. The lead SEAL member carries a standard M16A2 with a M203 grenade launcher attachment.

wounded. SEALs have also been involved in counter-narcotic operations in Central and South American, particularly in Colombia.

There are approximately 4000 personnel in the US Navy Special Operations Forces, and of these about 2000 are SEALs. They are under the control of NAVSPECWARCOM, which is divided into two Naval Special Warfare Groups (NSWGs). NSWG 1 is based at Coronado, California (also home of the Naval Special Warfare Center, where the

SEALs Mission Profiles

The US Navy SEALs operate according to five basic mission profiles, that remain unchanged:

Direct Action – essentially combat operations, such as raiding, sabotage, hostage rescue and the capture of targets afloat or ashore.

Special Reconnaissance – a SEAL speciality, the reconnaissance and surveillance of hostile territory, particularly beachheads. SEAL teams make beach surveys and, like their predecessors (the UDTs), mark landing approaches and demolish obstacles and fortifications in preparation for an amphibious landing.

Foreign Internal Defence – the training of the military and security forces of friendly nations, usually in a non-combat environment.

Unconventional Warfare – this is very much one of the reasons for John Kennedy's support for special forces. If required, the SEALs train, equip and lead guerrilla forces behind enemy lines.

Counterterrorist Operations – the SEALs, particularly DEVGRU, conduct anti-terrorist operations, both reactive and preventative.

SEALs are trained). NSWG 1 is responsible for the Pacific, the Persian Gulf and Asia. It consists of SEAL Teams One, Three and Five, SDV Team One and Special Boat Squadron One, made up of SB Units 11, 12 and 13. Each SEAL team has a specific area of responsibility.

The larger command is NSWG 2, which is based at Little Creek, Norfolk, Virginia. Its area of operations includes Europe, the Atlantic and Latin America. It consists of SEAL Team Two (responsible for Europe, Africa and some of the Middle East); SEAL Team Four (Southern Theater, including all of South America); and SEAL Team Eight. SEAL Team Eight is the newest formation, activated in 1988, and it shares responsibility for Africa and the Mediterranean with SEAL Team Two. These teams are supported by SBS 2, which is made up of SB Units 20, 22, 24 and 26, and SDV Team Two.

To enable these forces to be deployed forwards, NAVSPEC-WARCOM has five Naval Special Warfare (NSW) units outside the mainland United States: NSWU-1 is situated in Guam; NSWU-2 is in Stuttgart, Germany; NSWU-4 and NSWU-8 (formerly at Panama) are in Rossey Roads, Puerto Rico; and NSWU-10 is in Rota, Spain. There are also training detachments in Hawaii and Alaska.

In theory, a full SEAL Team is made up of 10 platoons of SEALs. In practice, it is roughly 30 officers and 200 enlisted men strong. There is also a small support staff of non-SEALs – about 20 naval personnel. There is a command element, including the CO, executive officer and operations officer, who are all fully qualified SEALs. Each platoon is 16 men strong (two officers and 14 men). The platoon divides into two squads (each with one officer and seven men), the

squad being the preferred size for operations. A squad further breaks down into two four-man fire teams. At the lowest level, the fire team is made up of two swim pairs.

SEAL Team Six, the maritime counterterrorist unit, was closed down in the late 1980s after its founder and commander, Richard Marcinko, was convicted on various charges of unlawful acts while in charge. The unit was later was reconstituted as the Naval Special Warfare Development

Above: Clad in neoprene and carrying Dräger LAR V rebreathers, a SEAL Team swim pair armed with M16A2s emerges from the surf.

Group (DEVGRU), to evaluate new tactics, weapons and equipment; however, it also maintains a maritime counterterrorist role. DEVGRU is divided into three assault groups: Red, Blue and Gold. Gray is the special boat unit, operating fast insertion boats, SDVs and the like. There is also a

Above: The SPIE (Special Purpose Insertion and Extraction) rig demonstrated is a spectacular method of extracting or inserting SEAL operators.

Green unit of new members, who are being prepared for service in the other groups. There are about 300 members of DEVGRU, which is based at Little Creek, Virginia.

THE SBS AND SDV TEAMS

Key to the whole US naval special forces set-up are the Special Boat Squadrons, also known as the 'Brown Water Navy'. They are responsible for operating a variety of special operations craft, from 52m (170ft) patrol boat coastal (PBC) to rigid inflatable boats such as the 5m (15ft) combat rubber raiding craft (CRRC), capable of

reaching 20 knots. The SBS has broadly three roles:

Coastal Patrol and Interdiction – this requires a reasonably big boat, so the mainstay of such missions is the PBC, which is large enough to carry a large weapons package and support fairly large numbers of SEAL and Naval Special Warfare forces for extended periods of time. It can reach 35 knots and has a range of 2000 nautical miles at a moderate cruise speed of 12 knots. There are 13 PBCs (starting with PC-1, USS *Cyclone*). These vessels have a crew of four officers and 24 men, and berthing facilities for additional special forces personnel. There is a platform at the rear for launching and recovering combat swimmers, and two CRRCs are carried. For operations closer to the shore, there is the 65ft (20m) MK III Swift Patrol Boat, a veteran of the 1960s, which requires a crew of 11 and can make 30 knots. It is nearing the end of its service and is in the process of being replaced by the more modern Mk IV Patrol Boat.

Special Operations Support – clandestine operations, such as the insertion of SEALS, need smaller boats with low radar signature. A key craft for these missions are rigid inflatable boats (RIBs), a variety of which are used by the SBS. The 24ft (7m) RIB can carry half a squad, as well as radar, an M60 and a Volvo inboard/outboard engine, which can make 25 knots; while the 32ft (10m) RIB can carry a whole squad. However, the boat of choice for stealth operations is the CRRC (usually a Zodiac), versions of which are used across the US special forces. The CRRC weighs 265 pounds (120kg) and can be launched from submarines and surface craft, or dropped along with its crew from helicopters or C-130s. It is 15ft (5m) long and has a 55 hp engine, although it can be paddled in if required.

Although SEALs can deploy from the US Navy's submarines, some are specially fitted to carry the naval commandos more safely and efficiently. They are fitted with a dry deck shelter (DDS). This is a small hanger, which can carry a swimmer delivery vehicle (SDV). The SDV Mk VIII is one of the more interesting and secretive vehicles of the US Naval special forces, and it is used to make sub-surface insertions. It has been described as essentially 'a little speed boat that operates underwater'. It uses an electric motor for propulsion. Like all submarines, it is steered blind, on sensors alone. Although an air supply is provided, the SEALs wear their scuba gear, as they are carried in a fully flooded compartment. It can carry six swimmers and their equipment, including the two crew. The crew (driver and navigator) plus the vehicle's support and maintenance team are part of a special unit of NAVWARCOM, the SDV Team. The driver and operator are SEAL-qualified. An Advanced SEAL Delivery System with a dry crew compartment should soon be entering service.

Riverine Patrol and Interdiction – this was very much a staple of US special forces in the Vietnam War, and the SEALs and SBS still operate in similar environments in Latin America, often with foreign military and law enforcement personnel. The standard craft used by the SBS are the Patrol Boat River (PBR), a 10m (32ft), well-armed and armoured vessel, which is portable by C-5 Galaxy transport aircraft; and the Patrol Boat Light (PBL), a 8m (25ft) version of the Boston whaler. Both PBR and PBL are Vietnam veterans that have given sterling service.

MARINE RECON

Although the US Marine Corps is regarded as an elite fighting force, the US Marine Recon Battalions are a much neglected special forces group within the US military, probably because they are not part of USSOCOM. Yet, to quote a British SBS officer, 'The Recce Marines are a class above and beyond the definition of special forces!' USMC is responsible for providing pre-assault intelligence and preparatory operations for the main weight of a Marine expeditionary force. Small-scale raiding also falls within these battalions' remit.

They date from World War II, when raider battalions were formed to provide the Corps with a small raiding capacity and the 1st Division's

---

Weapons

The SEALs use a wide variety of weaponry, dependent on mission type and, to an extent, personal preference. Pistols used by the SEALs include the 9mm SIG Sauer P226; the .45mm M1911A1; .357 Smith and Wesson revolver; 9mm H&K P9S; and the .45 H&K Mk23 Mod 0 Special Operations Forces Offensive Handgun, designed specially for USSOCOM. The primary choice of rifle is the CAR-15, often fitted with an M203 grenade launcher attachment; its larger brother, the M16A2, is also carried; and the veteran 7.62mm M14, with its larger round and more impressive stopping power, is still used. The mainstay submachine gun is the Heckler and Koch MP5 family. Although a wide variety of H&K submachine guns is used, the MP5K-PDW is designed specifically for NAVWARCOM use. For ship-boarding, jungle and close-quarters work, 12-gauge shotguns such as the Remington Model 870 are popular. Squad support weapons include the 7.62mm M-60 machine gun, and the M2HB .50 calibre HMG is a popular armament for vehicles and boats. The principal sniper weapons are the 7.62mm Remington M40A1; the 7.62mm M86; the M24; the 7.62mm M21 (an accurized M14); and the .50 Calibre McMillan SASR.

Heckler and Koch MP5K

Below: An elite within an elite, Marine Recon provide intelligence, reconnaissance and a preparatory raiding capability for the main weight of the US Marine Corps.

Left: The United States Marine Corps shoulder patch. The USMC is something of an elite in itself and the US Marines have been involved in just about all of America's wars and military operations.

Observation Group (later the Amphibious Recon Company) was tasked with providing beach reconnaissance and forward observation missions for the main force. The unit saw extensive service in Korea, often penetrating deep into North Korea. After the Korean War, the Corps underwent considerable restructuring, and, in 1957, the 1st Company 'Force' Recon Marines was formed, followed by the 2nd Company a year later. Marine Recon was deployed to Vietnam in 1965 to provide much needed intelligence for the Marines. It was involved in Grenada; the 1987–8 Persian Gulf Crisis; the rescue of US aircrew who ejected in a raid over Libya; and Desert Storm. More recently Marine Recon has seen service in Somalia, Liberia and Bosnia.

Prior to 1998, two units made up the Marine Corps reconnaissance capability – Recon and Force Recon. Recon provided support for divisional operations, while Force Recon was tasked with deep penetration and reconnaissance patrols. On the recommendation of the Defence Department, the two groups merged into a single

Right: An illustration depicting a Marine Recon member cautiously probing his way forward. He wears standard Woodland-camouflage, a green bandana and carries an XM17 submachine gun.

Reconnaissance battalion for each active division. Each Recon Battalion is divided into three companies: A Coy is responsible for training of new recon Marines before they are sent on to the battalion's other companies; B Coy operates in support of larger divisional actions, much in the role of the old recon

battalions; and C Coy, where the most experienced marines operate, undertakes the long-range penetration and raiding that had formerly been performed by Force Recon.

Recruits to the Marine Corps Recon are expected to have at least three to four years' experience and pass the 'Army Airborne Test' to test physical capabilities. Training continues at the Recon Indoctrination Platoon, followed by scuba diving courses at Coronado, parachute training (HALO and HAHO) at Fort Benning, and advanced ground combat training at the Infantry School. Specialized training, such as escape and evasion, jungle survival and sniper skills, continues at the recruit's Recon Battalion. The Marine Corps Combat Diver course was instigated at Naval Diving and Salvage Training Center in Panama City, Florida, in 1993.

The Recon Marines' standard weapon is the M16A2, often with the M203 grenade launcher. The CAR-15 is also used, as are the MP5 family of submachine guns and the Beretta M-9 and M-1911A1 pistols. Support weapons include the M249 SAW and M60 machine gun. Snipers carry the 7.62mm (0.3in) Remington M40 and .50 Iver Johnson SAR.

Right: A US Marine Corps recon team on exercise braces against the blast of rotor wash from a CH-53E Sea Stallion as it lifts off from the desert floor of the Marine Corps Air Ground Combat Center, Twenty-Nine Palms, California.

VENEZUELA
Compemi Turiamo

Copemi Turiamo is the elite unit of the Venezuelan Marine Corps. It has gained considerable experience in Venezuela's long and difficult struggle against drugs gangs and guerrilla groups.

Given Venezuela's long coastline, important oil reserves and the problems the region has with drug trafficking, the country has much need of a naval special forces capability. Thus within the Comando Anfibio (Amphibious Commandos) of the Venezuelan Marines is the Compemi Turiamo, the Marines' elite unit.

It is 200 men strong and is trained in the usual disciplines: commando operations, maritime reconnaissance, underwater demolitions and maritime counterterrorism and hostage rescue. Its main areas of operational activity are anti-narcotic operations and counterinsurgency on Venezuela's border with Colombia. However, it has also involved itself in Venezuelan politics, particularly in 1993, when the unit's commander, Hugo Chávez Frías, led a failed coup attempt. The Compemi Turiamo was subsequently disbanded, but such was Venezuela's need for a maritime special forces unit that it had to be reconstituted. As for Chávez Frías, he managed to get himself elected president in 1998.

Candidates for the Compemi Turiamo are selected from the Marine Corps, usually from men serving their two-year national service. Joining the unit will extend their service, but there are a number of benefits, not least increased pay. Training takes 10 months and features scuba, combat swimming, advanced combat and airborne courses.

The unit uses a mixture of assault rifles, including the M16A2, the FNC and the Steyr AUG. The favoured submachine gun is the 9mm (0.354in) Uzi; however, the counterterrorist section uses the Heckler and Koch MP5 family.

SPECIAL FORCES IN THE AIR

Airborne units were developed by Germany, Italy and Russia in the late 1930s and by the United Kingdom and United States during the early years of World War II. Airborne operations require individuals who can be dropped many miles behind enemy lines, often facing a life expectancy quantified in days or even hours. Such personnel must be resilient, intelligent and technically skilled in using their equipment. Airborne operations are no longer limited to static-line parachute jumps. They include helicopter insertion, high-altitude high-opening (HAHO) and high-altitude low-opening (HALO) parachute drops, rapid-exit airlanding operations, and even insertion by handglider or microlight. The expertise and toughness of airborne soldiers has made them much in demand. They are to be found at the front lines of both conventional conflicts and counterterrorism operations, and their bloody regimental histories stand as a mark of pride to all those who join their ranks.

Left: US airborne troops make a jump from a Hercules aircraft during exercise.

BELGIUM ▮▮
Paratroop Commando Brigade

*The Belgian Paratroop Commando Brigade has a prestigious lineage stretching back
to World War II. In the postwar world, its operational quality has been maintained in the former
Belgian colonies and during many international NATO operations.*

The Paratroop Commando Brigade is Belgium's main assault force, and it is currently assigned to the Multinational Division of the Allied Rapid Reaction Corps (ARRC). It consists of two parachute battalions and one commando battalion, each battalion having a strength of some 500 men. The brigade can deploy at very short notice along with its support element, which comprises a parachute armoured reconnaissance battalion (3rd Lancers), artillery battery (AA and field), logistics, engineers and medics.

The brigade dates from World War II, when the Belgian Government in exile formed paratroop and commando units to fight alongside the British against the occupying Germans. The first independent Belgian parachute company was formed in May 1942 as

Left: Like most paratroopers, the Belgian para-commandos have high-cut helmets designed to avoiding snagging on straps and lines during parachute jumps.

Above: Belgian paratroopers during urban warfare training. The training regimen is very similar to that used by the British Parachute Regiment.

part of the British 6th Division, but it later transferred to the British SAS Brigade for specialist commando training. Its new role involved performing clandestine operations in France and Belgium, typically hit-and-run, mainly against enemy lines of communication and troop formations.

Earlier, in 1940, independent commando units were formed, and these, after training in the United Kingdom, saw action in Norway later

that year. In 1942, they carried out raids in Madagascar, Bruneval, St Nazaire and Dieppe before becoming part of the international No. 10 Commando. As part of this new force, it saw action in the Far East, Greece, Italy and northwest Europe.

Unlike many units that were disbanded after the end of the war, the Paratroop Commando Brigade continued to operate at almost its wartime strength. Only at the end of the Cold

Weapons

Weapons used by the Paratroop Commando Brigade include virtually the entire range of weapons from Belgium's Fabrique National arms company, as well as mortars, Milan anti-tank missiles, 105mm (4.13in) field guns and Scorpion light tanks.

War was this reduced to a single brigade of some 3000 men.

The Paratroop Commando Brigade's most spectacular operation took place on 10 November 1964, in the town of Stanleyville, which is located in the Belgian Congo. The unit was required to parachute in and save the lives of 800 non-Congolese, who had been threatened with execution by the Congolese Army. The mission was a successful one.

All members of the Paratroop Commando Brigade are volunteers, and, before they are allowed to wear the red beret, they must undergo five months of commando training, followed by a month-long parachute course (which involves seven jumps, including one at night). Of particular interest is the 1st Battalion, the members of which wear not only the red beret, but also the British SAS 'Winged Dagger' cap badge to signify their wartime connections to the British SAS.

FRANCE
11th Parachute Division
Commando Parachutiste de l'Air No. 10

Paratroopers have been at the vanguard of almost every major French operation since World War II, from major combat drops in Indochina to peacekeeping in Beirut. They have also performed more postwar large-unit parachute missions than any other unit.

Based at Tarbes in the Midi-Pyrénées region of southern France is the French 11th Parachute Division, a unit that comprises some 11,000 personnel. The division primarily consists of long-service professionals, who are highly experienced and well motivated to continue France's long tradition of parachute-based operations.

The 11th Parachute Division is currently part of the French rapid intervention force, which also consists of the 6th Light Armoured Division, 4th Airmobile Division, 27th Alpine Division and the 9th Marine Light Infantry Division.

Right: Today the helicopter is the mainstay of airborne operations. Here a group of French paras have disembarked from an Aérospatiale SA330 Puma.

The 11th Parachute Division is split between two brigades and consists of seven battalion-sized units: the 1 RPIMa; 2 REP from the Legion étrangère; 1 and 9 RCP (Light Infantry); and 3, 6 and 8 RPIMa.

Weapons used by the 11th Parachute Division include the FAMAS assault rifle; HK MP5 submachine gun; FN Minimi light machine gun; 81mm (3.19in) mortar; 120mm (4.72in) mortar; Milan anti-tank missile system; and Mistral air defence system.

COMMANDO PARACHUTISTE DE L'AIR NO. 10

Commando Parachutiste de l'Air No. 10 (CPA 10) is a small, highly specialized unit that is tasked with missions such

Right: High-altitude parachute equipment includes oxygen tank, thermal mittens, a wrist-mounted altimeter and a barometric pressure-operated ripcord.

as laser target designation, restoration of airfield facilities, reconnaissance, and the securing and marking of landing zones and drop zones for airborne operations. The unit is of company strength and consists of some 125 personnel, who are divided between a HQ, three combat detachments and a logistics and training element.

One of the combat detachments has a HALO/HAHO capability and saw action in the Gulf, Bosnia and Kosovo, where it was used in the target designation role.

ISRAEL
Unit 5707
Shaldag (Unit 5101)
Parachute Reconnaissance Sayeret

Israel's airborne units played key roles in the Israeli victories during the Six-Day War (1967) and Yom Kippur War (1973). Since then they have had constant combat experience dealing with terrorism and civil disturbance.

Based at Palmahim Air Force Base, Unit 5707 is a highly effective army unit that specializes in both pre-bombardment intelligence and post-bombardment bomb damage assessments. The unit was formed in 1996 following air operations in the Lebanon, where it was proving difficult to bomb terrorists who fired their ground-to-ground rockets at Israeli targets, then went into hiding in highly populated areas, where

Right: The 7.62mm FN FAL rifle shown here has been replaced in most Israeli units by the indigenous 5.56mm Galil.

retaliation carpet bombing by the Israelis was impossible.

The role of Unit 5707 is to infiltrate populated areas and gather intelligence on where terrorists are hiding. Once a target has been positively identified, the unit waits until there are

Below: A private of the 202nd Parachute Brigade patrols the Gaza Strip armed with an M16A2 assault rifle fitted with an M203 40mm (1.57in) grenade launcher.

no civilians about, then calls in a precision air strike. The unit uses state-of-the-art infrared and low light level imaging systems to provide real-time BDAs (bomb damage assessments) to aircrew and operational command centres. On occasion, the presence of Unit 5707 personnel on the ground has meant that terrorists fleeing safe houses in vehicles could be targeted by both ground and air units.

The unit is also tasked, where the tactical situation warrants it, with searching building wreckage and bodies of dead terrorists for useful intelligence. Unit 5707 consists of four teams, each manned by eight soldiers who are armed with either Colt M4 assault rifles or M16 assault rifles with M203 grenade launchers. The unit is probably unique in its operational capabilities and operates primarily in Lebanon.

SHALDAG

Unit 5101, or Shaldag as it is more commonly known, is tasked primarily with identifying enemy fixed facilities – such as buildings, communications towers, bunkers and ammunition dumps – for Israeli ground attack aircraft and helicopter gunships. Shaldag can also target moving targets, such as boats and vehicles. For precision air strikes, Shaldag uses high-energy laser designators, which paint potential targets with a beam that can be tracked by aircraft-launched laser-guided bombs or Hellfire missiles fired from the AH-64 Apache helicopter. Because of the unit's excellent infiltration skills, they are often used for roles such as long-range reconnaissance, counterterrorism and hostage rescue.

Shaldag is based at Palmahim Air Force Base and consists of some 40 soldiers, who are divided into five

Above: A first lieutenant of the Sayeret Tzanhanim, the elite reconnaissance arm of the Israeli parachute brigade.

teams, each manned by eight operators. Shaldag is considered an elite unit, and all of its members have to undergo a rigorous selection and training programme, which is comparable to that of Sayeret Mat'kal and Sayeret Tzanhanim. Shaldag's training course lasts for almost 20

Left: *An Israeli para armed for both assault and support roles. He carries a standard 5.56mm (0.22in) Galil assault rifle and a belt-fed 7.62mm (0.3in) FN MAG machine gun.*

months and consists of long marches, navigation, communications, weapons handling, and tactical forward air control. The unit proved its worth during the 1996 Lebanon operation, when it located mobile rocket launchers that had been firing on Israeli settlements located near the border. Once the targets were identified, air strikes were called in and the launchers destroyed.

Weapons used by Shaldag include the M16 assault rifle with M203 40mm grenade launcher; Colt M4 assault rifle; Mauser SR 82 sniper rifle; Glock 17 pistol; and SIG Sauer P228 pistol.

PARACHUTE RECONNAISSANCE (SAYERET)

Israel's first cadre of budding paratroopers was trained in Czechoslovakia in 1948, with the first IDF parachute unit forming in 1949. In 1955, the first Parachute Reconnaissance Sayeret was created, following the formation of the first Parachute Brigade, the 202nd. Most of the unit's initial volunteers came from the disbanded Unit 101 and 890th Parachute Battalion. The unit lost no time in gaining its operational spurs, for it soon found itself involved in a number of anti-terrorist operations. During the 1956 Sinai Campaign, the unit fought as a separate force in the fierce battle for the Mitla Pass.

Following the formation of the 35th Parachute Brigade in 1964, the unit became an elite within an elite. In 1967, the 35th Parachute Brigade fought in a series of battles around Rafa Junction, with the Parachute Reconnaissance Sayeret leading from the front. However, it was the War of Attrition that brought the Sayeret into prominence, following a number of daring commando raids deep within Egypt (in some cases almost 300km (186 miles) into enemy territory).

During the Yom Kippur War, the Sayeret fought alongside the brigade in the Sinai against the Egyptian A-Saiqa. These actions often took place on both sides of the Suez Canal and were very costly in human terms. In 1976, the unit joined other Sayerets to launch a raid on Entebbe. During the 1982 war in Lebanon, the Sayeret used boats to infiltrate enemy territory via the Awali River, and they encountered stiff resistance from the Palestine Liberation Organization (PLO) while moving towards Beirut. Like many of Israel's special units, the Parachute Reconnaissance Sayeret is engaged in continual operations against both PLO and Hizbollah guerillas.

ITALY ▮▮
Folgore Parachute Brigade

Italy was one of the first countries to develop military parachute units – the Folgore Parachute Brigade's own history dates back to 1938. Today it takes 16 months of training to produce a para worthy of this tradition.

Based at Pisa, Italy's Folgore Parachute Brigade is a permanent part of the Italian field army. It is composed of a parachute infantry regiment (two battalions), an artillery battalion, a Carabinieri battalion, an aviation flight, an engineer company, a signal company, and an administrative support unit, all of which are air-portable or parachutable. The airborne Carabinieri, like the Folgore, have a long and proud history that dates back to World War I. (They were disbanded

Above: A stick of Folgore paras exit from the back of a C-130 Hercules transporter during free-fall para training.

Left: A sergeant major of the Folgore Brigade seen in the Lebanon in 1982 and armed with a Beretta BM-59 Ital para rifle with folding stock.

Above: The badge of the Folgore Brigade, a winged dagger set against a parachute and framed by wings – a typical para design.

in 1942 and reformed in 1951, but their history since has been stable.) In 1975, the unit was named the Tuscania 1st Airborne Carabinieri Battalion and shortly after became part of the Folgore Airborne Brigade.

Although an airborne unit, most of its operations have been conducted against the Mafia, and for this purpose it has a fleet of armoured personnel carriers (APCs), which is highly unusual for paratroopers, but very necessary under the circumstances.

The unit is also trained in anti-terrorist and anti-guerilla warfare, and it has participated in UN peacekeeping missions, where these skills have proved very useful.

Weapons used by the Folgore Parachute Brigade include the Beretta SCP 90 assault rifle; Beretta AR70/90 light machine gun; Beretta 92F pistol; and M2 .50 heavy machine gun.

THE NETHERLANDS ▬
11th Air Mobile Brigade

*Created in 1992, but with an ancestry reaching back to the 1960s, the
11th Air Mobile Brigade is one of the new breed of NATO rapid reaction forces. It contains
three air-transportable battalions of combat soldiers.*

The Netherlands 11th Air Mobile Brigade is a modern, well-equipped airborne force that operates as part of NATO's Multinational Division (Central). This in turn is an element of the Allied Rapid Reaction Corps (ARRC). The unit is comparable to the British 16 Air Assault Brigade: its modus operandi is virtually identical, and it operates both the CH-47 Chinook and AH-64 Apache in the same tactical way.

The 11th Air Mobile Brigade comprises three infantry battalions, which are supported by a heavy mortar company (equipped with 12

120mm (4.72in) mortars), an engineer company, a maintenance company, a medical company and a transport section that provides all-terrain vehicles (ATVs) for mobility during operational deployment.

Equipped with state-of-the-art communication and navigation systems, the brigade also has heavy fire support weapons, including mortars, anti-tank missiles (TOW, AT-4 and Dragon) and Stinger MANPADS.

Helicopter assets are provided by the Netherlands Air Force Tactical Helicopter Group when required, although a small fleet is on permanent

stand-by to allow the deployment of a battalion-sized unit at short notice. This was amply demonstrated during the crisis in Bosnia, when all three battalions were deployed in support of the UN Protection Force from January 1994 to July 1995.

The 11th Air Mobile Brigade was formed on 14 November 1960, when the 11th Brigade was formed for infantry-based operations. Barely five years years later, it was given a new role and became the 11th Mechanized Infantry Brigade. Finally, in 1992, its role was changed again, this time for the airmobile role.

RUSSIA ▬
Airborne Assault Troops (VDV)

*Russian Airborne Assault Troops numbered over 100,000 men in the 1980s.
Since then, their numbers have declined, but they remain the most capable of Russian troops,
heavily involved in fighting in Chechnya.*

In terms of size and capability, there is no force in the West that compares to the VDV (Russian Airborne Assault Troops. Their operational role is to provide Russia with a unit that can respond quickly in times of crisis and which is both self-contained and self-deployable. Although impressive in size and numbers by Western standards, the VDV is small by traditional Soviet military standards, each division containing some 6000 lightly armed troops plus their armoured support

vehicles. The troops, however, are a strategically valuable force, for they have special training in airborne assault tactics and can deploy anywhere in the world at very short notice from long-range transport aircraft.

The VDV also has a significant parachute assault capability, which dispenses with the need for an air base – if necessary, troops can be inserted anywhere within airlift range in a matter of hours. However, they lack the self-sustaining combat and logistical support of regular ground

forces and must therefore be resupplied and reinforced within days of deployment.

In the mid-1990s, the Airborne Assault Troops comprised eight air assault brigades and five airborne divisions (there were seven in the Soviet era). All were based in European Russia: one division in the Northern Military District, two in the Moscow Military District, and one each in the Volga and North Caucasus Military Districts (the latter division participated in the Chechen conflict).

Left: Russian parachute soldiers check and assemble weapons prior to an assault against a Chechen rebel position.

emerged that this decision was not due to any military requirement, but was rather a response to internal politics: the Russian leadership did not want airborne forces under the control of the General Staff or, indeed, the ground forces.

In 1992, Moscow carried out a review of its military capabilities and found to its horror that Russia had little or no military reserves and could deploy to potential trouble spots with only limited forces. In response, Boris Yeltsin, Russia's then president, ordered the creation of a new mobile force. This was to be similar in capability to the Airborne Assault Troops, but also comparable in terms

Right: Soldiers of an airborne paratroop division stand before an Mil Mi-24 Hind, the standard Russian assault helicopter.

It should be noted that the airborne assault brigades have a lesser combat capability than the divisions, for they lack artillery and armour assets, which greatly limits both their firepower and speed of advance. Once deployed by parachute or helicopter (their preferred method of deployment), the airborne assault brigades have to rely on speed and aggression to overcome their adversaries because reinforcements are likely to be days away.

In 1991, the Airborne Assault Troops were designated a separate service with direct responsibility to the Ministry of Defence, via Airborne Troop HQ rather than via ground forces command and control. The official reason given for this reorganization was that the airborne troops could not respond quickly enough under the control of a ground forces command structure. However, it later

Left: A Russian para in Afghanistan, 1979. His blue-and-white striped T-shirt is worn by all Russian elite forces.

of quality and quantity with the American mobile forces. However, this elite force never materialized, and instead the Airborne Assault Troops were reorganized once more. The result, unfortunately, was a reduction in performance, not an enhancement.

And still Russia needed an instant deployment force (capable of deploying in 3–5 days) and a rapid deployment Force (capable of deploying in 30 days). To rival NATO's rapid deployment forces, such as the Allied Rapid Reaction Corps (ARRC), these would have to comprise some 100,000–150,000 men. In 1996 came the concept of a mobile force, which on paper had some 100,000 men (of which 60,000 were Airborne Assault Troops), plus motor rifle formations, naval infantry, transport aircraft and

Below: A para exercise near Viazma for the 60th anniversary of an assault against German forces there in 1942.

logistical support. To make this concept a reality, four of the eight independent airborne brigades and two of the five airborne divisions were placed under the command of their respective district commanders, while the three remaining divisions became part of the strategic reserve.

In late 1996, two of the airborne divisions were disbanded, reducing the total strength of the VDV from 64,300 to 48,500 personnel. Although still an impressive figure by Western standards, this new Russian force was a mere shadow of the once mighty airborne forces of the former Soviet Union.

By Russian military standards, the VDV is considered an elite force because each member of the unit is individually selected from volunteer recruits. Selection criteria is based upon intelligence, loyalty and physical fitness, and candidates must go through a series of psychological and physical tests before being accepted for airborne training. Once accepted for parachute training, candidates are subjected to a daily routine of long and arduous physical training work-outs,

which are designed to build up stamina and general fitness. Discipline is harsh within the airborne forces, and it needs to be: these are Russia's shock troops, and their operational role is extremely demanding.

Every soldier is trained to a very high standard in personal weapons handling. Great emphasis is placed on both marksmanship and ammunition usage – key issues during operations behind enemy lines because resupply is likely to take several days. Soldiers are also trained in hand-to-hand combat, which is an indispensable skill for airborne forces.

To help build confidence and also dispel the natural fear of parachuting, each soldier packs his own parachute after he has completed just three jumps, the theory being that this focuses the soldiers' minds. Training jumps are carried out by day and night from fixed-wing aircraft in highly realistic combat conditions, and these training sessions include the use of live rounds and explosives.

The VDV has seen action in many places, including Czechoslovakia, Hungary, Afghanistan and Chechnya. It almost saw action in Kosovo, where a Mexican stand-off developed between its forces and NATO forces protecting the airfield at Pristina. Thankfully, this incident was resolved peacefully after intense political negotiations were conducted between Russia and NATO.

Above: Russian paras arrive in Bosnia in 1996, part of some 1600 Russian troops deployed in Bosnian peacekeeping.

Weapons and equipment used by the VDV include light tanks; armoured personnel carriers (mainly BMD-3s); self-propelled artillery; anti-tank and anti-aircraft artillery; MANPADS; mortars; and light, medium and heavy machine guns.

ORBAT

The current ORBAT for the Airborne Assault Troops is as follows:
THE 106TH GUARDS PARACHUTE DIVISION, holding the order of the Red Banner and the order of Kutunoz of the 2nd degree.
THE 76TH GUARDS PARACHUTE RED BANNER DIVISION of Chernigov.
THE 98TH GUARDS SVIRSK PARACHUTE DIVISION, holding the order of the Red Banner and the order of Kutuzov of the 2nd degree.
THE 7TH GUARDS PARACHUTE DIVISION
THE 104TH GUARDS PARACHUTE DIVISION.

Military Schools –
THE 242ND CENTRE OF TRAINING FOR PARACHUTE TROOPS

SPAIN
Spanish Airborne Brigade (SAB)

*The Spanish Airborne Brigade takes its place alongside the Spanish Legion
and Marine units to create a rapid reaction force. It is an elite amongst Spanish forces,
with a solid profile of combat and peacekeeping operations.*

The Spanish Airborne Brigade, or SAB, consists of three parachute battalions (Roger de Flor, Roger de Lauria, and Ortiz de Zarate); an artillery, engineer, and support battalion; and a highly skilled pathfinder company. The SAB is part of Spain's commitment to the Allied Rapid Reaction Corps (ARRC) and is known as the Fuerzo de Accion Rapide (FAR – Rapid Action Force).

Spain's first parachute battalion, the 1st Airborne Bandera, was originally part of the Spanish Air Force until handed over to the Army. It was an excellent unit, which was highly capable in special forces work and free-fall infiltration, and it saw action in the Spanish Sahara in 1956 and again in Morocco in 1958.

Weapons used by the Spanish Airborne Brigade include the CETME LC assault rifle; Colt Commando assault rifle; CETME Ameli light machine gun; 40mm (1.57in) grenade launcher, 60mm (2.36in) mortar and 81mm (3.19in) mortar.

UNITED KINGDOM
16 Air Assault Brigade (AAB)
Pathfinder Platoon
Parachute Regiment
No.47 Squadron (Special Forces Flight) RAF

*Airborne units are at the forefront of the British Army's combat response. The 16 Air Assault
Brigade is the Army's latest self-contained fully airmobile military unit.*

Based in Colchester is Britain's elite 16 Air Assault Brigade and its reconnaissance force, the Pathfinder Platoon. The 16 Air Assault Brigade was formed in 2000 and is a lethal combination of air assault infantry and attack helicopters. Its awesome capabilities bring a new meaning to the term 'manoeuvre warfare', as it has both the means and method of rapidly

**Right: Soldiers of 16 Air Assault Brigade
disembark from a Chinook helicopter
during a training exercise. The 16 AAB has
18 Chinooks and 18 Pumas for mobilizing
over 1000 troops in one airlift.**

Right: A 16 AAB soldier practises using the 5.56mm (0.22in) Light Support Weapon (LSW). The LSW is the long-barrelled support version of the SA80 rifle.

Right: A 16 AAB soldier practises using the 5.56mm (0.22in) Light Support Weapon (LSW). The LSW is the long-barrelled support version of the SA80 rifle.

inserting a large, well-equipped force deep behind enemy lines, at very short notice by day or night, and in all weathers. Although originally conceived as a hard-hitting mobile tank-killing force (it was known as 24 Airmobile), it has grown considerably since and now has capabilities such as hostage rescue, seizure of strategic assets, infiltration and extraction of allied forces, counterpenetration, flank protection, raids on key targets, and humanitarian and civil aid.

The unique capabilities of 16 Air Assault Brigade allow it to attack from any direction; concentrate, disperse or redeploy rapidly; delay a larger force without becoming decisively engaged; provide responsive reserve and reaction forces; react rapidly to tactical opportunities; place forces at natural choke points; provide surveillance and target acquisition; react to rear threats;

bypass enemy positions; facilitate surprise and deception; and rapidly reinforce committed areas.

The 16 Air Assault Brigade has an operational strength of some 10,000 personnel and comprises an HQ and

Signals squadron. HQ is responsible for all direction and coordination of air assault operations, while the parachute-deployable 216 Signal Squadron is responsible for establishing and maintaining communications between all elements of 16 AAB.

An integral part of the brigade is the Pathfinder Platoon, responsible for reconnaissance and the marking of helicopter landing zones and parachute drop zones. The 3rd, 4th and 9th Army Air Corps Regiments are responsible for reconnaissance (using Gazelles), anti-tank operations (Lynx and Apache) and light utility support (using Lynx). At present, 16 AAB is scaled for 48 Apache Longbow attack helicopters (with each regiment operating two squadrons of eight helicopters).

Three Air Assault Infantry Battalions are assigned to 16 AAB, of which two are always from the Parachute Regiment. Within each battalion there are five companies: three rifle companies, one support company and an HQ company.

16 AAB Support

The brigade is also supported by:

7TH PARA, RHA – providing three batteries (each with six guns) of 105mm (4.13in) light guns.

21ST DEFENCE BATTERY, RA – providing air defence for the Brigade (with Javelin and Starstreak MANPADS).

9TH PARACHUTE SQUADRON, RE – providing engineering support.

HOUSEHOLD CAVALRY REGIMENT (HCR) – providing medium reconnaissance as and when required, with three troops of four Scimitar armoured reconnaissance vehicles.

47 AIR DESPATCH REGIMENT – responsible for managing and packing equipment into aircraft.

THE PARACHUTE REGIMENT – providing two of the three infantry battalions assigned to 16 AAB.

RAF SUPPORT HELICOPTER FORCE – providing 18 Chinooks and 18 Pumas for mobility. The RAF also provides 16 AAB with C-130 Hercules transport aircraft as and when required.

The firepower levels are extremely impressive, as each battalion has 80 GPMGs, 14 .50 cal. Browning heavy machine guns, nine 81mm (3.19in) mortars and 16 MILAN anti-tank missile systems.

PATHFINDER PLATOON

By any normal military criteria, the Pathfinder Platoon would be deemed a special forces unit; however, with typical British understatement it is classed only as an elite specialist unit. The members of the Pathfinder Platoon are unconcerned, insisting that they are expert in the art of covert reconnaissance only and not a fighting force. They are being unduly modest, however, as they are members of the Parachute Regiment, a unit that has a fearsome fighting reputation around the world – in effect, they are an elite within an elite. Their excellent skills make them obvious candidates for the SAS, and for many the Pathfinders are simply a stepping stone between the Parachute Regiment and the SAS.

Originally formed during World War II, the Pathfinder unit had the unenviable role of jumping ahead of the main force of Paratroopers and securing a drop zone (DZ) for them.

In September 1944, Pathfinders of the 21st Independent Company parachuted into Arnhem to find and secure a DZ for Operation Market Garden. Although their part of the operation was a complete success, the unit was disbanded after the end of the war.

In 1981, 2 Para recognized the need for a pathfinder platoon and set about creating a modern equivalent, to have more or less the same role as the original Pathfinders of World War II. Despite the fact that it was only platoon strength (16 men), the new unit was known in 2 Para as C Company and effectively became the eyes and ears of the regiment.

In 1982, 2 Para's Pathfinder Platoon was split up and reformed into two platoons, Recce Platoon and Patrol Platoon. The title of platoon was somewhat ironic because the unit was now operating at company strength. In 1985, the Pathfinder Platoon became part of 5 Airborne Brigade and took on additional operational roles, which involved covert reconnaissance and sabotage. Again, the title platoon was retained, even though the unit was at company strength.

The selection of Pathfinder candidates is very similar to that of the SAS, with only the best passing through the rigorous assessment phase. New recruits to the Pathfinders are placed on a year's probation before they are officially accepted into the unit's ranks. Any soldier not already parachute-qualified must attend the basic parachute training course at RAF Brize Norton. Once qualified, the soldiers must undergo HALO training, with some going on to complete the more advanced HAHO course. The soldiers are then assigned to either Air

Left: A British para makes a drop. All British Army parachute training is conducted at No. 1 Parachute Training School, RAF Brize Norton.

Above: A British soldier gives a boy a glimpse through the Sight Unit Small Arms Trilux (SUSAT) optical sight, a standard fitting on the SA80 rifle.

or Mountain Platoon, where they will be posted to one of the five 4-man platoons. The essential difference between the two platoons is that all Air Platoon troops are both HALO and HAHO trained, while Mountain Platoon is trained in HALO only and specializes in arctic warfare.

Being a Para can be demanding, but serving as a Pathfinder is on another plane entirely because there is a constant demand on each soldier to

both maintain and acquire new skills. Soldiers learn survival and Escape & Evasion techniques until they become second nature because most of their time in conflict will be spent operating behind enemy lines. Although their prime mission is to operate covertly, they are trained, if compromised, to defend themselves in a devastating manner: each four-man team carries two M249 Minimis, two M16A2s fitted with M203 grenade launchers, and copious amounts of hand grenades.

Soldiers serving in the Pathfinders are expected to complete at least three years' service, with the option of an

extension, while officers serve for two years only. The idea behind these short-service postings is to ensure that both the officers and soldiers have a chance to share their knowledge and experience with other units and regiments. The Pathfinders also have links with many foreign units, including the Jordanian Special Forces; US Army Rangers; US 82nd Airborne Pathfinders; and the 2nd REP, French Foreign Legion.

For HALO operations, the Pathfinders use the GQ360 Ram Air Parachute, which gives them a greater amount of control and features an automatic chute-deployment device

Recent Operations

In 1999, the Pathfinders played an important role in Kosovo, where they were tasked with identifying safe and secure landing zones for helicopters bringing in British spearhead forces prior to the arrival of the main allied invasion force. In September 2000, the Pathfinders deployed to Sierra Leone and participated in a spectacular hostage rescue operation that involved 2 Para, the SAS and elements of the SBS. The rescue operation was sanctioned after a group of British peacekeeping soldiers was taken hostage by a group of drug-crazed rebels, known locally as the 'West Side Boys'. Although aspects of this operation still remain classified, the role of the Pathfinders was significant: they identified suitable helicopter assault points for 2 Para, then provided fire support as they fast-roped onto the drop zone. This was, in fact, the Pathfinders' second combat action in Sierra Leone, as they were involved in a skirmish with rebels while on a peacekeeping mission in 1999.

In 2002, they were deployed with 2 Para to Kabul, Afghanistan, for a short peacekeeping operation. The Pathfinders Platoon is now part of the newly formed 16 Air Assault Brigade, and it acts as the Brigade's advance force. Its operational roles include covert reconnaissance and the location and marking of drop zones, tactical landing zones and helicopter landing zones for subsequent air assault operations. After the main force has landed, the platoon takes on the role of tactical intelligence gathering and works very closely with the Brigade's HQ.

Pathfinders wear standard British Army combat uniforms, but tend to wear either Para or SAS smocks depending on personal preference. They also wear the famous Para Red Beret with its distinctive cap badge.

Equipment used by the Pathfinders Platoon includes state-of-the-art GPS and NVG systems, portable satellite communications, Land Rover 110 SOVs, Land Rover 90s, quad bikes, and Argocat all-terrain vehicles (ATVs). The Pathfinders make extensive use of the Land Rovers for long-range reconnaissance patrols and greatly value their ability to carry a large variety of weapons, including the GPMG, Mk-19 40mm (1.57in) automatic grenade launcher, and Browning .50 heavy machine gun.

Weapons used by the Pathfinder Platoon include the M16 A2 with

Below: A unit of the 16 Air Assault Brigade drives away from its Hercules transport aircraft on arrival at Skopje airport, Macedonia, in August 2001.

that opens the parachute at a preset altitude using the Hitefinder opening instrument. The standard height for HALO jumps is 7620 metres (25,000ft), with the parachute set to deploy at around 762 metres (2500ft). These heights offer the aircraft protection from radar detection and also give the soldier a chance to deploy his reserve chute in the event of a failure – or Roman Candle, as the Pathfinders would say.

For HAHO missions, the soldier needs to jump with oxygen as his jump and chute deployment height is 9144 metres (30,000ft). This height allows the soldier to glide for almost 90 minutes before hitting the ground. In good wind conditions, a soldier can glide for a considerable distance, which reduces the chances of radar detection for both him and the insertion aircraft.

Above: A Pathfinder unit on patrol. Its long-wheelbase Land Rover mounts a Browning 0.5 and a 7.62mm (0.3in) GPMG.

M203 grenade launcher; M249 Minimi; 7.62mm GPMG; Browning HP; Colt Commando; and SA-80 A2.

PARACHUTE REGIMENT

Based at Colchester, the Parachute Regiment provides the 16 Air Assault Brigade with most of its infantry component. The regiment is made up of three battalions – 1, 2 and 3 – two of which are always assigned to the brigade's air assault infantry. Unlike Russia, Germany and Italy – countries

with a long history of parachute-based operations – Britain was slow to realize the potential of airborne forces and formed a capability only in 1940. However, once a unit was formed, volunteers from the existing commando forces were quick to come forwards, leading to the formation of the 2nd Airborne Brigade.

They were not airdropped for their first action, which was in Tunisia, where they earned from the Germans the nickname of *Die Roten Teufel*, 'The Red Devils' – a name that they still bear. By 1943, the 2nd Airborne Brigade had grown considerably in size and capability, and now had its

own gliderborne force. Following a change of name to the 1st Airborne Division, the Paras were dropped into Sicily wearing their Pegasus airborne insignia and red berets. (This action was a precursor to the ambitious but ill-fated Market Garden Operation, where the paras fought a valiant action at Arnhem, Holland, in September 1944.) While the action in Sicily was taking place, a new formation known as the 6th Airborne Division was preparing for the D-Day invasion of Normandy. Since the war, the Paras have been involved in numerous conflicts and internal security operations in Palestine, Malaya, Suez,

Aden, Borneo, Northern Ireland and the Falklands Islands.

In 1999, it was the Paras that led the way into Kosovo for NATO, and they also participated in a spectacular hostage rescue operation in Sierra Leone. On their return to the United Kingdom, they were permanently assigned to the newly formed 16 Air Assault Brigade. Following the events of 11 September 2001, however, a small force that did not involve 16 Air Assault Brigade was sent to Afghanistan

No. 47 Squadron (Special Forces Flight) RAF

Based at RAF Lyneham, 47 Squadron RAF (Royal Air Force) is tasked with providing the United Kingdom's special forces with a dedicated long-range transport capability. The squadron operates a small fleet of specially modified C-130 Hercules transport aircraft, which are equipped with TFR (terrain-following radar) systems that enable their aircraft to fly at very low level and in all weathers. Aircrews assigned to 47 Squadron are screened for their ability to fly at low level for prolonged periods of time, as this type of flying can cause severe disorientation for some pilots. Those pilots that do make the grade work with the SAS and SBS, which can be very rewarding because there are numerous opportunities to travel and develop new skills.

Techniques regularly practised by 47 Squadron include TALO; ghost insertion, a technique whereby aircraft fly so close together that they appear on radar as one image; and JATO, a technique practised in the United States.

Known as the 22 SAS taxi service, No. 7 Special Forces Flight is responsible for the covert insertion and extraction of the United Kingdom's special forces. No. 7 SFF operates a small fleet of heavily modified Chinook HC Mk 2s, which feature air-to-air refuelling probes, state-of-the-art navigation systems, missile jamming devices, long-range fuel tanks, mini-guns and M60 machine guns. Many of its operations are secret, but it is known to have operated in the Gulf, Bosnia, Kosovo, Sierra Leone and Afghanistan. Selection and training standards for No. 7 SFF are extremely demanding, as much of the squadron's flying is carried out at low level and at night using third-generation NVGs.

as part of an international peacekeeping force.

All officers and men of the Parachute Regiment are volunteers, and they have to attend a rigorous two-day preselection course before attempting the much-feared training course. This lasts for some 23 weeks. The first eight weeks concentrate on basic military training, which includes drill, weapons handling and fieldcraft. Next come leadership training, rock climbing, canoeing and abseiling. Finally, it's the big one – 'P Company'

Left: A soldier of the Parachute Regiment wearing the Combat Soldier 95 uniform, the airborne red beret and carrying the much-troubled 5.56mm SA80 rifle.

(Pre-Parachute Selection Company). This part of the course is the most physically demanding, and it is comparable to that of the Royal Marines Commando course. For the 35 per cent who do pass, a basic parachuting course awaits them, their final hurdle before receiving their Parachute Wings.

Weapons used by the Parachute Regiment include the SA-80 A2 assault rifle; M16A2 assault rifle with M203 40mm grenade launcher; SA-80 A2 LSW light support weapon; M249 Minimi light machine gun; GPMG medium machine gun; M2.50 heavy machine gun; 81mm (3.19in) mortar; LAW 80 anti-tank missile; Milan anti-tank missile; and Starstreak MANPADS.

UNITED STATES OF AMERICA 🇺🇸
82nd Airborne Division
101st Airborne Division (Air Assault) –
'The Screaming Eagles'
160th Special Operations Aviation Regiment (SOAR)

The US Army contains the most powerful airborne forces in the world. Units such as the 82nd Airborne and 101st Airborne divisions provide large-scale assault options, while Special Operations para units concentrate on covert or precision airborne insertions.

The illustrious 82nd Airborne Division is based at Fort Bragg, North Carolina. The 82nd is made up of a divisional headquarters, a divisional support command and three airborne brigades. Each brigade consists of three parachute battalions, plus an HQ and support element that is equipped with mortars, anti-tank missiles and heavy machine guns. Entry into the 82nd Airborne Division is either by direct application or by volunteering from another unit. Before entering the Airborne brotherhood, all candidates must first pass a tough selection procedure, followed by a rigorous training programme and parachute course, after which they get their 'Wings' and maroon beret.

The primary role of the 82nd Airborne Division is to arrive by air, take control of the ground, and hold it until relieved by a main force unit. At any given time, one parachute battalion is on an 18-hour stand-by, with one of its companies on two-hour stand-by. The ready brigade rotates around the division and is on 24-hour notice to move. Airlift capability for the 82nd Airborne

Above: The divisional badge of the US 82nd Airborne Division. The double A stands for 'All American'.

Division is provided by Boeing C-17 Globemasters, Lockheed C-141 Starlifters and C-130 Hercules of the US Air Force. During operations, each soldier is issued with enough food rations, water and ammunition to last for three days; after that, a resupply becomes necessary.

The 82nd has seen action in many countries, including Vietnam, Grenada, Panama and Afghanistan.

Weapons used by the 82nd Airborne include the M16A2 assault rifle; Colt M4 assault rifle; M249 SAW light machine gun; M60 medium

Left: A soldier of the 82nd Airborne Division wearing the standard US Army General Purpose (Woodland) uniform.

Left: US airborne troops board a flight of Blackhawks. An individual Blackhawk can carry 11 troops.

machine gun; M2 .50 cal. heavy machine gun; M203 40mm grenade launcher and 81mm (3.19in) mortar.

101ST AIRBORNE DIVISION (AIR ASSAULT) – 'THE SCREAMING EAGLES'

Based at Fort Campbell, Kentucky, is the world's only air assault division – hence the designation 101st Airborne Division (Air Assault). It is not deemed a special forces unit, unlike its neighbour, the 160th Special Operations Aviation Regiment (SOAR). Nevertheless, the 101st Airborne Division is an elite unit by any military standards and has no equal in terms of its size and operational capability. The 101st Airborne Division (Air Assault) is formed of three brigades, plus Division Artillery, Division Support Command, the 101st Aviation Brigade, 159th Aviation Brigade, and 101st Corps Support Group, as well as several separate commands.

In terms of military personnel, the 101st currently has 26,819 men directly within its ranks and 18,166

Right: Soldiers of the 101st Airborne Division airlift equipment using a CH-47 with a three-ton payload.

support troops, making Fort Campbell the third-largest military population in the US Army and the seventh largest in the Department of Defense.

The mission of the 101st is to deploy within 36 hours worldwide to close with the enemy by means of fire and manoeuvre to destroy or capture him, or to repel his assault by fire, close combat or counterattack. The unit grew out of World War II, the unit being formed on 15 August 1942.

Within days of its activation, its first commander, Major General William C. Lee, promised his new recruits that the 101st has a 'rendezvous with destiny'. He was right. The 101st Airborne Division led the night drop prior to the D-Day invasion. And when surrounded at Bastogne by the Germans and asked to surrender, Brigadier General Anthony McAuliffe gave the answer that has since became famous — 'Nuts!' Then, despite being outgunned and outnumbered, the 'Screaming Eagles' bravely fought on until the siege ended. For this, they were awarded four campaign streamers and two Presidential Unit Citations.

Following the end of World War II, the 101st faced an uncertain future; there was little need for such a large airborne force during peacetime. However, in 1948 and again in 1950, the unit was temporarily reactivated as a training unit at Camp Breckinridge, Kentucky. Finally, in March 1956, the 101st was transferred (minus most of

its personnel and equipment) to Fort Campbell, Kentucky, where it was reorganized as a combat division.

In the mid-1960s, the 1st Brigade and its support troops were deployed to Vietnam, the rest of the division joining them in 1967 to form the world's first airmobile division. Vietnam was the birthplace of the concept of 'air cavalry', and the 101st was instrumental in its success, proving that helicopters and light infantry made for a deadly combination. During its seven years in Vietnam, the 101st Airborne Division participated in 15 campaigns, earning itself additional laurels.

In October 1974, the 101st was re-designated as the 101st Airborne Division (Air Assault), resulting in the 3rd Brigade changing its operational capabilities from that of parachute to air assault. In addition, and to ensure maximum operational efficiency, the 101st created an Air Assault school, specifically to teach new soldiers about the art of helicopter-based warfare. This new generation of air assault soldiers was also given permission to wear the new emblem of the 101st, the Air Assault Badge.

In the mid-1970s, the 101st conducted numerous training and readiness exercises as part of its work-up phase. It also opened its Air Assault School to other US Army units, to ensure a better understanding of helicopter assault tactics and techniques, and the procedures used by infantry during combat operations. This training proved highly valuable and put the 101st in good stead for forthcoming operations.

On 12 December 1985, tragedy struck the 101st Airborne Division when 248 members of the division

Units

The 101st Airborne Division (Air Assault) is made up of the following units:
- 1st Brigade – 1st, 2nd, and 3rd Battalions 327th Infantry
- 2nd Brigade – 1st, 2nd, and 3rd Battalions 502nd Infantry
- 3rd Brigade – 1st, 2nd and 3rd Battalions 187th Infantry
- 101st Aviation Brigade – 2nd Battalion, 17th Cavalry Squadron, and 1st, 2nd, 3rd and 6th Battalions 101st Aviation Regiment
- 159th Aviation Brigade – 4th, 5th, 7th and 9th Battalions 101st Aviation Regiment

The Division's supporting units are:
- 1st, 2nd and 3rd Battalion, 320th Field Artillery;106th Transportation Battalion; 129th and 561st Combat Support Battalions; C Company, 1st Battalion 377th Field Artillery; 63rd Chemical Company, the 101st Division Band, and several support companies.

were killed in a plane crash near Gander, Newfoundland, while returning to Fort Campbell from a routine tour of duty in the Sinai peninsula. On a personal level, this was a major setback for the division.

Still, the 101st had a job to do. On 17 August 1990, elements of the 101st arrived in Saudi Arabia as part of the Allied Coalition force. Their mission:

to support Allied Forces in their operations against Iraq. The first units of the 101st deployed in Saudi Arabia comprised 2700 troops, 117 helicopters and 487 vehicles, which were transported on board 110 USAF C-5 and C-141 transport aircraft. The remainder of the division was transported by sea to the Saudi port of Ad Daman, a journey that took 46 days.

Fort Campbell, Kentucky

At 425 sq. km (164 sq. miles), the installation is one of the world's largest. About 48.5 sq. km (18.7 sq. miles) have been developed into the cantonment. The remaining area is dedicated to training and firing ranges.

Ranges	52	MOUT Facilities	3
Major Drop Zones	5	Impact Areas	3
Assault Landing Strip	1	Demo Areas	1
A2C2 Air Sectors	10	Maneuver Areas	20
Bayonet Assault Course	1	Artillery Firing Points	340
Rappel Tower	1		

Above: Two members of the 101st Airborne use laser engagement systems on their rifles during training.

Once in theatre, the 101st Airborne established its base camp at King Fahd Airport, which was known to the 101st as 'Camp Eagle II'. After a period of working up, the 101st deployed to a forward operating base (FOB), codenamed 'Bastogne' after one of the division's finest showings. From here, its members mounted round-the-clock training operations, which involved practising night assaults, urban assaults and street fighting.

On 17 January 1991, Operation Desert Storm began, its purpose to liberate Kuwait. The 101st Aviation Regiment drew first blood. The initial attacks were carried out by eight AH-64 Apache helicopters against two Iraqi early warning radar sites that were key targets for the Coalition Forces. Once these were destroyed, Allied strike aircraft were able to bomb Baghdad with little fear of interception from Iraqi fighters. As these attacks went in, Blackhawk helicopters of 1st Battalion were flying CSAR patrols nearby, in case any Allied aircraft were shot down.

Throughout the air campaign, the 101st flew hundreds of sorties against Iraqi positions until ordered to stand down in preparation for the ground war. On 24 February 1991, the ground war began. The 101st and the French 6th Light Armoured Division advanced on the left flank of the Coalition line towards Baghdad and the Euphrates River valley. The first stage of the operation involved 300 helicopters lifting the 101st Airborne to their first objective – FOB Cobra, located 175km (110 miles) inside Iraq.

The arrival of the 101st at Cobra took the Iraqis completely by surprise, and, after a short firefight, they surrendered. By the end of the day, the 101st had consolidated their positions and cut Highway 8, which was Iraq's key supply route. This helicopter assault was the largest in modern warfare history.

The following day, 3rd Brigade moved north to occupy positions on the southern bank of the Euphrates River, where it encountered little resistance. While this operation was taking place, the remaining elements of the 101st maintained their positions at Highway 8 and Cobra, effectively acting as a blocking force in the event of an Iraqi counterattack.

On 26 February, the 101st began accepting the surrender of Iraqi soldiers en masse – the war was over. Desert Storm had been a remarkable success story for the 101st Airborne Division, which had completed the largest helicopter assault in history without a single loss of life.

At the end of the war, the 101st Airborne Division returned to Fort Campbell. Subsequently, it embarked on a number of peacekeeping and humanitarian missions in such countries as Rwanda, Somalia, Haiti and Bosnia.

Following the events of 11 September 2001, the 101st Airborne was deployed to Afghanistan in January 2002 to relieve the 26th Marine Expeditionary Unit. Its mission: to destroy the Al Qaeda terrorist network and Taliban regime. As the 101st commenced operations in Afghanistan, it took its first casualties, when one soldier was killed and several wounded following a raid on a terrorist cave complex near Gardez.

On 2 March 2002, the United States launched Operation Anaconda to find, capture or kill Osama bin Laden and his Al Qaeda and Taliban supporters. The mission, which was located in the eastern mountain ranges of Afghanistan, was to last for 16 days and involved some 1000 US troops, including special forces and elements of the 101st Airborne Division and 10th Mountain Division.

Above: A US soldier on patrol in Kosovo during 2001, helping to prevent cross-border arms shipments.

'Rendezvous with Destiny'

General Order Number Five, which gave birth to the division, reads: The 101st Airborne Division, activated at Camp Claiborne, Louisiana, has no history, but it has a rendezvous with destiny. Like the early American pioneers whose invincible courage was the foundation stone of this nation, we have broken with the past and its traditions in order to establish our claim to the future.

Due to the nature of our armament, and the tactics in which we shall perfect ourselves, we shall be called upon to carry out operations of far-reaching military importance, and we shall habitually go into action when the need is immediate and extreme.

Let me call your attention to the fact that our badge is the great American eagle. This is a fitting emblem for a division that will crush its enemies by falling upon them like a thunderbolt from the skies.

The history we shall make, the record of high achievement we hope to write in the annals of the American Army and the American people, depends wholly and completely on the men of this division. Each individual, each officer and each enlisted man, must therefore regard himself as a necessary part of a complex and powerful instrument for the overcoming of the enemies of the nation. Each, in his own job, must realize that he is not only a means, but an indispensable means for obtaining the goal of victory. It is, therefore, not too much to say that the future itself, in whose molding we expect to have our share, is in the hands of the soldiers of the 101st Airborne Division.

Anaconda hit problems right from the start: the 101st Airborne were landed right in the middle of enemy positions, rather than in a valley running parallel to that position. As a result, the American forces were ambushed by a massive enemy force and suffered many casualties, including eight fatalities and 73 wounded. The firefight was of such intensity that every helicopter involved in supporting the ground forces was hit by effective enemy fire, with the result that two Chinooks were lost and several others so badly damaged that they were unable to used again. Despite these setbacks, the 101st fought back with great determination and killed hundreds of Al Qaeda soldiers before withdrawing. Although the American forces failed to find Osama bin Laden or, indeed, any of his lieutenants, the operation was deemed successful because it forced the remaining Al Qaeda and Taliban forces out of Afghanistan and into neighbouring Pakistan.

The unit's primary weapons systems are infantry, attack helicopters, support helicopters, field artillery and air defence artillery. Helicopters used by the unit include:

AH-64 Apache – for close support, light strike, anti-tank and escort missions.

OH-58D Kiowa Warrior – for armed reconnaissance and scouting missions.

UH-60 Blackhawk – for short-range infiltration/exfiltration missions, plus Medevac.

CH-47 Chinook – medium range support, infiltration/exfiltration type missions

160TH SPECIAL OPERATIONS AVIATION REGIMENT (SOAR)

Following the failure of Operation Eagle Claw in 1980, the US Army decided to form its own dedicated special operations aviation regiment, the 160th SOAR. Known as the Night Stalkers, who live by the motto 'Night Stalkers Don't Quit', the 160th SOAR

is responsible for supporting SOF personnel worldwide and is capable of carrying out a wide range of missions, including armed attack, force insertion and extraction, aerial security, electronic warfare, and command and control support.

Pilots serving in the 160th SOAR are among the best in the world and train constantly to keep up their proficiency. Since their formation, the 160th has seen action in Grenada, Panama, Iran, the Gulf, Somalia and Afghanistan. The 160th SOAR operates some of the most sophisticated helicopters in the world, including the A/MH-6 Little Bird, used for short-range infiltration/ exfiltration, reconnaissance, resupply, liaison duties and light strike; MH-60 K/L Blackhawk, used for medium-range day and night insertion/extraction missions, resupply, MEDEVAC, rescue and recovery, and short-range CSAR; and MH-47 D/E Chinook, used for medium- to long-range all-weather infiltration/exfiltration missions, refuelling operations, rescue and recovery missions, and resupply missions in hostile areas.

Above: The regimental badge of the 160th Special Operations Aviation Regiment (SOAR). Other badges bear the motto 'Night Stalkers Don't Quit'.

THE AIR FORCE SPECIAL OPERATIONS COMMAND (AFSOC)

Under the umbrella of USSOCOM, AFSOC was established on 22 May 1990 and is the United States' specialized air power, capable of delivering special operations combat power 'anytime, anywhere'. AFSOC comprises some 10,000 personnel, of which 22 per cent are based overseas. AFSOC's aircrew are highly trained professionals, who operate with cool, calm precision and are amongst the most respected aviators in the world today. The unit is capable of rapid deployment at short notice and operates with some of the best rotary and fixed-wing aircraft available today, giving SOF mobility, forward presence and engagement precision. AFSOC has the following active Air National Guard (ANG) and Air Force Reserve units assigned to it:

Left: A soldier of the 101st Airborne Division enjoys a coffee at Kandahar airport, Afghanistan, during Operation Enduring Freedom.

16th Special Operations Wing (SOW) – operating with eight special operations squadrons, five fixed-wing and one rotary wing, an aviation foreign internal defence (FID) unit, and a fixed-wing training squadron.

352nd and 353rd Special Operations Groups – based in the United Kingdom and Japan, this is a theatre-orientated group comprising two fixed-wing and one rotary wing special operations squadrons, plus a special tactics squadron.

919th AF Reserve Special Operations Wing – operates with two fixed wing special operations squadrons.

193rd Special Operations Wing (ANG) – operates with a fixed-wing special operations squadron.

Right: Helicopters of the 160th Special Operations Aviation Regiment (SOAR) aboard a US aircraft carrier during training manoeuvres.

Below: The 160th SOAR specializes in high-risk rescue and recovery of important personnel, including airmen downed at sea.

720th Special Tactics Group – a unit with special operations combat controllers and para-rescue men, who work jointly in special tactics teams. Their mission includes air traffic control to establish air assault landing zones; close air support for strike aircraft and gunship missions; establishing casualty collection stations; and providing trauma care for injured personnel.

16th Special Operations Wing – the oldest unit in AFSOC, this is responsible for deploying specially trained and equipped forces from each service on national security objectives. The Wing focuses on unconventional warfare, including counterinsurgency and psychological operations during low-intensity conflicts. It also provides precise, reliable and timely support to SOF worldwide. The squadron operates a mix of aircraft types.

18th Flight Test Squadron - the Air Force Special Operations School. The school provides education in special operations subjects to personnel from all branches of the Department of Defense, governmental agencies and allied nations. Subjects covered include regional affairs and cross-cultural communications, anti-terrorism awareness, revolutionary warfare and psychological operations.

SPECIAL FORCES TRAINING

Special forces training usually falls into three sections. First, soldiers are tested for physical fitness. During a series of punishing exercises, the candidate will reveal his psychological determination and character. Secondly, soldiers are instructed in the key skills of their unit, such as covert insertion, weapons handling and night fighting. Finally, the candidate will usually specialize within the unit. Specialist roles include communications officer, sniper, demolitions expert or CRW operative. Candidates can be rejected at any stage during the process, and some selection courses last well over a year. A typical rejection rate for special forces is around 80 per cent. The upshot of such rigorous selection is that only self-reliant, determined, tough and intelligent individuals emerge at the end to uphold the standards of an elite force.

Left: High Altitude Low Opening (HALO) freefall training on an 'Aerodium' vertical fan trainer.

SPECIAL FORCES TRAINING

*Irregular warfare requires highly skilled individuals capable of independent action
and innovative thinking. The history of special forces shows that small teams of such people
can have a military effect out of all proportion to their numbers.*

Ask anyone to describe a special forces soldier and you will probably get a description of someone who is a cross between Sylvester Stallone in *Rambo* and Arnold Schwarzenegger in *Commando*. Indeed, over the years, the movie industry has been working in overdrive to make action films that portray special forces as muscle-bound meatheads who walk around with large-calibre weapons slung around their person, along with coils of ammunition belts and dozens of grenades. The truth of the matter is that special forces soldiers are not at all like their screen image in terms of both physical and mental stature: far from being loud-mouthed and arrogant, they are generally quiet and unassuming men. As you read through this book, you will see a common thread that links special forces world-wide – the stringent entry criteria. Special forces want the best of the best and can afford to be selective about who they recruit, as these men – and, in some cases, women – may one day be required to serve their country.

Operators from many countries around the world are highly trained and extremely professional in their work; however, apart from looking fit and healthy, there is nothing to distinguish them as special forces personnel. Indeed, many could walk into a bar or shopping mall without anyone looking at them twice – the ultimate test for those who want to be a grey man (a person who does not attract attention, but blends into the surroundings).

Many people often ask questions about special operations and special forces, querying what their role in modern warfare is. According to the United States Special Operations Posture Statement 2000, the term 'special operations' describes actions which are conducted by specially organized, trained and equipped military or paramilitary forces in order to achieve military, political, economic or psychological objectives by unconventional means in hostile, denied or politically sensitive areas.

They may be conducted in peacetime, in periods of conflict or during all-out war, either independently

> It is not the critic who counts, not the man who points out how the strong man stumbled, or where the doer of deeds could have done better. The credit belongs to the man who is actually in the arena; whose face is marred by the dust and sweat and blood; who strives valiantly; who errs and comes short again and again; who knows the great enthusiasms, the great devotions and spends himself in a worthy course; who, at the best, knows in the end the triumph of high achievement, and who, at worst, if he fails, at least fails while daring greatly; so that his place shall never be those cold and timid souls who know neither victory nor defeat.
>
> *Theodore Roosevelt (Paris Sorbonne, 1910)*

Left: In special forces, a signaller is responsible for secure team–base communications and has specialized in encoding and decoding technologies.

or in coordination with conventional forces. The military and political situation frequently dictates such special operations, and such operations usually differ from conventional operations in their degree of risk, the operational techniques involved, their modus operandi, independence from friendly support and dependence upon essential operational intelligence, and the knowledge of the indigenous assets available.

UNCONVENTIONAL WARFARE

The idea of special forces is nothing new. There have been numerous examples throughout history of men performing unconventional operations that either ended or shortened a conflict. Examples include the ploy of the Trojan Horse, used by the Greeks to insert soldiers into Troy, the city they were besieging; and the American General Roy Rogers, who formed the Rangers, an elite group of men who waged an unconventional war with great success against the

French and their allies, the North American Indians. In fact, some of his famous military standing orders and tactics are valid to this day (see Special Forces on Land, United States).

Modern warfare wears many guises, ranging from large conventional forces operating on peacekeeping missions to Stealth aircraft bombing targets deep behind enemy lines without detection. The special forces soldier, however, has no face – this anonymity is what keeps him alive.

Throughout history, small bands of warriors have waged war by using unconventional weapons, tactics and techniques to fight and defeat larger conventional forces. These groups were generally crude and often behaved in an unlawful way, which is not the way modern special forces operate.

MODERN WARRIORS

Today, special forces operators have high personal goals: a second-best performance is often considered to be no performance at all. As the British

Above: Two British SAS soldiers undergo jungle survival training in Borneo. The course, which is also conducted in Belize, usually last six weeks.

Below: Lieutenant Colonel David Stirling, the founder of the British SAS. Stirling's original force numbered 60 men and was termed 'L Detachment'.

SAS say, 'Perfect planning prevents poor performance' – a statement that all professional soldiers respect and understand. Moreover, it is not enough for the special forces operator to be the most useful, resourceful and feared person on the battlefield; he also wants to work within a moral framework.

In Afghanistan, the role of the special forces soldier came under intense scrutiny. Here was a war where aircraft such as the mighty B-52 were being used for close-support bombing missions – an idea that would have been ridiculous just 10 years ago and which is made possible only by small teams of highly trained and well-equipped men operating amongst the enemy forces, directing air attacks with deadly accuracy, without being detected. Special forces are also a great tool for governments that want a foothold on the ground where conventional forces would be vulnerable to attack. A good example of this dates from the 1970s, when the British SAS waged a low-intensity war in Oman against overwhelming guerilla forces and defeated them. In Britain, meantime, the war barely rated a mention, partly because only 80 British SAS soldiers were there at any given time.

Special forces operators are men – and, in some cases, women – who have been specially selected, specially trained and specially equipped to carry out special missions. Their use in a crisis is always considered because they give politicians a chance to resolve a problem quietly and discreetly. You simply need to compare this to the media spotlight in which a conventional battle group deploys.

What's more, in the event of things going wrong, the sensitive issue of casualties is minimized, as a small force cannot, by definition, produce large-scale losses, and the media never knows in the first place exactly how many were deployed.

The role of special forces is growing all the time, as their ability to carry out seemingly impossible missions is increasingly recognized. During the Gulf War, British SAS and US Delta Force operators located and destroyed Iraqi mobile Scud missile launchers, which had been causing severe problems for the Allied coalition. After the war ended, there was a great impetus to create more special forces operators, but they cannot be mass-produced, as their type is a very rare breed indeed: many receive the calling, but only a few are chosen.

GERMANY
Kommando Spezialkrafte (KSK)

The training programme for the Kommando Spezialkrafte (KSK) is the longest of any special forces training regime, lasting up to three years. The length of course permits every KSK operative to receive instruction in advanced military specializations.

Unlike many special forces units, the KSK is remarkably open about its selection criteria, as most of its training courses were developed in consultation with the United Kingdom, France and the United States. To become a KSK operator takes about three years and includes HALO, HAHO and scuba training.

The initial selection process and basic training phase lasts for three months and is broadly based on the British SAS and US Delta Force system. Einzelkaempferlehrgang 1 is an advanced training course which all combat officers and senior NCOs must complete successfully. The selection process takes place at the KSK's Blackwood training centre, which is located at Calw, and it involves the following:

1. A one-day psychological test with a computer-assisted assessment;
2. A one-week selection phase;
3. Two days' physical fitness testing, including a minute of maximum

KSK Criteria

Before a potential recruit can undergo KSK training, he must meet the following criteria:
1. Be airborne-qualified.
2. Be already serving in the Army.
3. Volunteer for at least 6 years of service with the KSK.
4. Officers must be under 30 years of age, and NCOs under 32.

sit-ups, a minute of maximum press-ups, three 10m (33ft) sprints, stand jumping, and 12-minute run.

4. A 500m (1640ft) swim in under 15 minutes.

5. Standard German military assault course, to be completed in less than 100 minutes.

6. 7km (4-mile) field run with 20kg (45-pound) bergan, to be completed in under 52 minutes.

7. Three days of additional psychological tests.

Candidates who successfully pass the basic screening and selection course go on to more advanced specialized training courses, including:

BASIC COMMANDO TRAINING

One week of SERE training under extreme and demanding conditions, which requires the candidate to complete a 100km (62-mile) march in four days with full combat kit. During this march, candidates will be required to carry out abseiling, river crossings,

Above: A KSK soldier on patrol. He carries the Heckler & Koch 7.62mm G3 rifle, although today most German soldiers use the updated 5.56mm HK33.

Left: A unit of KSK performs a static-line parachute jump. KSK parachute training also includes HAHO, HALO, night jumps and amphibious jumps.

map reading by day and night, and contact drills. This is followed by further psychological screening.

BASIC COMMANDO TRAINING II

Three-week combat survival course at the International Long Range Recon Patrol School, located at Pfullendorf.

Once this training is completed, candidates are assigned to an operational KSK team, where they will have many opportunities to work with other special forces units, including the British SAS and US Delta Force.

SOUTH AFRICA
Special Forces Brigade

Selection for South Africa's Special Forces Brigade weeds out over 95 per cent of applicants, such is the severity of the programme. Much of the training focuses on survival skills in South Africa's unforgiving landscape.

The South African Special Forces selection course is one of the toughest in the world and has been described as the 'ultimate challenge' by those who have undertaken it. Both the selection procedure and the actual training for the 'Recces' is extremely tough, even by South African standards. The unit is keen to avoid 'loudmouths' or 'body builders', who rarely fit in and seldom pass the initial selection phase. Although physical fitness is important, it is not the be all and end all – the personality of candidates comes under scrutiny, too. What the instructors are looking for is a candidate who is fit, intelligent, patient, determined, flexible and tenacious. During training phase, there are just two key requirements that a potential recruit must demonstrate: initiative and guts. In a typical year, more than 700 potential recruits will undergo the selection procedure, but fewer than 50 will make the grade.

The Special Forces Brigade holds two selection courses each year. Even before this, potential recruits visit a number of units to find out more about their training and operational roles. The recruiting team shows potential candidates film footage of the actual selection and training course so that they are under no illusions of what is required. If this film fails to frighten them away, they move on to the PT test, which they must pass. For those that pass the initial PT test and medical examinations, a three-week preselection course awaits them. This phase starts with two weeks of tough

PT sessions, which last for eight hours a day and are designed to prepare candidates for the full selection programme. Even at this early stage, some 20 per cent of the candidates drop out, mainly because of the harshness of the physical training. For those remaining, there is no let-up in the punishing schedule: candidates are sent to Zululand for a one-week water

Above: A unit of South African Recon Commandos on patrol. Recon Commandos specialize in counterinsurgency warfare, long-range surveillance operations and parachute insertions.

orientation course that tests out their watermanship skills and instructs them in the use of two-seater canoes, kayaks and small motor boats.

The Requirements

Before a soldier attends selection, he must first meet the following requirements:
1. Be a South African Citizen (although exceptions are often made for British subjects).
2. Be a high school graduate.
3. Have at least one year's service in any of the following forces – active, reserve, voluntary or police.
4. Speak at least three languages.
5. Have no serious criminal record.
6. Be between 18 and 28 before selection.
7. Ranks: NCO; private to staff sergeant.
8. Officers: candidate officer to captain.

Following this phase of boat training, candidates carry out navigation exercises in swampy terrain, then have to take part in an 8km (5-mile) race, which requires candidates to team up in pairs and carry a heavy pole between them without dropping it. The catch in this exercise, however, is that each pole is very heavy and normally requires a four-man lift. The candidates are watched throughout this exercise by their eagle-eyed instructors, who are looking for teamwork and initiative, and for those that show leadership skills. By the end of the week, candidates will have noticed a reduction in their rations and will have been assessed for adaptability, coordination, fitness, claustrophobia, resistance to cold, and their ability to work in difficult and demanding circumstances. For some, this week proves too much for them, and they quit.

Those left on the course receive no rest, but are quickly flown to an operational area for the final part of the selection programme. The first week of this final phase involves bush orientation and survival training, as many of the candidates will have little or no experience in this area. One of

the first tasks for the instructors is to search each candidate for tobacco, sweets, food and toiletries – all items that are strictly forbidden. The only item of personal kit allowed is a first-aid kit. During the survival phase, candidates are taught about plants, obtaining water, starting fires and techniques for dealing with animals such as elephants and lions.

Once the candidates have received their survival lesson, they are on their own and have to build a shelter using only their ground sheet and brushwood. The candidates' shelters are then judged for their practicality, neatness and camouflage. At this stage,

their rations are reduced again and each man is restricted to 5 litres (9 pints) of water per day. Candidates are still subjected to at least an hour of PT each morning before they are allowed breakfast, and at this stage it consists of little more than a biscuit and a small amount of water.

Once through the survival element of the course, the candidates move on to the observation test. On a set route, 10 items are hidden, which they must find and correctly identify. An assault course then awaits them, and it must be completed three times, twice without kit and once with a 35kg (77-pound) cement-filled mortar-bomb container. After completing this task, the candidates go for a 5km (3-mile) run along a gully strewn with loose rocks. At the end of the run, they have to pick up a tree trunk and carry it back to their camp without dropping it. Those successfully completing this phase of selection are evaluated for their performance during the previous week and are assessed on their water discipline; ability to cope with heights; navigation; observation skills; ability to take in information; weapons handling; leadership skills; and ability to work with others while under stress.

As the candidates ponder their fate, they come under automatic gunfire, which tests both their reflexes and

The PT Test

Candidates are required to complete a 30km (19-mile) course in 6 hours with normal kit and rifle, carrying a 30kg (66-pound) sand-bag; an 8km (5-mile) run, wearing boots and carrying a rifle, in under 45 minutes; 40 push-ups, 8 chin pulls and 68 sit-ups in a set time; 40 shuttle runs of 7m (23ft) each in under 90 seconds; and a freestyle 45m (148ft) swim. If they pass this test, they are then considered as serious candidates and undergo a thorough medical and psychological examination, in which they are questioned about their reasons for joining the Special Forces Brigade and more importantly what they have to offer the Recces.

Left: During the first weeks of basic training for the Special Forces Brigade, PT sessions can last for eight hours a day. The candidates are advised to begin training six months before arrival on the course.

condensed milk, half of a 24-hour ration pack, and 12 biscuits (8 of which are contaminated with petrol). Throughout the five days, the candidates are subjected to numerous problems, such as dealing with wild animals, brush fires and insects, to name just a few. As they reach their final rendezvous, they are told that there has been a mistake and that they have to continue walking for a further 30km (19 miles).

At this point, some candidates lose their tempers and quit. Those who continue, usually find the instructors waiting nearby for them with copious amounts of fresh food and cold drinks. Generally, only 17 per cent of each recruitment cadre makes it through selection.

their reactions. For those who survive this gruelling test, the final and most difficult challenge awaits them.

The remaining candidates are gathered together and given a magnetic bearing and rendezvous point that is some 38km (24 miles) away. They must rendezvous at a set time if they want to eat; however, they are not told that the ration biscuits are contaminated with petrol. As they make their way towards the rendezvous point, they pass a checkpoint where they receive some water, while their instructors drink ice-cold cans of soft drink in front of them. At the rendezvous point, there is plenty of good food, but only for the instructors and those who want to quit the course.

The remaining candidates are then briefed on their final exercise: five days in the bush with just a can of

After Selection

Once a candidate has passed selection, he must attend and pass a parachute course before being accepted into the Recces. Further training lasts for some 42 weeks and includes survival, tracking, explosives, weapons handling, unarmed combat, navigation, first aid, unconventional warfare, bushcraft, guerilla tactics, and signalling. In addition to learning about Western weapons, the candidates are also taught how to handle enemy equipment, usually Russian or Chinese. They are also subjected to regular PT and are expected to better their physical standards. The final test for the candidates is a night out in lion country with only a rifle, ammunition and a box of matches.

Once qualified, the new Recces joins an existing team and specialize in whatever subject they were best at during selection. After a period of time, the Recces can further refine their skills by joining a dedicated specialist unit, such as the combat divers or maritime assault unit. Whatever element of the Recces a candidate joins, he knows that he is serving in one of the world's most respected units and that a great deal will be expected of him throughout his career.

UNITED KINGDOM 🇬🇧
Special Air Service (SAS)

Special Air Service training forms the benchmark for many elite units. The training has two stages: Selection Training tests the candidate's physical fitness to the limits, while Continuation Training teaches and assesses elite military skills.

The British SAS has one of the most demanding selection courses in the world. It is designed to challenge a candidate both physically and mentally to the point of absolute exhaustion, for this is the only way in which to judge if a candidate has the right aptitude for SAS training. The regular SAS Regiment considers only applicants already serving in the British Army who have completed at least three years' service. The TA (Territorial Army Reserve Force) SAS, however, accepts potential candidates from both serving members of the reserve forces and outside civilian volunteers. They are looking for men with physical and mental strength, initiative, self-reliance and the intelligence to work through highly complex issues while exhausted and under extreme stress.

SELECTION

The selection process is designed to weed out the unsuitable as soon as possible. There are always dreamers and

Above: The Bergen pack worn by the SAS usually weighs around 25kg (55lb) during Selection Training.

Left: The winged dagger badge of the SAS and its renowned motto. The dagger itself is meant to represent King Arthur's sword, Excalibur.

time wasters, who apply for SAS service without realizing what is required. Typical candidates are generally in their mid-twenties, although older applicants do apply for selection. Selection courses are run twice a year, once in summer and once in winter, and candidates have

no choice about which one they attend. As to which one is the easier to pass, both have their good and bad points, but the ratio of success on each course is more or less the same.

It is assumed that if a man feels confident enough to apply for the SAS, he must also appreciate the physical and mental tasks that lie ahead and therefore be preparing for them as best he can. The Selection Training programme lasts for one month and is run by the Training Wing of 22 SAS at Credenhill, Hereford. The selection programme was originally designed in 1953 and has changed very little since then. It commences with a build-up period of two weeks for officers and three weeks for all other ranks.

The reason why the officers work-up period is shorter than the other ranks is simple: SAS officers are expected to outperform their men in every aspect of military knowledge and skills. If not, they have no business being officers in this regiment.

THE FIRST WEEKS

To attend Selection, all candidates must first undergo a medical at their parent unit and be certified fit by their regimental medical officer. When they do begin the course, candidates are given a chance to work up their strength because some may have been on operational tours and had little time to prepare. So, during the first week, candidates complete training runs that become longer each day.

Each candidate must also be capable of passing the standard Battle Fitness Test (BFT) in the same time as an average infantrymen – any longer and he will fail.

Above: Most route marches during Selection are conducted in the Welsh Brecon Beacons, a mountain chain with extremely variable weather conditions.

As the programme continues, the candidates are sent on a series of long, hard forced marches over the Brecon Beacons and Black Mountains of South Wales. The marches are designed to test their navigation and map-reading skills, as well as their physical strength. The marches place relentless demands on the candidates, who are given ever more complex and daunting problems to solve in all weather and by day or night, carrying a pack that starts off weighing 24 pounds (11kg) and will increase to 55 pounds (25kg) by the week's end.

During the winter months, the Welsh mountains are often covered in mist and snow, making navigation extremely difficult because the candidates cannot see visual reference points. The winds blowing over the mountains can frequently reach gale-force, making it very difficult for a man to stand upright, let alone walk. Another problem for the candidates is the ground itself, particularly after hard rain, which will make the ground marshy and the going very tough indeed. Although Selection is designed to test candidates to their physical limits, there are frequent checkpoints along the route. These checkpoints serve three purposes: they prevent cheating; they provide information about the candidates' next route; and they ensure the candidates' safety, a priority as there have been numerous

fatalities on the Brecon Beacons over the years, mainly due to hypothermia and severe falls. (At one stage, the SAS even trialled satellite tracking devices as an additional safety measure.)

Throughout Selection, the emphasis is on the individual candidate and not the entire cadre, which generally numbers 120 men. Each candidate must rely on himself for motivation, as the instructors neither help nor hinder, but provide information and safety cover only. At no time will they give a candidate any indication of how he is doing or how much time he has left to complete a task. Throughout Selection, candidates drop out or are told that they have failed. Indeed, it is only when candidates report for the next march and see their name on the

instructors' list that they know that they are still okay. For those not on the list, a short journey back to the base camp awaits them, and there they will be thanked for attempting Selection and given a travel warrant back to their respective unit. Some of the candidates will be given a second chance to attempt Selection, but this will be the end of the line for most. The SAS makes a point of talking to those who have failed Selection to reassure them that they are still good soldiers with many good qualities – just not those which the SAS is seeking.

Below: A view of Pen-Y-Fan, the highest peak in the Brecon Beacons at 886m (2900ft) and the focus of the infamous route march known as the 'Fan Dance'.

Above: Around 70 per cent of candidates are weeded out of SAS Selection during the gruelling physical tests of the first 12 weeks of the course.

Below: Hypothermia is one of the biggest dangers during SAS Selection. In 1979, an SAS major actually died of exposure on the Brecon Beacons.

As the remaining candidates ponder their fate each morning, they take some comfort from the fact that they are still in the programme and a day closer to passing. As each day begins, the candidates are given a new route and a series of rendezvous points where they will gain further information. They are not allowed to write anything down and are forbidden from marking their maps in any way – in enemy hands, any marks on a map could give away valuable information. As they are on their own at all times and have no idea of their timings from checkpoint to check-point, they simply have to push as hard and as fast as they can until they are told to stop by the instructors.

On occasions, the instructors will order a candidate to stop and strip his weapon down, then reassemble it. They usually pick a time when the candidate is cold and exhausted, and therefore vulnerable because his coordination will be slower than normal. One favourite trick of the instructors is to place a map and a magnetic compass on a vehicle's metal hood, which will distort the compass reading. They brief the candidates, issuing them with a new bearing to march on. Once the compass is lifted from the hood, the bearing will of course change significantly, and if the candidates fail to notice this, they are likely to become lost.

Below: The SAS do not use the British Army SA80 because of questions regarding its reliability. Instead, they select the US M16A2 with M203 grenade launcher.

FINAL WEEK

During one exercise on the final week, the instructors take away the maps from the candidates and provide them instead with a poorly drawn sketch map that has little on it apart from a few marked points. The candidates then have to use all their navigational skills to find the checkpoints that will provide the missing data.

On another exercise known as the 'Fan Dance', the candidates must negotiate an extremely difficult geographical feature known as Pen-Y-Fan (or 'The Fan') three times in four hours from three different points. However, at no point are they told the

number of times they must climb the 2900ft (884m) peak or how much time has been allocated for the task. All of the climbs are very difficult, especially when carrying a heavy pack and a rifle, and it comes as no surprise that this exercise is the most demanding in Selection phase.

As the Selection phase reaches its climax, the candidates are marching all day and even through most of the night, ending on the final day with a 50-mile (81km) march across the Brecon Beacons; this march includes 'The Fan' and other local geographical nasties. Bearing in mind that an average person walks at a pace of two

Left: An SAS trooper makes a trap for rainwater from a palm leaf and sticks during the Jungle Survival section of Continuation Training.

recruits move on to the combat and survival element of Continuation, which teaches new SAS members how to fight and survive behind enemy lines with little or no support. They are taught how to find and build shelters, locate food and water, and escape and evade enemy capture.

Once this training is completed, the recruits embark on a five-day escape and evasion exercise in the Brecon Beacons, in which they have to evade capture by an enemy force. The enemy is usually played by a local infantry battalion or, on occasion, a NATO battalion if it happens to be in the United Kingdom on exercise at the time. No matter how good the recruits are throughout the exercise, the instructors ensure that they are caught at some time, as they cannot move forward without completing the 'Resistance to Interrogation' (RTI) phase of Continuation.

JUNGLE SURVIVAL

After the RTI phase is over, recruits are sent on a jungle survival course, which lasts for up to six weeks. This course is normally held in the Far East (usually in Brunei) and trains recruits in survival, building shelters, finding food and water, navigation and jungle warfare. The SAS places great emphasis on its jungle warfare training, as it has fought many of its most remarkable campaigns in the jungle, including in Malaya and Borneo.

Those that pass the jungle phase move to RAF Brize Norton in Oxfordshire to undergo parachute training with No. 1 Parachute Training School. Many recruits are ex-paras and are excused this course. However, the others will have to undergo four weeks of static-line training, followed by eight jumps, including one at night.

to three miles (3–5km) per hour on flat ground, and that these already exhausted men have to carry a 55lb (25kg) pack and a rifle across very high and treacherous terrain in less than 20 hours, it is a daunting task, to say the least. No surprise, then, that the failure rate is very high indeed: on average only 7 to 15 per cent of each cadre completes it successfully.

CONTINUATION

For those few passing the Selection phase, the worst is yet to come. Now they must complete a six-month training period, known simply as Continuation. The first phase lasts for 14 weeks and is designed to teach new recruits basic SAS skills, including movement behind enemy lines; contact drills; signalling; and the operational roles of the standard SAS four-man team. All recruits have to reach basic signaller standard, regardless of rank and future specialization, as communications play a key part in special forces operations. In addition, all recruits learn basic field medicine; sniping; ground control of air, mortar and artillery fire; survival skills; sabotage and demolition skills; and foreign weapons handling. After completing the skills phase, the

Resistance to Interrogation

The RTI phase lasts for around 24 hours and is one of the harshest elements of Continuation. It has to be: the SAS must be sure of its men at all times because much of their work is behind enemy lines. The Regiment has to be confident that they will not crack under pressure and betray their fellow operators, and RTI is probably the best means of revealing a weak link. Much of the RTI phase is classified, but it is no secret that it is both physically and mentally challenging. Although no physical torture takes place, there is no shortage of mind games that border on severe mental torture. The instructors and expert interrogators do their utmost to unhinge the recruit and have many ways of breaking a man down without so much as touching him. This can be done in many ways: subjecting the recruit to constant deafening white noise, which can shear metal if the decibel level is high enough; blindfolding recruits, then handcuffing them to active railway lines; pouring petrol over them and leaving them near an open fire. Again, it must be stressed that no physical harm comes to recruits from these methods. But for those who ask why the SAS subjects its men to such barbaric treatment in this day and age, there is a very simple answer: it works.

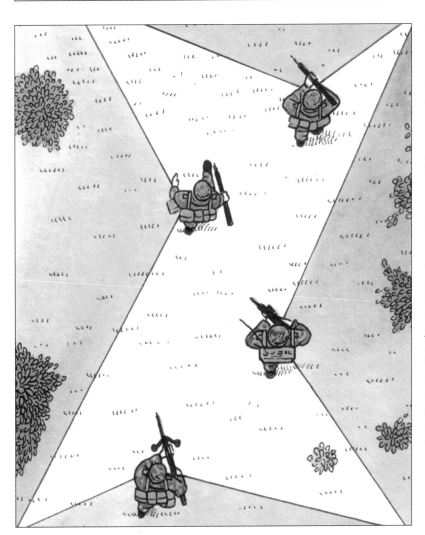

After passing parachute training, the recruits are awarded their Sabre wings and return to Hereford. They are presented with their sand-coloured beret, complete with winged-dagger badge. They are now members of the Special Air Service Regiment.

AFTER SELECTION

Regardless of previous rank, all recruits revert to the lowest rank in the SAS (that of trooper), but continue to be paid according to their rank. Although they have been accepted into the SAS, they are on probation for their first year and can still be dismissed at any point during this time. The new soldiers are assigned to one of 22 SAS Regiment squadrons and have a choice between joining Boat, Air, Mountain or Mobility Troop. Those selecting Boat Troop learn about maritime operations and how to handle small boats, including rigid raiders, kayaks and submersibles. Troopers also undergo scuba and specialist diving training, which includes underwater demolition and

Left: A typical four-man SAS patrol configuration. Each man has responsibility for a dedicated field of fire, these adding up to 360 degrees of protection and cover.

235

Above: Typical equipment carried by an SAS trooper during operations, including a Stinger anti-aircraft missile, an MP5 submachine gun and the basic survival belt kit.

including survival training, climbing techniques and the use of equipment such as skis, sledges and skidoos. Troopers joining Mobility Troop train in all aspects of vehicle operation, both in conventional and unconventional roles, including deep reconnaissance and hit-and-run missions, for which the SAS is renowned. Troopers learn how to drive defensively and offensively in different types of terrain, ranging from woodland to desert, and practise ambush and counterambush techniques until they are second nature. At some point, each trooper will rotate through counterterrorist training, as the SAS is the United Kingdom's primary counter-terrorist unit. Training includes close-quarter battle, sniping, fast-roping, insertion techniques, tubular work and unarmed combat. As the SAS is the world's most feared and respected special forces unit, there are many opportunities for troopers to crosstrain with other units around the world, including the US Delta Force, German GSG-9 and KSK, and both the Australian and New Zealand SAS.

Below: SAS soldiers train at the 'Killing House', the centre at Hereford for live-fire instruction in hostage rescue and urban assault techniques.

maritime counterterrorist operations. Troopers joining Air Troop undergo specialist training in HALO/HAHO techniques, in the United Kingdom and overseas. In addition, they learn about all aspects of airborne insertion, both conventional and unconventional, including the use of heavily modified long-range helicopters. Those joining Mountain Troop learn about all aspects of mountain and arctic warfare,

UNITED STATES OF AMERICA
Delta Force

*Delta Force soldiers are selected for training based on their prior military performance.
There are no volunteers. Training places a high emphasis on the candidate being able to operate
under conditions of constant isolation.*

Unlike the US Navy SEALs, who are very open and frank about their selection and training process, Delta refuses to discuss its requirements. What is known about Delta is that, twice a year, representatives from the unit make a trip to the Army's main personnel centre in St Louis, Missouri, to examine soldiers' military records. Their mission is to find those outstanding captains and sergeants among the Green Berets and Rangers who have skills that are of interest to Delta.

They then send a letter, telling them that Delta is interested. If the feeling is mutual, there is a telephone number to call. If not, there are instructions to destroy the letter. For those that make the call, an interview follows which quickly weeds out unsuitable candidates. Potential candidates are then subjected to a tough PT test, which is more demanding than the normal Army test. Those that pass who are not already parachute-qualified must undertake a course at an airborne school before they can go any further. Before commencing Selection, each soldier is put through an intensive week of PT that involves running, swimming and forced marches with heavy packs. The idea behind this PT week is that it gives candidates a chance to improve their physical fitness and also highlights any

injuries or medical issues that need to be addressed before Selection proper.

Once past these initial hurdles, the candidates go to Camp Dawson, an Army National Guard post in West Virginia's Appalachian Mountains, for a one-month assessment phase. This

part of the course is very similar to that of the British SAS, as Delta's founder Colonel Charles Beckwith felt that it was the best in the world for sorting the wheat from the chaff. Like SAS selection, only a small percentage of each intake passes; this number rarely

Right: A special forces soldier on a route march in full combat gear. Route marches require excellent navigation skills performed under extreme fatigue and any weather conditions.

The Psychology Test

One of the most interesting and controversial aspects of Delta's selection process is the psychological examination that each candidate must undergo before being considered as a potential operator, or 'D' man. During the psychological phase, candidates are subjected to a barrage of questions from a number of different doctors: describe your relationship with your family; do you like foreigners; do you do drugs; are you running away from something; how do you feel about gays in the army; do you feel that you are ugly; do you look in the mirror and see Rambo; are you scared of the dark; and so on. The questioning is relentless because the doctors want to build up a detailed psychological profile on each candidate and weed out any potential psychopaths. The ideal candidate is a stable individual who has an emotional anchor in life, such as a family or religion. What Delta does not want are loner types or misfits, and definitely no one with criminal tendencies. The other key area of a candidate's profile relates to the ability to handle extreme stress while carrying a gun. What Delta is looking for is a fine balance – someone who is not too ready to pull a trigger, but not too hesitant either.

reaches double figures. During selection, candidates are subjected to long marches with heavy packs over areas that are both mentally and physically demanding. They are never given timings or any information regarding their progress, and they learn from day to day whether they are in or out.

THE SELECTION

Although Delta's original selection course was modelled on that of the British SAS, it has been slightly changed over the years to better reflect American requirements for course health and safety issues. One of the toughest aspects for all the candidates is the isolation factor, as they have little contact with anyone, apart from the instructors. Many candidates adjust to this only with difficulty because they are used to working as part of a team, and the whole idea of being a loner goes against the grain. Testing this is exactly the purpose of the exercise because Delta wants operators who can react quickly to change.

Left: Patrolling is a basic Delta Force skill. More advanced abilities taught during training include combat driving, lock picking, skiing, evasion and covert surveillance techniques.

Right: One Delta route march lasts 36 hours with only one hot meal. The candidate is otherwise expected to feed himself using his own resources.

After the psychological evaluation is completed, each candidate is asked to write a short autobiography, which must be frank and honest. During the second week of the preselection phase, candidates are physically worn down by seemingly endless forced marches, which eventually end with a tough 18-mile (29km) march at night through dense woodland. The idea behind this phase is to exhaust candidates before they begin the next 18 days of formal selection.

At the beginning of this formal part, candidates are given a number and a colour. The number identifies the individual, and the colour designates their squad. They are not allowed to talk to other candidates, and the Delta instructors say little to them as individuals. When addressing the candidates, the instructors are very matter-of-fact and do not engage them in conversation nor give them any clue as to how they are doing. The instructors never shout at the candidates, but they never praise them either; they neither frown nor smile, which often unnerves the candidates, who have no idea of their progress at any given time.

A typical day begins with a self wake-up at 0600 – there is no reveille. Within each barrack room is a blackboard with the day's instructions written on it – for example, Red 3 report to vehicle 6 at 0700 with full kit and a 40-pound (18kg) pack. No two days are alike: the reporting times differ, as do the weights. During the day itself, the weights can be changed, sometimes in the candidate's favour, but mostly not. Any candidates found with underweight packs are punished on the spot by instructors who give

them a heavy rock to carry. Generally, candidates receive two hot meals a day, one in the morning and one at night; however, at some point they will receive nothing because the instructors want to see which candidates have prepared for such an event.

A typical candidate's march will start with a truck picking him up shortly after breakfast and dropping him off on a back road somewhere in the forest as part of a four-man group. He will then be given a point on a map and told to make his way to it as quickly as possible. As he makes his way towards the checkpoint, he has no idea of what the expected reporting

time is, and this will play on his mind throughout the journey.

Once he arrives at the checkpoint, he will be tired and blistered, and also anxious, not knowing if he has passed or failed this particular exercise. The impassive instructors give nothing away as they mark their notebooks and speak only to advise the candidate of his next checkpoint – 'Red 7, these are your next coordinates, the standard is best effort.'

The candidate has to keep going until he reaches the next checkpoint, where he will hopefully receive some food and rest. Before bedding down, he will be given a time for meeting up

Left: Fast-rope training – Delta has several dedicated assault-training centres, but also conducts training operations on public buildings, airports and installations.

with the rest of the cadre next morning. If he oversleeps, however, there will be nobody to wake him up, which means that he will miss the truck and fail selection.

Throughout the next few days, the routine varies from eight hours of marching with three MRE (Meals Ready to Eat) packets, to 36 hours of marching with only one MRE. To disorient the candidate, his number and colours are changed on a frequent basis so that he never feels safe or secure. At any point, he can be stopped by an instructor and ordered to strip and reassemble a foreign weapon, while being asked to solve difficult mathematical questions.

On occasion, he will be approached by doctors, who briefly observe and scribble notes without saying a word. Little does the candidate know that he will also be photographed by Delta instructors, who want to make sure that he is ploughing his way through the woodland and not cheating by using the paths. If caught once by the instructors on a path or road, he will receive an official warning; caught twice and he is out. For many of the candidates, the stress is just too much and they quit, while others have already failed, but do not know it yet. To help sow further confusion in the cadre, instructors often place failed candidates within their ranks so that they have no way of accurately gauging the general standards of the other candidates.

Every candidate is allowed a number of lives, but they are never told how many of them they have left or indeed how many they had when they began. If a soldier drops out or is failed during selection, he receives a pep talk from the Delta instructors, who praise his efforts and point out his good points, as well as his bad ones. They try to let the failed candidate down as softly as possible, anxious not to damage his confidence or future career. In addition, Delta also makes a point of writing to the candidate's parent unit, thanking it for providing a good soldier who is a credit to his unit. This process may seem a little over the top, but it is done for the very good reason that one day Delta may need the support of this soldier during an operation, and they want no ill feelings, which could cause friction.

Right: Amphibious warfare forms a key element of Delta Force training. Apart from boat deployment, amphibious parachute drops and scuba diving are also taught.

Below: Most Delta Force combat skills are taught in the six-month Operators Training Course, concentrating on covert operations and assault tactics in various environments.

Left: Free-fall parachuting is taught to all Delta operatives. It is perfected to altitudes of 10,000m (30,000ft), with parachute openings as low as 1000m (3280ft).

FINAL PHASE

When a candidate is failed during selection, he is whisked away very quietly, without a scene, and the remaining candidates are never told why. For them, each day that goes by is a victory, for many of their fellow cadre members will have been failed or dismissed, leaving for the final phase of selection only about 20 per cent of the original intake.

The last phase of selection involves a march of 40 miles (64km) in two days along the open and winding

Below: Special Forces paras make a static-line jump. Static-line missions are used when an aircraft must deploy parachutists at heights as low as 150m (500ft).

Above: Firearms training forms a large section of Delta training. Here recruits practise fire-on-the-move techniques using 5.56mm Colt M4 carbines.

Appalachian Trail with full kit. It is a difficult, gruelling march which breaks many of the candidates; however, for those who pass, a hot meal and a warm shower awaits them at the base camp.

Once back at the barracks, the remaining candidates are told to read a number of books, all of which are intellectually challenging. They then have just 18 hours to write a detailed report on the contents of each book. The instructors set this exercise as a means of evaluating how alert candidates are after two days without sleep.

After handing in their reports, the candidates are then subjected to a further series of interviews, in which they have to answer numerous questions on their childhood, family, military career and the selection course itself. Those that survive this

interview move on to the final hurdle, the commander's board.

During this interview, the candidate sits in a chair surrounded by Delta's commander and his five squadron leaders. The board reads through all of the candidate's psychiatric reports and starts asking difficult questions: would you give up your child's life for your country; on a mission, would you be prepared to kill a young shepherd who has stumbled across your hide; would you be willing to obey an order from the President to kill one of his political rivals? The idea behind such questioning is to see how a candidate reacts to pressure from a higher authority: is he easily flustered; does he panic while under pressure; can he be trusted with secret information?

On some occasions, a candidate will be asked if he cheated at any point on the course by using roads or paths. If he did so and admits to it, he may be kept on. If he lies, however, photographic proof will be shown to him,

and this will result in his instant dismissal. After the candidate's interview is over, the senior Delta officers meet in private to discuss him.

All aspects of the candidate's performance throughout selection are evaluated. If there are any lingering doubts about a candidate at this stage, he will be rejected. In theory, Delta's commander can overrule any rejection decision; however, he rarely does. The decision to accept a candidate is made by majority vote only.

Once a candidate is accepted into Delta, his selection and assessment reports are sealed for eternity. Nobody, including the candidate himself, is allowed to see the scores or indeed know what the pass mark was on this selection course.

OTC

After passing this phase, the candidate is sent on the Operators Training Course (OTC), which consists of six months of instruction in covert

Above: Sentry removal techniques are taught during the close-quarter battle (CQB) training. The number of techniques taught are fairly small, but all emphasize lethality.

Left: Helicopters offer the advantages of excellent low-level manoeuvrability, producing limited or no radar signature, and precision deployment and extraction.

operations, commando assaults, close-quarter battle, and sniping.

The pace of the OTC is relaxed compared to that of selection, although all new students are on probation for the first year. A typical training course sees students spending more than 1000 hours in the Delta shooting house alone, where they will learn about every aspect of combat shooting until it becomes second nature. In addition to the practical exercises, students attend numerous lectures on subjects such as psychology, combat theory, world politics and terrorism. They also receive detailed instruction on clandestine operations and image projection – in other words, how to dress while working undercover. But it's not all just theory: they learn how to ride motorcycles as part of vehicle familiarization training.

After this phase is over, the students then spend six weeks studying communications, combat medicine

and advanced infantry skills, followed by nine weeks of assault and rescue operation training, which includes two- and four-man assaults, how to enter buildings, rope work and helicopter insertion. The students then work with the CIA on real tasks such as VIP protection and intelligence-gathering operations, usually against low-level criminals.

Once this training is over, they move on to what Delta Force is all

about: they are now trained operators. They will, however, receive additional training, in subjects such as explosive ordnance demolition (EOD), scuba and HALO/HAHO parachute infiltration.

Delta operators also frequently crosstrain with other counterterrorist units around the world, including the German GSG-9, French GIGN, Australian SASR and, of course, the British SAS, with whom they work particularly closely.

Delta Force Officer Requirements

Joining a special forces unit as an ordinary soldier is hard enough, but becoming an officer is something else again – exceptional qualities are needed to lead the best of the best.

Shown here are the requirements for becoming an officer in the US Army's 1st Special Forces Operational Detachment-Delta (1st-SFOD), as described by US Army PERSCOM Online:

The U.S. Army's 1st Special Forces Operational Detachment-Delta (1st SFOD) plans and conducts a broad range of special operations across the operational continuum. Delta is organized for the conduct of missions requiring rapid response with surgical applications of a wide variety of unique skills, while maintaining the lowest possible profile of US involvement.

Assignment to 1st SFOD-D involves an extensive prescreening process, successful completion of a 3- to 4-week mentally and physically demanding Assessment and Selection Course, and a 6-month operator training course. Upon successful completion of these courses, officers are assigned to an operational position within the unit.

As an officer in 1st SFOD-D, you will have added opportunities to command at the Captain, Major and Lieutenant Colonel levels. You may also serve as an Operations Officer. After service with 1st SFOD-D, there are a wide variety of staff positions available to you at DOD, JCS, DA, USASOC, USSOCOM and Joint Headquarters because of

your training and experience. In addition, there are interagency positions available to you as well.

The prerequisites for an officer are:
Volunteer
U.S. citizen
Pass a modified Class II Flight Physical
Airborne qualified or volunteer for airborne training
Pass a background security investigation and have at least a secret clearance
Pass the Army Physical Fitness Test (APFT), FM 21–20, 75 points each event in the 22–26 age group, (55 push-ups in two minutes, 62 sit-ups in two minutes and a 2-mile run in 15:06 or less), wearing your unit PT uniform
Minimum of two years' active service remaining upon selection into the unit
Captain or Major (Branch immaterial)
Advance course graduate
College graduate (BA or BS)
Minimum of 12 months successful command (as a Captain)

1st SFOD-D conducts worldwide recruiting twice a year to process potential candidates for the Assessment and Selection course. Processing for the September course is from October through January. Processing for the September course takes place from April through July. Assignments with 1st SFOD-D provide realistic training and experiences that are both personally and professionally rewarding.

GLOSSARY

AAA – Anti-aircraft artillery

AFV – Armoured Fighting Vehicle

AMTRAC – Amphibious Tracked vehicle - such as the LVTP-7

ARVN – Army of the Republic of Vietnam

AUG – *Armee Universal Gewehr* (Army Universal Rifle) Assault Rifle manufactured by Steyr

Brown Water Navy – nickname for US Special Boat Squadrons

BUD/S –Basic Underwater Demolitions/SEAL

CDB – Clearance Diver Branch

C^2 – Command and Control

C^4I – Command and Control and Information and Intelligence

CO – Commanding Officer

COFUSCO – *Commandment des Fusilieriers Marins Commandos* (Marine Infantry and Special Forces Command)

COS – *Commandement des Opérations Spéciales* (Special Operations Command).

Coy – Company

CQB – Close Quarter Battle

CONOPS – Concept of Operations

CRRC – Combat Rubber Raiding Craft

CSAR – Combat Search and Rescue

CT – Counterterrorism

CTR – Covert Tactical Reconnaissance

DEVGRU – Naval Special Warfare Development Group

DDS – Dry Deck Shelter

DGSE – *Direction General de la Securite Exterieure* (General Directorate of External Security).

DINOPS – *Détachment d'Intervention Opérationnelle Subaquatique* (Underwater Special Intervention Detachment)

DoD – Department of Defense

DPM – Disruptive Pattern Material

DZ – Drop Zone

EOD – Explosive Ordnance Disposal

EXFIL – Exfiltration

FIBUA – Fighting in built up areas

FN – *Fabrique Nationale d'Armes de Guerre* – Belgian arms manufacturer

GI – Government (or General) Issue (term used for US soldiers)

GIGN –*Groupe d'Intervention de Gendarmerie Nationale* (Intervention Group of the National Gendarmerie)

GPMG – General Purpose Machine Gun

GRU – Chief Intelligence Directorate of the General Staff – Soviet/Russian Military Intelligence

HAHO – High Altitude High Opening (method of parachuting)

HALO – High Altitude Low Opening (method of parachuting)

HELOPS – Helicopter Operations

H&K – Heckler and Koch (firearms manufacturer)

HMG – Heavy Machine Gun

HMS – Her Majesty's Ship

HP –Horsepower or Hi Power (9mm Browning Pistol)

HSB – High Speed Boat

IDF – Israeli Defence Force

IFOR – Implementation Force (Peacekeeping force in Bosnia)

INFIL – Infiltration

JATO – Jet Assisted Take Off

Klepper – kayak manufacturer of Rosenheim, Germany. Klepper kayaks are prized for their lightness and durability and are standard equipment, particularly in the two-man versions, with western naval special forces units.

LAW – Light Anti-Tank Weapon

LMG – Light Machine Gun

LRRP – Long Range Reconnaissance Patrol

LSV – Light Strike Vehicle

LSW – Light Support Weapon

LZ – Landing Zone

MAG – *Mitrailleuse d'Appui Général* (general purpose machine gun)

Maiale (Pig) – two man Italian mini-submarine from the Second World War

MCF – Marine Commando Force

MOD – Ministry of Defence

MRE – Meal Ready to Eat

NAVART – Naval Artillery

NATO – North Atlantic Treaty Organisation

NAVSPECWARCOM – Naval Special Warfare Command

NBC – Nuclear Biological Chemical

NCO – Non-Commissioned Officer

NSWG – Naval Special Warfare Group

NSWU – Naval Special Warfare Unit

NCDU – Naval Combat Divers Unit

NVG – Night Vision Goggles

OBUA – Operations in built up areas

OP – Observations Post

Operation 'Brightlight' – US POW recovery missions in
Vietnam, 1970–72

Operation Desert Shield – the build of US forces in the Gulf
after the 1990 Iraqi invasion of Kuwait

Operation Desert Storm – the coalition assault on Iraqi forces,
1991

Operation Enduring Freedom – the coalition assault against
the Taliban regime in Afghanistan 2002

Operation Frankton – Royal Marine commando operation
against the Bordeaux Docks in December 1942

Operation Just Cause – US invasion of Panama, 1989

OPSEC – Operational Security

ORBAT – Order of Battle

PBC – Patrol Boat Coastal

PBL – Patrol Boat Light

PBR – Patrol Boat River

PDF – Panamanian Defence Force

PDSS – *protivodiversionniye sili i srredtava* (Russian UDT unit)

Phoenix Program – US pacification campaign against the Viet
Cong infrastructure in South Vietnam.

Platoon – traditionally lowest level of military organization
that an officer routinely commanded. Usually 30–40 men
strong.

POW – Prisoner of War

PSM – *propulseur sous-marin* (see SDV)

PSYOPS – Psychological Operations

RAN – Royal Australian Navy

Rebreathing gear – a closed circuit breathing device, which
recycles and purifies the diver's exhaled gases rather than
expelling then as bubbles. Its military advantages are
obvious. Dräger LAR V and Oxymax are amongst the most
popular modules used by western naval special forces.

Recce – Reconnaissance

REG – *Régiment Étranger de Génie* (Foreign Engineer
Regiment)

REP – *Régiment Étranger de Parachutiste*

RIB – Rigid Inflatable Boat

ROK – Republic of Korea

RM – Royal Marine

RMBPD – Royal Marine Boom Patrol Detachment

RN – Royal Navy

RSM – Regimental Sergeant Major

SAS – Special Air Service (UK)

SASR – Special Air Service Regiment (Australian)

SAW – Squad Automatic Weapon (M-249 light machine gun)

SBU – Special Boat Unit

SCUBA – Self-Contained Underwater Breathing Apparatus

SBS – Special Boat Squadron (US), Special Boat Section,
Special Boat Service (UK)

SEAL – Sea-Air-Land (US Navy special forces unit)

SDV – SEAL Delivery Vehicle or Swimmer Delivery Vehicle

SF – Special Forces

SFOR – Stabilisation Force

SMG – Submachine Gun

SO – Special Operations

SOE – Special Operations Executive

SOF – Special Operations Forces

SOU – Special Operations Unit

SOV – Special Operations Vehicle

Spetsnaz – *Voyska Spetsial' Nogo Nazrachenniya* (Forces of
Special Designation)

SWAT – Special Weapons and Tactics

TA – Territorial Army

TAB – Tactical Advance to Battle

TACAIR – Tactical Air Support

TAG/OAT – Tactical Assault Group/Offshore Assault Team

TALO – Tactical Air Landing Operations

Tubular Work – Operations carried out in cylindrical objects,
i.e. aircrafts, trains and coaches

UAR – Underwater Assault Rifle

UAV – Unmanned Air Vehicle

UCAV – Uninhabited Combat Air Vehicle

UDT – Underwater Demolitions Team

UKNLAF – United Kingdom/Netherlands Amphibious Force

UN – United Nations

Unimog – A type of vehicle known by its manufacturer

UOU – Underwater Operations Unit

USN – United States Navy

USMC – United States Marine Corps

USSOCOM – United States Special Operations Command

Vietcong – Vietnamese communist insurgents

Zodiac – a make of RIB used by Western naval special forces

USSOCOM ORGANIZATION

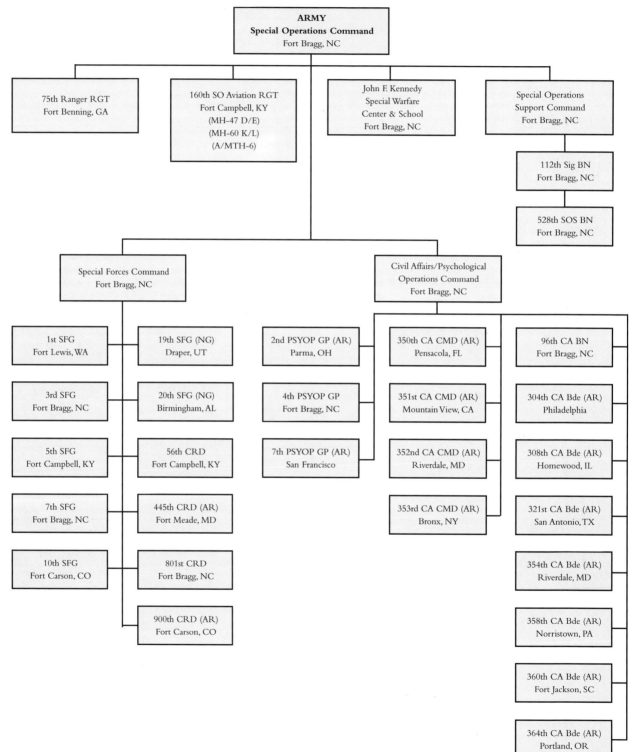

ARMY
Special Operations Command
Fort Bragg, NC

75th Ranger RGT
Fort Benning, GA

160th SO Aviation RGT
Fort Campbell, KY
(MH-47 D/E)
(MH-60 K/L)
(A/MTH-6)

John F. Kennedy
Special Warfare
Center & School
Fort Bragg, NC

Special Operations
Support Command
Fort Bragg, NC

112th Sig BN
Fort Bragg, NC

528th SOS BN
Fort Bragg, NC

Special Forces Command
Fort Bragg, NC

Civil Affairs/Psychological
Operations Command
Fort Bragg, NC

1st SFG
Fort Lewis, WA

19th SFG (NG)
Draper, UT

3rd SFG
Fort Bragg, NC

20th SFG (NG)
Birmingham, AL

5th SFG
Fort Campbell, KY

56th CRD
Fort Campbell, KY

7th SFG
Fort Bragg, NC

445th CRD (AR)
Fort Meade, MD

10th SFG
Fort Carson, CO

801st CRD
Fort Bragg, NC

900th CRD (AR)
Fort Carson, CO

2nd PSYOP GP (AR)
Parma, OH

350th CA CMD (AR)
Pensacola, FL

96th CA BN
Fort Bragg, NC

4th PSYOP GP
Fort Bragg, NC

351st CA CMD (AR)
Mountain View, CA

304th CA Bde (AR)
Philadelphia

7th PSYOP GP (AR)
San Francisco

352nd CA CMD (AR)
Riverdale, MD

308th CA Bde (AR)
Homewood, IL

353rd CA CMD (AR)
Bronx, NY

321st CA Bde (AR)
San Antonio, TX

354th CA Bde (AR)
Riverdale, MD

358th CA Bde (AR)
Norristown, PA

360th CA Bde (AR)
Fort Jackson, SC

364th CA Bde (AR)
Portland, OR

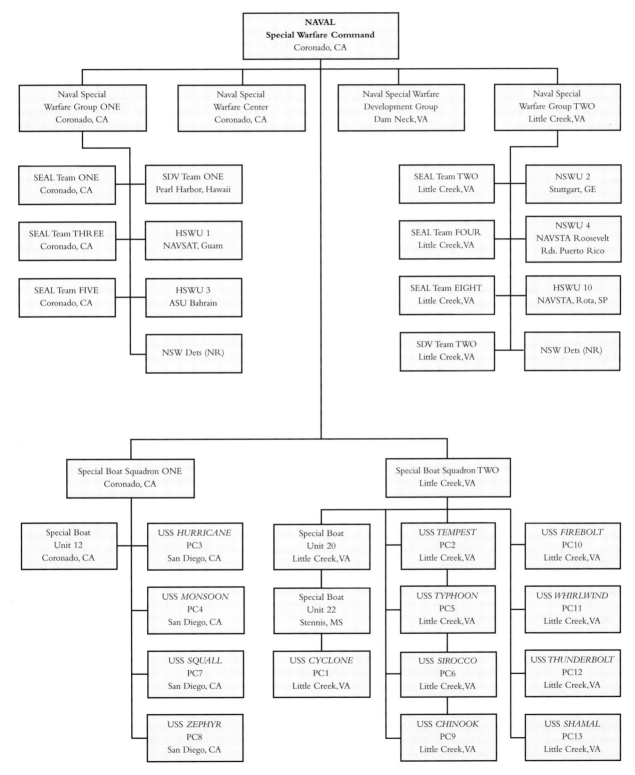

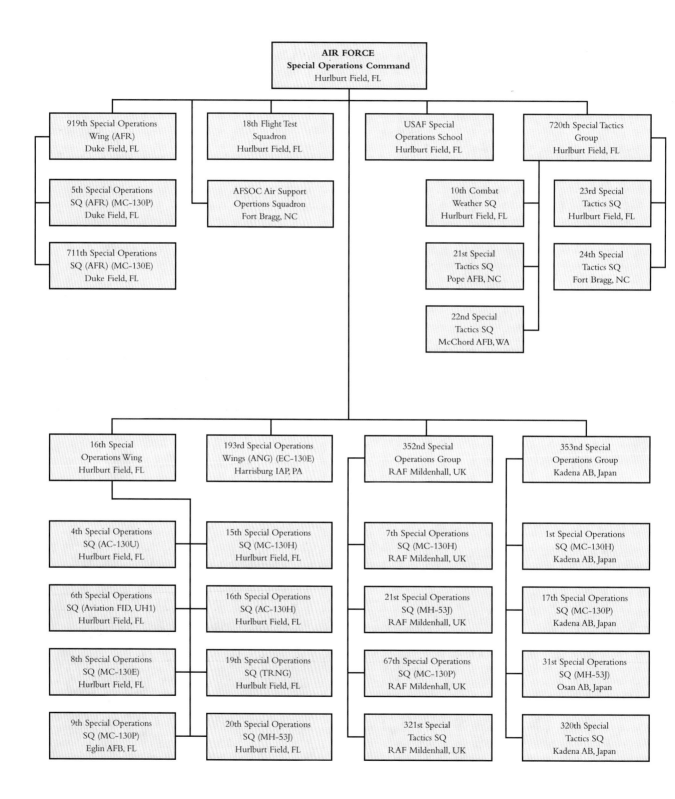

AIR FORCE
Special Operations Command
Hurlburt Field, FL

919th Special Operations
Wing (AFR)
Duke Field, FL

18th Flight Test
Squadron
Hurlburt Field, FL

USAF Special
Operations School
Hurlburt Field, FL

720th Special Tactics
Group
Hurlburt Field, FL

5th Special Operations
SQ (AFR) (MC-130P)
Duke Field, FL

AFSOC Air Support
Opertions Squadron
Fort Bragg, NC

10th Combat
Weather SQ
Hurlburt Field, FL

23rd Special
Tactics SQ
Hurlburt Field, FL

711th Special Operations
SQ (AFR) (MC-130E)
Duke Field, FL

21st Special
Tactics SQ
Pope AFB, NC

24th Special
Tactics SQ
Fort Bragg, NC

22nd Special
Tactics SQ
McChord AFB, WA

16th Special
Operations Wing
Hurlburt Field, FL

193rd Special Operations
Wings (ANG) (EC-130E)
Harrisburg IAP, PA

352nd Special
Operations Group
RAF Mildenhall, UK

353nd Special
Operations Group
Kadena AB, Japan

4th Special Operations
SQ (AC-130U)
Hurlburt Field, FL

15th Special Operations
SQ (MC-130H)
Hurlburt Field, FL

7th Special Operations
SQ (MC-130H)
RAF Mildenhall, UK

1st Special Operations
SQ (MC-130H)
Kadena AB, Japan

6th Special Operations
SQ (Aviation FID, UH1)
Hurlburt Field, FL

16th Special Operations
SQ (AC-130H)
Hurlburt Field, FL

21st Special Operations
SQ (MH-53J)
RAF Mildenhall, UK

17th Special Operations
SQ (MC-130P)
Kadena AB, Japan

8th Special Operations
SQ (MC-130E)
Hurlburt Field, FL

19th Special Operations
SQ (TRNG)
Hurlbult Field, FL

67th Special Operations
SQ (MC-130P)
RAF Mildenhall, UK

31st Special Operations
SQ (MH-53J)
Osan AB, Japan

9th Special Operations
SQ (MC-130P)
Eglin AFB, FL

20th Special Operations
SQ (MH-53J)
Hurlburt Field, FL

321st Special
Tactics SQ
RAF Mildenhall, UK

320th Special
Tactics SQ
Kadena AB, Japan

SAS ORGANIZATION

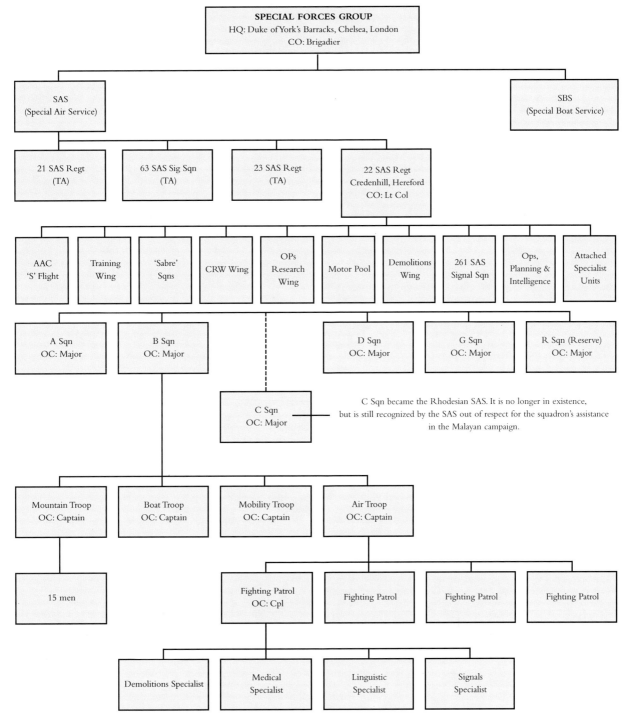

SPECIAL FORCES GROUP
HQ: Duke of York's Barracks, Chelsea, London
CO: Brigadier

SAS
(Special Air Service)

SBS
(Special Boat Service)

21 SAS Regt
(TA)

63 SAS Sig Sqn
(TA)

23 SAS Regt
(TA)

22 SAS Regt
Credenhill, Hereford
CO: Lt Col

AAC
'S' Flight

Training
Wing

'Sabre'
Sqns

CRW Wing

OPs
Research
Wing

Motor Pool

Demolitions
Wing

261 SAS
Signal Sqn

Ops,
Planning &
Intelligence

Attached
Specialist
Units

A Sqn
OC: Major

B Sqn
OC: Major

D Sqn
OC: Major

G Sqn
OC: Major

R Sqn (Reserve)
OC: Major

C Sqn
OC: Major

C Sqn became the Rhodesian SAS. It is no longer in existence,
but is still recognized by the SAS out of respect for the squadron's assistance
in the Malayan campaign.

Mountain Troop
OC: Captain

Boat Troop
OC: Captain

Mobility Troop
OC: Captain

Air Troop
OC: Captain

15 men

Fighting Patrol
OC: Cpl

Fighting Patrol

Fighting Patrol

Fighting Patrol

Demolitions Specialist

Medical
Specialist

Linguistic
Specialist

Signals
Specialist

INDEX OF UNITS

INDEX